WALLED IN LIGHT
SAINT COLETTE

To my sisters,

the Poor Clare Nuns

WALLED IN LIGHT
Saint Colette

by MOTHER MARY FRANCIS
Poor Clare Nun

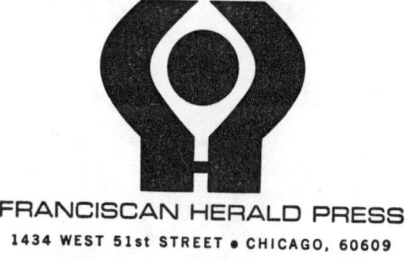

FRANCISCAN HERALD PRESS
1434 WEST 51st STREET • CHICAGO, 60609

WALLED IN LIGHT, Saint Colette by Mother Mary
Francis, P.C.C., published by Sheed and Ward, New
York, 1959. Copyright 1985 by Franciscan Herald Press,
1434 West 51st Street, Chicago, Illinois 60609. All rights
reserved.

Library of Congress Cataloging in Publication Data

Mary Francis, Mother, 1921-
    Walled in light, Saint Colette.

    Reprint. Originally published: New York: Sheed and
Ward, c1959.
    1. Colette, Saint, 1381-1447.   2. Christian saints—
France—Biography.   I. Title.
BX4700.C67M3   1985   282'.092'4 [B]   85-4394
ISBN 0-8199-0889-6

Contents

"It was the hour of the flaming out of the sun from the fogs of the
   North
When Colette, as a grain full-ripe, sees the shell burst forth
Of the narrow cell she had built twelve feet from the altar of God,
Its sill no more to be trod.
But now the voice of heaven has sounded: 'Forth, and abroad!'
No need of enclosure now in the shell of stone;
She is free in the salt of heaven, she is walled in light alone."
                              —Paul Claudel, trans. George O'Neill[1]

[1] Reprinted with permission from Mme. Ste. Marie Perrine, *St. Colette and Her Reform*, trans. Mrs. Conor Maguire (St. Louis, Herder; London, Sands, 1924).

Foreword

A saint least likely to be obscured by the centuries would appear to be the woman who was confidante and mentor to French royalty in the tumultuous fifteenth century, who propped up the sagging structure of primitive Franciscanism and restored it to its original spiritual grandeur, whose miracles all but defy their numbering. Yet St. Colette of Corbie, a favorite saint of Europe, has become the forgotten saint in America. Everyone knows of St. Francis and St. Clare. Not so many know that the saints of Assisi form a Franciscan triumvirate with the saint of Corbie. She has been lost in their glory. But that, in fact, was always her aim.

Many French biographers have written her remarkable story. A few English writers have told it, too. Most authentic, however, and certainly most charming, are the two simple expositions left us by St. Colette's confessor, Father Pierre de Vaux, and her secretary, Sister Perrine de la Baume. When dying, Perrine solemnly attested the truth of all she had written of Sister Colette in her "notebook," adding that she must have omitted many things but that she had certainly added none.

Shortly before his death, Father de Vaux likewise swore to the truth of his longer biography. He did this in the presence of his superior and immediately after he had celebrated Mass, standing with his hand over his heart to indicate that he testified to his veracity by the Body and Blood of Christ. Both biographers were evidently at pains that their readers should have no least doubt about what they had written. So great a spiritual genius as Colette Boellet perhaps needed these formal attestations, for few women have accomplished as much or been as completely lovable. Relying primarily on these two indisputable sources on the saint, I have also borrowed from the works of Father Sellier, Abbé Douillet, and Abbé St. Laurent.

This is her story, the work of our community. For no Poor Clare can write a book alone. It requires the charity of many Poor Clares who type manuscripts, help with difficult translations, lift the burden of many other small chores from the author, share her difficulties and encourage her efforts. It needs also an abbess who does not merely say: "Write this book," but whose wisdom and understanding extend over the obedience to its conclusion. Thus, I want to thank my Mother Abbess and my Sisters in Roswell, as well as those in the other Colettine Poor Clare monasteries in the United States and Europe who have given so generously of their priceless manuscripts and books, along with their encouragement and their prayers. My gratitude is also due to several of the Franciscan friars who helped and advised me in the writing, especially Father Leo Ohleyer, O.F.M., whose criticisms and suggestions have been invaluable.

SISTER MARY FRANCIS, Poor Clare

July 16, 1959

765th birthday of St. Clare

1 The Boellets of Corbie

The little house of M. and Mme. Boellet on the Rue de la Chaulcie was typical of most dwellings in fourteenth-century Corbie of Picardy. It was low and humble, set well back from the street, and perhaps even neater than the neighboring cottages because it held no children. Evidently it never would. For in 1380 Mme. Boellet was in her sixtieth year, and her husband a few years older.

Widowed Margaret Moyon had borne no children to her first husband, and her second marriage to Robert Boellet was also barren. It was the same suffering known to many a loving and disappointed couple, but with this difference: Margaret Boellet was the kind of Frenchwoman whose faith seems to grow stouter on the fare of impossibility. At fifty-nine, she still prayed daily before a little wooden shrine of St. Nicholas which her carpenter husband had built in their childless home to the patron of children. "St. Nicholas, give me a son!" she stubbornly pleaded. Either Boellet's hope was the equal of his wife's or his affection was eager to indulge her dream, for the ageing couple had agreed that if God sent them a child it would be called Nicholas. And they went together on pilgrimage, springtime after springtime, to the shrine of Notre Dame de Brebières to enlist the kind offices of the Mother of God. Meanwhile the sorrow of their childlessness was not allowed to feed upon itself.

Robert Boellet had brought down upon himself and his wife the gossip and criticism of many in Corbie by establishing a house for the spiritual rehabilitation of fallen women. It was a singular charity in his time, one born out of the compassion which only the very pure can feel for the very sinful. In fourteenth-century Corbie, as in every other century and city, the pharisees who sinned carefully and prudently held as objects of revulsion those who sinned for a liveli-

1

hood. It was otherwise with Boellet. Father Pierre de Vaux writes that "to him [Boellet] was given the grace to have pity and compassion on the poor, and to help and comfort poor women of dissolute life." He goes on to tell how Robert "established a house in Corbie to receive fallen women and to comfort them and provide for their necessities." The recurrence of the word "comfort" provides most revealing evidence about M. Boellet. How many understand that comfort is the first alms such profligates need?

It would never be Boellet to dole out his money and reserve his heart. The poor creatures he gathered up out of the back lanes of Corbie touched the deepest chords of his chivalry. And these women who had never before known disinterested kindness in a man could not at first believe in it. Gradually, however, his persevering goodness reached down into unsuspected depths of their womanhood. Treated like ladies, they began to behave surprisingly like ladies. It was not easy to be less than M. Boellet seemed so sure one was, under the crust of vice. And then there was the fact that Margaret Boellet, too, so often visited their house of refuge, bringing much of love and nothing of reproaches.

Sometimes, as might be expected, Robert's efforts proved thankless enough, for some who lived by his charity only waited to draw fresh breath for a return to the familiar wallow. But there were others who never returned to the old ways, those whom Pierre de Vaux describes as "retrieved for a better life." The Boellets experienced both the bitterness and the blessedness of the work of reform, and for them one taste of the blessedness obviously outweighed whole chalices of the bitterness, since there is no evidence that this charity of theirs ever flagged. The experience was one of the richest heritages they were to bequeath to another reformer.

Perhaps some of the wretched women the Boellets reclaimed guessed the reason for the shadows of sadness in the eyes of the old couple; outcasts often enough preserve the one delicacy which is a feeling for the sorrow of others so refined as to become an intuition. If they knew of the little carved shrine of St. Nicholas and why it stood in the Boellets' home, they must have discovered at least one prayer they could make without anguish: "St. Nicholas, send them a child of their own." But then, it could not be. Margaret was already an old woman.

It would be quite a feat, however, to persist in being old when springtime comes to Picardy and its famous roses take possession of the land. The farmers in Corbie of Picardy plant their early wheat and watch for the reawakening of their grapevines. They do not hurry. The awaited spring is always unexpected in its wonders, and Corbians understand the importance of savoring April.

Corbie was famous in the late fourteenth century only because of its imposing abbey church of Saint-Pierre and the great community of Benedictine monks whose abbot was as much lord of the town as of its abbey. But the sleepy little place had many charms of its own. Cradled in the junction of the river Corbe (now Encre) and the Somme, the flat countryside unrolled rich carpets of meadows which were its chief wealth. Then, in that spring of 1380, God sent Corbie a different kind of wealth and its most enduring claim to fame. By September, the whole town was buzzing with excitement over it. And the Boellets' neighbors were round-eyed with marvelling reverence as they watched fifty-nine-year-old Mme. Boellet growing great with child.

"Miracle! Miracle!" flew from lip to lip. "The child shall be called Nicholas," Margaret promised as she knelt before the little wooden shrine. And Robert agreed. But on January 13, 1381, the smiling midwife placed a small bundle of daughter in M. Boellet's arms; and Margaret whispered: "Nicolette!" Robert agreed again. "She will be called Nicolette," he pronounced.

That Sunday in January when Nicolette Boellet first opened her eyes upon the France she was in some measure to transform flung a real sense of awe over Corbie. After five centuries, the little girl's presence is still vibrant there, and even today the people of the town will lead you enthusiastically to the site of the Boellets' dwelling on the Rue de la Chaulcie (now de la Chausée). The little house became a place of pilgrimage, and a chapel was built to enclose the rooms where small Mlle. Boellet had laughed and cried and composed ditties for her playmates to sing. During the chaos following the French Revolution, the simple shrine fell into hopeless disrepair. There were sporadic attempts at reconstruction, but no really successful one until 1938. Then war interrupted the work again, and bombs and shrapnel demolished the new chapel. But the Corbians are not easily daunted. They began still another chapel in 1947. And so strongly have they cherished their traditions of their saint that they will show you today what appears to you a mere remnant of tiling around an ancient hearth and tell you proudly that "this is the room of the cradle." The old well of the Boellets is still there, too. It is covered over now, but the townsfolk will assure you that St. Colette saw her face mirrored in that very well when she went to draw water for her mother. As though they had often seen her at the task, they will tell you it was a very pretty face she saw, and with the same conviction that their forebears in 1381 had solemnly declared at Nicolette's birth that "God hath visited His people."

It required no master exegete to bring the Scriptures to play upon the youngest citizen of Corbie and her aged parents. It had been proved often enough that "no word is impossible with God." There was the flinty faith of Sara and Abraham striking off the spark of their son, Isaac, from what had seemed the stony silences of heaven. There was ancient Anna praying unceasingly in the temple until she wrested the boy Samuel out of the mercy of God into the shelter of her womb. And there were aged Elizabeth and mute Zachary gazing upon their small son cradled in the young arms of their cousin, Mary. "What an one, think you, will this child be?" the people of Ain Karim had asked one another at the christening of John. The god-fearing folk of little Corbie in Picardy wondered what manner of child Nicolette Boellet would be. What mysterious destiny lived in the mind of God for this little girl born so far out of the natural course of things? Margaret and Robert did not know. The jubilant old pair were content to await the hour of God's manifestation of His plans and pray not to be a hindrance to them.

About Margaret's advanced age at the birth of her only child, there can be no doubt. We have the testimony of her daughter. Sister Perrine de la Baume writes: "I have myself heard our glorious Mother [St. Colette] tell many times how her mother was approaching her sixtieth birthday when she was conceived and born, and had passed the age [for childbearing] in the natural course of things." The immemorial cult of St. Colette as patron of childless couples springs from her own birth of a sexagenarian mother.

Nicolette's birth was a miracle, everyone in Corbie agreed. All right, then, let it be, the calmness of the Boellets seemed to say. Were not miracles commonplace with the good God? These days, there were very dear and homespun miracles all around them, and in these Margaret and Robert found the joys for which their hearts had hungered for forty childless years.

2 *Colette's Childhood*

Robert Boellet was a master carpenter employed mainly by the Benedictine monks at the abbey of Saint-Pierre. By the time his daughter was three, he had learned to accommodate his stride to Nicolette's jogging steps as she walked by his side on his frequent trips to deliver his work to the abbey and to receive new orders from Abbot Raoul de Raye.

The great Benedictine abbey over which de Raye presided was not only the pride of Corbie but its very *raison d'être*. Founded in 657 by the French Queen St. Bathilde, the widow of King Clovis II, it took its pioneer community from the world-famed abbey of Luxeuil, founded by the Irish Saint Columbanus in the sixth century. Under Dom Theofrid, first abbot of Corbie, monastic life quickly took shape there, enjoying lavish endowments from Queen Bathilde and singular privileges from Popes Benedict III and Nicholas I. The monastic school attached to the abbey became celebrated throughout France, especially under St. Adelhard, the ninth abbot; and the community made a foundation of its own in Westphalia in 820. When fire ravaged the clusters of monastic buildings in 1137, the new structure which rose like a phoenix out of the ruins far surpassed the original in grandeur.

There were great material advantages for the people of Corbie in all this; but there were hazards, too. And not only for the people. Perhaps more for the monks. When St. Bernard of Clairvaux visited the abbey of Corbie, he was far from being impressed by the magnificence of the place and the size of its revenues. There was little there to gladden the heart of a saint looking for monastic poverty and humble living. And, as so often happens, the people sometimes grew restive under the abnormal rule of religious become petty sovereigns.

Proud of their famous abbey, the people of Corbie at the same time fretted for independence, and in 1123 did actually obtain from King Louis VI a municipal charter granting them power to govern themselves. The attempt to break free of the lord abbot of Corbie came to grief in short time, however. The power and wealth of the abbey held the town tightly in their grip, and Corbie soon found itself on the brink of ruin. The municipal leaders were forced to humble themselves, throw themselves on the mercy of the abbot, and retreat into the old dependence. Apparently it was the last significant attempt of the townspeople to throw off the yoke of the abbot's rule. And when Nicolette Boellet was making her first trips there, the old spirit of pride in its famed abbey pervaded Corbie to the exclusion of more personal ambitions. The power of the abbot over them was taken for granted by the people and considered desirable.

Neither was the abbey of Corbie a lax house according to the standards of the time. If its great wealth troubled the heart of St. Bernard, its religious observance seems to have been laudable enough. Day and night the great chants of the Divine Office rose out of the enormous choir and spread like a humeral veil over Corbie. There had been a time before Nicolette's birth when the number of monks was so great that the Office was sung continuously day and night, the community dividing itself into shifts of chanters so that as one group finished the appointed canonical hour, another was waiting to repeat it in its turn. Whatever its shortcomings in other ways, it remained true that out of the heart of this magnificent abbey the Church's lifeblood of prayer still flowed down into the homes and shops and fields of the people of Corbie. Their lives took meaning and direction from the life that pulsed in the abbey. In 1387, Dom Raoul de Raye was their respected lord.

Unfortunately, Corbie's lord was one of that pathetic company of every century who are the almost-great. It is obviously this Benedictine abbot whom Father Pierre de Vaux describes with a circumspection so careful as to be only identifying: "He was a religious of great dignity and noble extractions, but a man of easy conscience . . . and all wrapped up in worldly affairs." Brilliant and forceful, the abbot could nevertheless be intimidated by the short-sighted and mediocre on occasion, as we shall see. But though he was sometimes throttled by the human respect against which he inveighed so eloquently to his monks in chapter, Dom Raoul was quick to recognize in others the greatness of soul he himself could never quite attain. That he was without the hauteur and arrogance that characterized some abbots of his time, when abbeys comprised whole towns on which the greed of nobles fastened, is witnessed by his friendship with Robert Boellet. He must have been a man of prayer to have so respected the simple goodness of his master carpenter. The heights of spiritual greatness which always just eluded Dom Raoul still fascinated him, and perhaps that is why he came more and more often to talk with Boellet when the carpenter's sweet-faced child was with him. At any rate, we are certain that the powerful abbot had not only a tender love for the little girl but a genuine respect; for, when he was later offered her guardianship, he accepted it with as much of humility as of devotedness.

Small Mlle. Boellet quickly became a favorite with many more in Corbie than my lord abbot. The child had a very affectionate nature, and the familiar diminutive "Colette" soon replaced her baptismal name of Nicolette forever. It must have seemed more fitting for the sprite of a girl with her dark, intelligent eyes and quick, shy smile. Margaret and Robert hid their respect for this child of Divine Providence under a sturdy French regime of parental authority. Colette was never encouraged to think of herself as a special kind of being, but was taught to consider herself very ordinary if she must consider herself at all.

Colette often recalled in later life how her devotion to the Passion of our Lord was enkindled by her mother "when I was very young." Sister Perrine has left us the saint's reminiscences of those early days in an account which points up Margaret's thrift and energy as well as her piety. She tells us it was "while she was sewing or weaving" that Mme. Boellet instructed her precocious child in religion. Pretty legends about the Child Jesus modelling clay birds and commanding them to take life and fly were beneath the notice of this woman whose own spiritual life was nourished on sterner fare, who was, as Colette herself said, "given to many penances." Margaret was given to much love, too, however; and it must certainly have been difficult not to sweep the small suffering figure of her daughter into her arms as she watched the child's tears splashing on her white apron. "She told me about our Lord's sufferings," Colette told Sister Perrine, "and I cried very much. I thought about His Passion every day."

When she was four, and with her reason entirely awakened ("I had understanding" is her own terse description), she had a poise that would have done credit to a woman. It is evident in a strange incident which took place about this time.

With all the normal curiosity of a small girl, Colette loved to pore over the tools in her father's carpenter shop and to watch Robert's strong hands fashion a handsome monastic lectern out of the stacks of boards. In his turn, Boellet enjoyed having his small, silent daughter with him as he worked; and Margaret had added spiritual overtones to Colette's liking for the shop by telling her of the Holy Family of Nazareth where St. Joseph had worked at the same trade as her own father, and where the Child Jesus had learned and labored at his father's side. Perhaps the carpenter shop was the seed-bed of that immense reverence for work which Colette would express in her Constitutions forty years later.

Why she should one day have taken Robert's heavy axe into her small hands while he was away is probably explained by that mysterious fascination which sharp tools hold for all children. Perhaps she tried to swing it in an arc, as she had seen her father do. At any rate, the axe slipped from her hands and the big blade came slashing down into the white flesh of her ankle. The foot was almost completely severed, hanging precariously by the outer skin. Blood spurted against the wall and flowed along the floor. Yet no screams of terror and pain rose to warn the Boellets of the plight of their little daughter. In silence, the child of four stood gazing at her nearly-severed foot.

Then, with a serenity that quite terrifies the rest of us, she took a clean white handkerchief from her apron pocket, bent down and bandaged the frightful wound tightly with it. She then stepped confidently forward on the foot that only a small handkerchief and thin layers of flesh held in place. The bleeding stopped, and the next day only the dark stains on the wall and the dried blood on the floor remained to testify to a miracle that seems part of a prophecy.

Did the little girl who stood with such miraculous calm watching her lifeblood flowing away feel a breath of the future blow across her heart? We do not know. Colette never offered any explanation of this miracle to the confidants of her adult life. The suggestion that she mystically entered upon her work of reform at that moment, and that the merciless cut of the axe forebode the bitter opposition and persecution she was to suffer, is mere speculation. On the other hand, the saint was very exact in describing the details of the accident to her confessor, Father Pierre de Vaux, many years later. "My foot was hanging only by a little piece of skin," she declared. ("La partie coupée ne tenait plus que par un peu de peau.") It may be the fact that Poor Clares traditionally use cheap colored handkerchiefs that led Colette to specify that the handkerchief she had at four was white! More amusing is her informing Father Pierre that the handkerchief was clean.

In her adult years, Colette was so sensitive on the point of ever being thought better or more gifted than others, that she often went to extremes in her efforts to belittle herself. "Useless servant of Sir St. Francis," "stupid girl" were two of her favorite descriptions of herself. We shall see later that her distaste for praise and her horror of being acclaimed as a worker of miracles led her to hide herself from her companions for days at a time, to scold her admiring friends with an asperity she never otherwise showed, and once to throw into the fire an account of her virtues and miracles written by her confessor.

In the face of all this, it seems quite safe to believe that when Colette told Sister Perrine that she had "infused knowledge" from her childhood, that at the age of four she had "a very high understanding of God which did not come to me from men," and that she was "almost continually united to God," she was giving us very accurate details. If she confided to Father Pierre that she cut her ankle with an axe and that the foot left hanging by a piece of skin was miraculously healed when she tied her handkerchief around it, it would seem that she attached a special importance to the incident. Tales of more astonishing miracles than this surely went into that fire which, Sister Perrine sadly writes, "burnt up the writings,

every bit, so that nothing remained." For us, though, the miracle
remains hung with mystery. We can only feel that at that hour
Colette returned her childhood to God. Little girls of four do not
endure the crushing pain of an axe-cut in silence. They do not watch
spurting blood (particularly their own!) with detachment.

Sister Perrine has recorded that it was Margaret Boellet's custom to attend daily Mass and to receive the sacraments of Penance
and Holy Communion once a week, thus much oftener than most
religious did in the fourteenth century. Colette told Father Pierre
de Vaux how she used to watch her mother's progress toward the
Communion table with unswerving gaze and then wrap her arms
tightly around Margaret when she returned to her place. It is tempt-
ing to speculate on what acts of thanksgiving Mme. Boellet must
have made those mornings, with two thin little arms ardently enclosing her and the God within her.

Despite her amazing gifts of mind and soul, however, Colette
seems to have had none of that aloofness associated with genius.
Though children will invariably avoid the one who is "different,"
the youngsters of Corbie were always clamoring for Colette Boellet
to come out and play with them. We are told she had a flair for
composing little songs to fit childish occasions, and that she sang
them in "a strong voice." Perhaps the early biographers relished this
bit of information because it established a minor natural kinship to
St. Francis, who was also frail of body and powerful of voice. That
the children of Corbie never guessed how much their clever leader
wished to be alone and away from the games she herself was invent-
ing for them surely gives evidence of Colette's early triumph over
herself, for she later admitted to Father Pierre that these childish
amusements "filled me with ennui." Before she was ten, the little
girl had learned and was practising the selfless detachment from
spiritual indulgence which can be the last outpost of renunciation
for many a middle-aged religious.

Sister Perrine writes of how "our glorious Mother, Sister Colette,
told me that she desired to live in the desert like St. John the Bap-
tist." Guileless Perrine explains to us that this excellent desire could
not be carried out because, unfortunately, "she was not a man." The
lanes of Corbie were the little girl's "desert"—surely a more burning
one for such a child than lonely stretches of sand and stars.

We have Colette's own words to Perrine that from the time she was seven years old she "meditated for at least one hour each day." And we know that Robert Boellet had testified to his faith in his daughter's extraordinary spirituality by building her a small oratory of her own. On the other hand, there is only tradition to support the stories of Colette's having been favored with infused knowledge of Spanish, Italian, German and Latin when she was nine. The tradition, however, is a strong one. And what is certain is that this child who never studied that ancient tongue later wrote Constitutions for the nuns of St. Clare in flawless, scholarly Latin. We shall also find Colette berating bandits in Heidelberg in such perfect German that they "were confounded." And we have Father Pierre de Vaux's calm assurance that "the Mother knew *all* languages"! When this knowledge was infused, he does not tell us, but he does say that she had it "like the glorious apostles," which may mean that she could speak any language as needed but did not have a permanent gift of tongues in the sense that the knowledge was abiding.

Yet, whether already at the age of nine or only later in her life, Colette was certainly a distinguished linguist on occasion. And her general knowledge astounded everyone from her confessor, Father Jean Guyot, to the simple townspeople. Her two closest friends from her early childhood were Jacquette Legrande and Guillemette Chrétien, children of the Boellets' neighbors and girls several years older than she. Both accepted their little friend as a teacher, a fact remarkable enough at an age when children are given to exhibiting a fierce superiority over those two or three years their juniors.

Colette's formal education was only the meager affair thought necessary for daughters of the lower middle-class of that century. A carpenter's daughter needed to know how to turn a fine seam, how to be thrifty in managing her kitchen, how to knit and spin, and little else. She learned to read and write and was also perhaps given some basic arithmetic, broad history and geography. Yet the child was learned, with knowledge "not given her by men." Little Mlle. Boellet with so much science in her pretty head was obviously God's instrument. But instrument for what? At sixty-nine, Margaret must have wondered what her own part in it all was to be and thought ruefully that God had better be quick in revealing it. And Robert? A man in his seventies is looking toward eternity. What of his daughter, already a woman in soul and mind, but still so much a child in her small, frail body? Then, when she was nine, according to her own testimony, a true Pentecostal wind swept across the mind of Colette Boellet.

With terrible and painstaking clarity, the history, spirit, and present state of the great Franciscan Order founded in the thirteenth century by St. Francis of Assisi was revealed to the little girl. Here was God's first intimation of His plans for this child of destiny; but as for her parents, the new knowledge infused into the fertile mind of their daughter could only have puzzled them the more. To Colette, it was overwhelming as no other of her preternatural gifts had been. She understood in an immense flash of knowledge the ideals of St. Francis and St. Clare when they founded their Orders of mendicant friars and contemplative nuns. And she understood what human weakness had made of those ideals in the less than two centuries that had elapsed since the saints' deaths. A French child's natural love of beauty and quick response to a spiritual ideal would reach out for the loveliness of the vision. It would revolt as quickly from the ruins of the Franciscan ideal. There is a tragic overtone in Colette's comment, recorded by Sister Perrine, after she had had quite sufficient natural evidence of the ruins.

"Many times," writes Perrine, "I have heard her say to her nuns: 'I tell you, my Sisters, that our Lord provided that such a great understanding of the religious Order of Sir St. Francis was given me when I was nine years old that it equalled the understanding I have at forty.' So I heard her say it many times." Why would Colette, always a woman of few words, have repeated it "many times," except that both the vision and the anguish it had caused her were continually being verified and renewed by practical experience? Colette had gone far beyond the confines of mere precocity when a nine she carried in her heart the burden of fifteenth-century Franciscanism.

3   *The Franciscan Order: Vision and Reality*

In his meager life span of forty-four years, St. Francis of Assisi had used the grace of God to transform society. To the luxury-loving early thirteenth century he preached the beauties of utter evangelical poverty; and all over Italy, men and women listened and followed him. Despising his own early dreams of military glory, Francis had elected to answer the strange summons of God in his soul. When he did, he found himself the guide and mentor of an increasingly large company. By the time of his death in 1226, he was the father of more than five thousand friars minor, or "lesser brothers," as he chose so charmingly to call his sons.

Europe was stale with war and pinched with avarice when the spirit of this little man of unimposing appearance blew across it like the breath of a long-forgotten spring. To men who had never known anything but wars and hatred between nations and towns and families, Francis talked of peace. "May the Lord give you peace" was his greeting to all who were fortunate enough to cross his path. There was something of God's own courtesy in the gentle benediction. Men listened and marveled. To an age of fierce coveting of lands, revenues, and church benefices, of child-cardinals and carnal-minded clergy, of ambition and distrust, came St. Francis who coveted nothing but men's souls; who loved the things of earth, even the savage beasts, with the utterly pure and detached love of those who live completely by the spirit; who begged as a favor to be considered the last and least of all men; whose love and trust reached out even to those most treacherous of men, the professedly religious who work out odious plans for their own advancement behind a screen of uprightness and respectability.

Francis upset the whole age. It became altogether too awkward to declare the Gospel out of date when this little barefoot man was living it with such obvious joy. And it was very difficult for those who took alarm at Francis' preaching of poverty and fraternal love and humility to find grounds for censuring him. How could they blame a man who wanted nothing! How could they punish him for wishing good to all other men? Had the frustrated pharisees of the thirteenth century known the colloquialisms of the twentieth, they would have complained that they could not get a handle on Francis. Worst of all, the more shabbily they treated him, the better he seemed to like them!

And so the strange message uttered by Francis began growing steadily in volume. Soon not only his native Assisi but scores of other towns were echoing the tremendous battle-cry of his war for souls: "Pax et bonum!" And, as is inevitable in the life of a very great man, a great woman caught his message and echoed it. In the life of St. Francis the woman was St. Clare. So perfectly did the soul of Clare fathom the vocation of Francis that even secular history has welded their names together.

As quickly as good men rallied to the side of St. Francis came the generous-hearted girls and women to the cloister of St. Clare. Together, the two Orders worked at the reform of society, the friars in the marketplace, the nuns on their knees. And the secret of their vast power over society was that both were true reformers in the original meaning of that beautiful and long-suffering word.

There had been many men before the time of Francis who deplored the relaxed state of religion. These were the self-appointed repairers of the Church. They called themselves reformers, but actually they were intensely dedicated deformers. Reviling and abusing men for their sins, they sought to deform the loveliness of the Gospel into harsh lines of their own rigorism. There was no room for Christ's compassion in their "gospel." They came to preach no "good news," but the very bad news of arrogance, and a pride which would recognize no authority that reproached it. When sinful men heard them, they became more sinful still, proving anew the ancient and awful truth that men will always live down to expectation. Told they were utterly sinful, their zeal to prove it was whetted. It seemed to become boundless.

Men were accustomed to coping with these "reformers" who told them how evil they were; but here was Francis, telling them how good they were! Here was a poor and humble man who blamed nobody for anything, but preached with a shining face of the love of God for all men, of the beauties of His creation, of the anguish of His redeeming Passion, of the joy of serving such a God. The little saint of Assisi never called himself a reformer, for the simple reason that he was one. He taught men in the gentle school of love how to form their lives over again out of the lines of hatred and avarice into the Gospel designs of love and mercy. Thus he was the true reformer, superimposing on the teaching of Christ nothing new, seeking only to restore and to form again the plan of life the God-Man had taught. While the deformers of religion were fiercely shouting: "Reform!", Francis was singing: "I am the herald of the great King!" That is how he happened to reform so many in so short a time.

But in the very size of Francis' and Clare's following was the seed of its destruction. The ever-increasing battalion of Francis' warriors of love was a motley group indeed. There were the polished men of wealth and standing like Bernard di Quintavalle, the learned and scholarly like Peter di Catanii. Beside them walked men such as Brother Giles, the unlettered farmer of the caustic wit, and that gentle priest, Leo, Francis' secretary and confidant whom he called "the little sheep of God." There was Brother John, that delightful man dubbed "the Simple" because of the singular way he chose to attain perfection: whatever Francis did, John did. This imitation included not only acts of virtue, but walking or sitting—and, as some not so favorably disposed toward John insist, sneezing. (But by the fine irony of God, this simple brother whom so many thought a fool could later be held up as a model of wisdom for those really hopelessly foolish ones who called themselves the sons of St. Francis while electing to imitate him in nothing.) There were men renowned in the wars like that grand old knight, Angelo Tancredi, and capable men of affairs like handsome Brother Masseo. All these men, in character so different and from backgrounds so utterly diverse, caught the flame of Francis' preaching and cherished the Franciscan ideal to the end.

Unfortunately, there were others who were only dazzled by the personality of Francis or caught on an upsurge of emotion by his preaching. Like the thorny ground of the Gospel parable which enfolded the seed only to choke its growth in the end, these men took the words of St. Francis into hearts from which they were soon crowded out by the clutter of worldly cares. One is tempted to wish St. Francis' words might have fallen by the wayside instead of into the thorny hearts of men incapable of living by his ideals.

Then, too, Francis' own credulousness led to the final sorrow of that day when the spectacle of so many sons faithless to his ideals of poverty and penance dragged from the saint's soul that terrible indictment: "Too many friars minor! Would that the world might marvel at their fewness!" St. Francis was no fool. In a sense, he knew men through and through. He knew who could stand hard testing, who could be pruned by trial to bring forth still richer fruits of virtue, and who must be led more tenderly in their weakness of soul. But, in another sense, Francis did not know men, because his own abysmal humility convinced him that all other men were not only as good as himself but far better. To conceive of himself as a man set apart from other men by reason of his gifts of soul and mind would have made Francis laugh with delight as over a piece of sheer nonsense. To walk barefoot in the cold, to feast on crusts and scraps, to consider being maltreated and abused as "perfect joy," to take the Gospel so literally that he needed no other rule of life, were things natural enough to a saint of the spiritual proportions of Francis of Assisi. He never considered that he was doing anything unusual, much less heroic.

St. Francis had also a boundless faith in the goodness of men. In very many cases, this faith did actually move mountains of pride and ambition and hatred in the hearts of those who heard him speak. In others, it did not. Even during the lifetime of the saint, the Franciscan ideal suffered some rough handling by certain of his comfort-loving and ambitious sons. After the first golden years, the Order passed into a period when those who cherished the primitive Rule of St. Francis and burned to keep it always "without gloss" had to wrestle with those who strove to establish a Franciscanism diminished by mitigations and privileges.

Yet this is not to say that all those who opposed a literal observance of St. Francis' plan of life were evil men. Some obviously were; others were merely those whom most persons would be apt to describe as prudent men. There was much to be said in support of their contention that such simplicity, such guileless faith, such an utterly spiritual way of life were wholly impracticable for the rank and file of friars. And the Popes very often agreed with them, granting dispensations from poverty and sanctioning many mitigations from the primitive Rule. Too, as the Order grew so prodigiously, the direct personal influence of St. Francis was necessarily weakened, and often entirely removed. Toward the end of Francis' life, hundreds of his friars had never even seen their father and founder. Without the personal contact that had enlivened the zeal of his earlier followers, these friars were easy prey for the arguments of the mitigants, whether specious or sincere. The Franciscan Order in its beginnings was not so much a foundation as a flame. And the flame was Francis. With the passing years, there were all too many in the Order who had never been happily set on fire by him.

This deepening division within the Franciscan Order was not equally apparent to the world among the cloistered daughters of Clare, but it was just as real. And perhaps it was all the more insidious for being shrouded in the obscurity of the enclosure. There was open contention among the friars. Among the nuns, there was only a gradual, quiet relaxing of discipline in many monasteries. Poverty became too burdensome; and annual revenues and property settlements began taking the place of the ideals of St. Clare who wished her nuns to live solely by the work of their own hands and on alms, "as pilgrims and strangers in this world." The lyric poverty of the first monastery of San Damiano never diminished in purity. Indeed, it was to San Damiano that Francis and, after his death, his faithful sons turned to comfort their souls and refresh their spirits. But it was not so in other places.

In 1250, three years before the death of St. Clare, the sister of St. Louis the King of France, Princess Isabella, founded a Poor Clare monastery at Longchamps. Isabella wanted to attract vocations from among the nobility of the French court, and she certainly succeeded. Nearly all the nuns of the numerous community at Longchamps were aristocrats. It was thought imprudent to expect these delicately reared and fragile young ladies to live the life of utter poverty and austerity ordained by St. Clare, although the foundress herself had had no such scruples about the duchesses who dwelt at

San Damiano in just such poverty and penance, or about the beautiful daughter of the King of Bohemia whose hand had been sought
in marriage by the Emperor Frederick but who was to go down in
history not as Empress Agnes but as Blessed Agnes, Poor Clare nun.

When Isabella established her monastery at Longchamps, St.
Bonaventure was the general of the Franciscan Order. He sanctioned the mitigations of the primitive Rule which Isabella sought,
not only on the score of poverty and austerity of life, but for
enclosure, too. Isabella herself did not scruple to leave the enclosure
whenever she judged that her excursions might benefit the monastery. And she had lay attendants within the enclosure. Longchamps
was a far cry from the first monastery of Poor Clares in France
founded in 1220, only eight years after St. Clare herself had made
profession of the Franciscan Rule and begun living it with her sister,
Agnes, in the crude little dwelling in San Damiano. At the invitation
of the Archbishop of Rheims, this little group of nuns led by Sister
Marie de Braye made its laborious way from Assisi to Rheims and
joyously set up monastic life in a huddle of small huts on the bank
of the Vesle. Marie de Braye had carried a cord of St. Clare in her
hands on this journey of poverty and love. Better still, she had
carried in her heart the seraphic ideals of the first daughter of St.
Francis.

Still, the monastery at Longchamps had, and deservedly, a reputation for piety and regularity. If the daughter of the King of
Bohemia became Blessed Agnes, we must not forget that the sister
of King St. Louis of France likewise became Blessed Isabella. Her
frequent trips out of the cloister were made for what she must surely
have considered "a reasonable, manifest, and approved cause," as
laid down in the Rule, and undoubtedly with the permission of higher
superiors. Having lay attendants within the enclosure is less easy to
explain; yet the integrity and personal holiness of the abbess whom
Holy Church has exalted forever as Blessed Isabella are certainly
beyond question. The fact that one of St. Francis' most illustrious
sons, himself a saint, thought it well to grant so many dispensations
to the nuns of the Second Order is in itself a résumé of the whole
unhappy situation.

As among the friars there were those who were undoubtedly moti-
vated by high ideals of their own in their efforts to modify the primi-

tive Rule of St. Francis, so there were many nuns of the Second Order who sincerely wished to embrace the way of life of St. Clare but who found her primitive Rule beyond their powers. For these, there were eventually to come into being the branches of the Order known as the Friars Minor Conventual and the Urbanist Poor Clares. They were earnest and devoted followers of St. Francis and Clare, and both groups have borne witness to their sincerity and holiness in the saints and blesseds they have given the Church. Apart from these, and in increasingly large numbers, were those who sought not only a modified but a relaxed form of Franciscanism. These were the "sons" whom the gentle St. Francis had cursed during his lifetime. These were the "daughters" over whom St. Clare wept.

By 1264, with St. Clare dead for only eleven years and already canonized for nine, Pope Urban IV granted St. Bonaventure's request that uniformity be established among all the Poor Clares. The papal reply was in the form of an entirely new Rule, embodying all the mitigations granted to Longchamps and a number of other monasteries. The Pope acted in all good faith and with the very best intentions, as undoubtedly St. Bonaventure did also. What they proposed became known as the Urbanist Rule alluded to above, and many monasteries accepted it, acceding to the wishes of the Franciscan General and the Pope. It still flourishes today in vigor and holiness as a separate branch of the Second Order and an embellishment of the Franciscan family. However, as also among the friars, there remained among the nuns many others who held fast to the first ideals of the Order. They clung tenaciously to the primitive Rule. To these was extended the "privilege of poverty" given by Pope Innocent IV to the first Poor Clare nuns of St. Clare's monastery. St. Francis had always considered it an inestimable privilege to imitate the poverty of Jesus Christ, but the term now acquired a new poignancy and even a certain irony.

In 1390, when God showed nine-year-old Colette Boellet in a panoramic sweep both the foundations of the Franciscan Order and its decline, the era of mitigation and relaxation was at its height. It was not the sincere Urbanists over whom she mourned, but the supposed "primitive Poor Clares" attached to the Queen of Portugal and living in her palace; certain Poor Clare abbesses vying with the rich abbesses of other non-mendicant Orders in making a display of pomp and dignity, and succeeding (or failing, according to the personal views of the onlooker) magnificently; Spanish Poor Clares with Moorish slaves in their service, and the words of St. Clare about "the grace of working" well forgotten.

Others of St. Clare's impassioned pleas to her daughters, words written into her Rule, likewise fell on deaf ears. "Let the Sisters be most sedulously on their guard lest they be seen by those who enter." Some monasteries now had "permanent visitors." "The abbess is bound to assign to each her manual labor, and this at the Chapter in the presence of all," St. Clare had written. But manual labor was too much to ask of great and delicate ladies. Most heartbreaking of all was the contrast of actual living to these words of the saint in the eighth chapter of her Rule: "The Sisters shall not appropriate anything to themselves, neither a house nor a place nor anything; and as strangers and pilgrims in this world, serving the Lord in poverty and humility, let them send for alms with confidence. Nor ought they to be ashamed of so doing, since the Lord made Himself poor in this world for our sake. This is the height of that most exalted poverty which has made you, my dearest Sisters, heiresses and queens of the heavenly kingdom, which has rendered you poor in things but enriched you with virtues. . . . To it, dearest Sisters, cleave with all your might, never wishing to possess anything else under heaven." But there were a considerable number of things which many of the highborn Poor Clares wished to possess under heaven besides poverty. They preferred to resemble heiresses and queens in a more ponderable fashion.

Great leaders were rising up among the friars at this time, though, who defended the primitive Rule with a burning eloquence and, better, with the purity of their own primitive Franciscan lives. St. John Capistran and St. Bernardine of Siena were reinvigorating Italy with the flame of their father St. Francis, and St. Catherine of Bologna was a living embodiment of the Franciscan spirit among the Italian Poor Clares. France had as yet no notable leader. And who would have looked for one on the Rue de la Chaulcie where a carpenter's daughter watched the squadrons of black crows ("les corbeaux" from which it is thought the town of Corbie took its name) flying over her home, filled her days with small, trivial tasks of domesticity, and trotted off to school quite obscured in the company of the other nine-year-olds of Corbie?

Surely none of the small girls who whispered their confidences into Colette's ears after school, nor the fortunate poor ones who were given her lunch when no one was looking on to espy her charity, guessed what confidences of heaven had been reposed in the heart of their little friend and benefactress. Even Guillemette Chrétien and Jacquette Legrande, Colette's closest friends, knew nothing of this supernatural intervention in her life. Quietly and mysteriously, the pieces of God's mosaic of Colette's future were being set into place. Fitted to her vision of affairs in the Franciscan Order was the love for the Divine Office which was steadily growing in the child's soul. Father Pierre de Vaux tells us how Colette from her childhood had loved "the psalms and the litanies" with a great love. Her famous Matins skirmish tells us, too.

It was a common practice among the more pious people of Corbie to assist at the night Office as well as at the daytime services in the abbey church. In their old age, Margaret and Robert Boellet still went occasionally to this Office, called Matins by reason of its being sung at the first breath of the new morning. Sometimes they let themselves be wheedled into taking Colette with them; and once she had established this privilege, their daughter could not bear to forego it for a single night. She marshalled all her arguments with the vigor of a general organizing his forces for battle or a lawyer presenting his brief; and evidently the Boellets could not resist her indefatigable logic, for they both capitulated. Colette went happily along to the midnight sacrifice of praise at the abbey each night.

All went well enough for some weeks, but then certain neighbors of the Boellets began clicking their tongues. Whoever heard of a twelve-year-old girl getting up every night and attending Offices long enough to exhaust a strong man! No wonder she was so undersized. Tsk! What kind of parents were Margaret and Robert Boellet? But that is the way old people will do, indulge every foolish whim of a child. Well, they would pay for their folly.

The Boellets could not resist this verbal persecution long. The day came when Robert forbade Colette to attend the night Offices. However, he did not consider it sufficient to make this solemn withdrawal of the permission. He took the precaution of moving Colette

into a different bedroom on the second floor of the house. From
there, she could not leave the house at night without waking her
parents. Evidently, M. Boellet had fears that his strong-minded child
might find it convenient to forget obedience in her zeal for what
seemed more perfect to her.

Among the Boellets' closest friends was an old man named Adam
Mannier. He had for Colette not only the tender, indulgent affection
which most people in Corbie felt for the child but also a deep sense
of reverence for what he felt sure were God's extraordinary graces
in her soul. So convinced was Mannier that Colette, being so obviously superior to ordinary children of her age, could not be judged
and treated by ordinary parental standards, that he coolly took it
upon himself to see that the little girl realized the desire her parents
had refused.

When Margaret and Robert were safely and soundly sleeping, the
old man would steady a ladder against the side of the Boellet home
just under the window of Colette's room on the second floor. Colette
would hurry to the window, manoeuvre her small person through it,
and scramble down the ladder, to be carried off triumphantly on
Mannier's shoulders through his own house next door, set down on
his front doorstep, and given his blessing on her midnight journey
to the abbey.

This episode in Colette's childhood need not cause embarrassment to any except those who will not tolerate any exhibition of
fallen humanity in a heroine. Only a woman of iron will could have
kept the faith to pray that her barrenness might be ended in her
sixtieth year. Colette was Margaret's daughter. We do the saints
no service by pretending that their sanctity was full-blown at their
first cry after birth. It is a very natural thing that a precocious, strong-
willed child should also occasionally be wilful; and Colette simply
forgot for a time that obedience is the greatest sacrifice when she
was under fire of that most subtle temptation, which is the lure of
the forbidden good.

Of course, Margaret and Robert heard of their daughter's esca-
pades; but this time they did not remonstrate. When the gossips of
Corbie began again to dispense their free advice and criticism, the
Boellets remained unperturbed and smiling. The fact is, old Mannier
had evidently suffered some qualms of conscience over his high-

handed action. He came to his friend and laid before Robert a case for Colette so convincing that her father could not fail to be moved. Adam grew eloquent in his defense of the little girl as a child of grace, chosen and guided by God. He reminded his neighbor that her preternatural gifts were obviously part of a large and mysterious design they would understand later and that this child of predilection could not be judged by common norms. Robert talked the matter over with Margaret, and no further objection was ever made to Colette's attending the night Office at the abbey church. Father Pierre writes that after this M. Boellet had only one answer for busybodies of Corbie who "did not know the difference between the will of God and the instigations of the devil." "I am certain that our child will do only what is good and right" was the reply Colette said her father repeated "many times," which indicates the perseverance of the cavillers.

Although the early biographers make no mention of it, it is difficult to suppose that Colette herself did not quickly repent of her wilfulness and throw herself into the arms of her parents with contrite tears. Nothing so swiftly loses its savor as the forbidden good illicitly seized. Perhaps Colette weighed the burden of being freely given the privilege she had commandeered against the burden of her self-imposed penances and learned even then that the tender blows of mercy can fall much harder than the rough swing of the discipline. At twelve, Colette was prepared to compare the two. She had already developed a thirst for practices of asceticism usually reserved to those three or four times her age. And in this realm of the spiritual, her parents seem never to have raised objections.

In later years, the saint told Father Pierre de Vaux of some of her penitential practices as a child. He describes them as mortifications "according to her little capacity," though they appear to us sufficient to indicate a quite impressive capacity for a delicate girl just entering her teens. She slept on a mat of straw instead of her comfortable feather bed. She wore a small iron chain around her waist. She ate very sparingly and gave to the poor with a free hand the sweets and delicacies so irresistible to most small girls. Chesterton says that St. Francis devoured fasting with as much gusto as other men might devour food. Colette was already St. Francis' true daughter. Her intuitions of the doctrine of the Mystical Body of

Christ were already so sharp as to give her a real delight in filling up in herself what was lacking in the dissolute and the carnal.

It would not have needed parents as devout and perspicacious as Margaret and Robert Boellet to recognize that these penances were inspired by God and not by caprice or pride. Their child-ascetic was as far removed from being a sadist or an exhibitionist as the truth is removed from the lie. She performed her mortifications as well as her acts of charity with a joyousness and a delicacy that themselves gave proof of the Spirit which guided her. The man who sets his jaw and goes shouldering his way through penances is a man who does not even suspect the real meaning of penance. Colette Boellet did more than suspect it, even at twelve.

Imprisoned in our ease and fettered by our poor little comforts, we are strangely drawn to the saints luxuriating in the freedom of their mortifications and singing in their penances. When St. Francis was disowned by his earthly father as a madman, he sang out: "Our Father, who art in heaven!" with the breathless joy of one suddenly making a great discovery. When he sat down to a banquet of broken crusts spread on a flat stone by a running stream, he launched into such enthusiastic praises of the repast provided by a good God that disgruntled Brother Masseo could not resist the contagion of his joy. Those who expect nothing are always being happily surprised at the bounty of anything. And Colette Boellet was so joyous in her mortifications because she was a child-ascetic attached to God and not to asceticism.

Colette's young body seems to have bent easily to God's inspirations. With her opinions, it was sometimes a different matter! Chastity attracted her as forcibly as carnality might draw another. But she was not content with espousing chastity for herself; she had a great and mistaken zeal for promoting it in others to a degree God had not inspired. She told Father Pierre how she once went so far as to take her mother to task for having married a second time. Perhaps her giving him the text of this amazing conversation so precisely indicates how often she later repented of reproaching her aged mother.

"I said to her," Colette recalled many years later: " 'I would like it much better if you had married only once.' My mother replied: 'Child, you would not be if I had not remarried'; and I said: 'Well,

God is all-powerful, and He could easily have made me to be the daughter of one of our neighbors who had married only once.'" Whether this exchange ended with Margaret's administering to Colette a few well-deserved spanks on her starched petticoats has not been recorded.

4 *Colette's Youth*

Colette's spiritual and mental growth continued apace. Not so her physical development. At fourteen she was no bigger than a normal child of nine, and her parents began to be genuinely anxious. Margaret was seventy-four now, and Robert looking towards eighty. They knew the day could scarcely be far off when they would have to leave their daughter alone in the world to fend for herself. How could such a tiny girl ever hope to make her way in a world of action and power? Even the meager physical gains of her early years seemed now to have stopped completely. It appeared that Colette would remain a dwarf of a woman. But while her parents fretted and prayed over her small stature, Colette herself remained unconcerned. Height was the last matter that could have troubled her mind, and she seemed as unconscious of her low stature as she was of the beauty of her face. Then one day she overheard her father expressing to her mother his distress at having so stunted a child. "How will she ever be able to take over the work of the household?" Dumbfounded for a moment by this revelation, Colette quickly rallied her forces. Her small stature embarrassed and distressed her parents? Very well, then, something mut be done about it. With characteristic energy Colette set out to do it.

It was an easy matter to get permission to make a pilgrimage to the church of Notre Dame de Brebières. It was a favorite haven for the

devotion of the people of Corbie and environs, and some close friends
or neighbors of the Boellets could always be found in the groups of
pilgrims. The lovely church housed a very ancient wooden statue
of the Blessed Virgin holding the Child Jesus, with a sheep frisking
at her feet. This delightful carving (destroyed along with the whole
church in World War I) had been discovered long before Colette's
birth by an old shepherd grazing his flocks on the pasture land of
Brebières. When it was brought into the town of Encre (later
renamed Albert in honor of the Marquis of Albert, Duke of Luynes,
to whom King Louis XIV had presented the place), the statue was
venerated as miraculous. Miracles did seem to blossom around it,
and eventually the great church of Notre Dame de Brebières was
built to house it.

Colette walked the ten miles from Corbie to Encre in the spring
of 1395 with a number of other pilgrims, each intent on some favor
he hoped to obtain through the kind maternal offices of Notre Dame
de Brebières. It is safe to wager, however, that Colette was the only
one in the party who hoped to return to Corbie taller than when she
left it. Arrived at Encre, she entered the church, made her way to
the altar, and (as she told Father Pierre) addressed our Lord without preamble: "Lord, do You wish me always to remain so small?"

The businesslike faith of this prayer and the guileless reproof it
implied would be calculated to move a far less tender heart than
the divine. Having stated the troublesome matter on the agenda
with such naive directness, Colette went on to enlarge her prayer
with charming trust. "Lord, if it is for Your glory and my salvation
that I remain always so small, it is all right with me, for I prefer that
You make me tall in paradise instead of in this world if my body
should be the occasion of offending You. But if it should please
You, safeguarding these two matters, to give pleasure to my father
by making this little body of mine grow, may Your will be accomplished in me and on me." Colette looked up into the ancient carved
face of the Madonna, at the Holy Child snuggled against her, at
the sheep frolicking before them. "Amen," she added with all the
finality of faith. With the same faith, she stood up. She was taller by
several inches. She must have observed it at once, either by the embarrassing shortness of her skirt or by discovering a changed eye-
level when she rose to thank our Lady and the Child Jesus, for

she was very definite about her increase in height when she described this incident to Father Pierre de Vaux many years later and gave him the text of her prayer. "I returned taller than I went," she said.

Her changed stature naturally caused a furor among the other pilgrims when the party gathered for the long walk home. When she arrived back in Corbie, it set the whole town buzzing. Within a year and some months, Colette's height reached its full measure of five feet, six inches, which is considerable for a French girl. Margaret and Robert were jubilant and more than ever awestruck by the wonders of grace in their child. The miracle is perpetuated at Brebières in a reliquary which shows a small girl kneeling before the famous statue of the Virgin and the Child. Even the sheep is there. And below the little girl's figure is inscribed the name "Colette."

The sudden practical realization of her small stature that her father's words had given her some months earlier was now followed by another distressing revelation. Colette was unexpectedly brought to a most unhappy realization of her beauty by the amorous whisperings of a young man, and this in the church while she was at prayer. She wheeled on him with a volley of reproaches, and her unfortunate admirer began shamefacedly to retreat. His escape, however, was not to be so easy. Although the doors of the church stood wide open, the would-be cavalier could not pass outside. He felt himself gripped in an invisible vise when he attempted to go out. Terrified, he returned to Colette's side and begged her pardon for his overtures. At her word of forgiveness, he was released from the unseen hold and fled from the church. One can suppose his enthusiasm for a lovely face was considerably dampened after this.

The matter ended Colette's abstraction from her beauty. Aware now that her loveliness might be an occasion of trouble for others, she returned to God with a second prayer about her appearance, one we may safely wager the Almighty rarely hears from a girl of sixteen. "Take away the beauty of my face, O Lord, lest it should cause You to be offended." Colette prayed with all the earnestness of her soul, sure that this request needed no restrictive clauses. However, God answered the plea with only a compromise. The bloom of her exquisite complexion faded, leaving her face austerely pale; but the lovely carven features remained the same. Sister Perrine writes that after this prayer Colette's "face, hands, and body became of a dull white color, and remained thus all her life." And Father Pierre de Vaux describes her as "very beautiful and pleasing both in face and figure . . . but of heavenly rather than earthly appearance."

A woman now in appearance as well as in intellect, Colette began to exhibit the remarkable eloquence which she kept all her life and before which formidable nobles and disapproving churchmen were to go down in defeat. Jacquette Legrande and Guillemette Chrétien had become her inseparable companions, loving nothing so much as to sit with her in the broad flowering fields of Corbie, hearing her tell of the mysteries of our Lord's life and Passion in the moving words of an eyewitness of those events. Marie Sénéchal, another neighbor, soon joined them. Then others came, and still others, until Colette had a very considerable audience. Older women joined the young girls, and before long news of this unusual preaching reached the ears of the Bishop of Amiens. "She begged everyone to love God," the old biographies tell us. And how characteristic of St. Francis is that phrase! No haranguing, no dramatic flights of fancy, no fierce reproofs. Only a sixteen-year-old girl begging everyone to love God, who is so good and lovable.

Her hearers were fascinated, and very many of them responded to her simple appeal by loving God to the extent of bettering their daily lives considerably. The bishop sent the curé of Colette's parish church, Father Jean Guyot, to sit in on these quaint gatherings. The curé went a number of times. He listened, observed, and concluded. His final conclusions to the Bishop of Amiens were that the young girl's learning was prodigious, her prudence and zeal praiseworthy in every respect. Father Guyot offered his own support to her without reserve.

Many of the later biographers insist that there was a great deal of protest from the neighboring clergy over Colette's preaching and that the Bishop of Amiens, although convinced of her sanctity and her genius, ordered her to cease her impromptu discourses. However, neither Pierre de Vaux nor Sister Perrine makes any mention of such a prohibition. Colette did greatly curtail, if not entirely stop, her preaching when she was seventeen, but probably only because this was the year of Margaret Boellet's death and the young girl now had the full care of a father past eighty.

As so often happens in the case of an aged couple who have preserved the first bloom of their love even on the warmth of its full ripening, Robert Boellet's life was, in a sense, already ended with the death of his wife. For years past, M. Boellet had been known as a master at peacemaking. The stubbornest wranglers could not long resist his gentle overtures. He was frequently called in to settle intimate family disputes as well as public quarrels. Even when not invited to arbitrate, he often went into the thick of domestic battles.

Father Pierre de Vaux has given us Colette's own description of her peace-loving father. "He was," the saint said, "a very sweet person, pleasant and amiable, to whom God had given the grace to pacify others and [especially] those who were in [a state of] division and discord." She added that "he used this grace very diligently, and worked and labored until he had left them in good peace." Peace was indeed "good" to Boellet, and now his patriarchal figure moved through the streets of Corbie like an angel of peace. Colette, always at his side with a firm young hand under his elbow, received an enviable education in the art of peacemaking. Years later it was to be said of her that she brought the peace and joy of God wherever she went.

They must have been a charming pair, the white-haired old carpenter with the gentle eyes and persuasive manner, and the girl whose pale beauty so far eclipsed the blooming prettiness of her childhood. Together, Boellet and his daughter made their trips to his house of refuge where the poor women struggling to lay firm hold on a new life received them with something of the awe due to heavenly visitants. Colette moved among them as an equal, smiling and loving, quite unmindful of any line of demarcation between herself and them. She told Father Pierre she was accustomed to visit these fallen women from the time she was fifteen. It is comment enough on the kind of training the Boellets considered suitable for their daughter.

Sometimes the two walked slowly together to the abbey for Vespers, and the squadrons of black crows flying above them would turn Robert's mind and conversation to the dark days that had come upon France and the Church. Little detailed news of the glittering world of Avignon or the tottering world of Rome reached Corbie,

but travellers brought piecemeal despatches of national and ecclesiastical affairs in both places. The despatches were increasingly
ominous.

The year before Colette's birth, 1380, had been a most unhappy
one for France. It robbed her of her king, Charles V, and one of her
noblest medieval warriors, Bertrand de Guesclin. During the half
century following Bertrand's death, his repeated exhortation to his
men at arms, "never to forget that in whatever country they might
be making war, churchmen, women, children, and the poor people
were not their enemies," was well forgotten in the devastating civil
wars that came upon the very heels of Charles VI's succession to the
throne at the age of twelve. While still very young, Charles married
the infamous Isabeau of Bavaria, scourge enough for any kingdom;
and shortly after this unfortunate marriage, the young king met with
two tragic accidents in succession, which left him mentally deranged.

The king's four uncles, among them the formidable Duke of
Burgundy, battled desperately to wrest the power from Charles; but
the favor of Isabeau rested on her brother-in-law, Louis, Duke of
Orleans. The irresponsible Charles was prevailed upon by his queen
to deliver a virtual regency to Louis. Alarmed and infuriated, the
king's counsellors forced him to recall this concession from the Duke
of Orleans and give it into the hands of the Duke of Burgundy. From
that day, the two powerful dukes were bitterest enemies; and the
situation became even more acute when the death of the Duke of
Burgundy left his royal claims and vast possessions to a son greedier
for power and fiercer in battle than himself. This was John the Fearless, who was to figure so largely in Colette's later life. One of the
early acts of John's admirers after the old duke's death was to
strengthen his heir's claims by the simple expedient of murdering
Louis, Duke of Orleans.

That might have been that, and John's rise to the heights of power
in France swift and sure, except for the fact that Louis's heir accomplished the master stroke of marrying the daughter of the most
capable as well as the most ambitious man in southern France, the
Count d'Armagnac. With d'Armagnac's espousal of the Orleanist
claims to the throne, the fierce war between Orleanists and Burgundians reached heights of almost incredible cruelty, and devastated
France. As if this were not enough, the legitimate heir to the throne,

the eldest son of the ill-fated Charles and the scheming Isabeau, grew old enough to assert his own just claims to the throne. The heir was the weak and wretched dauphin whose claims were to be upheld and vindicated by St. Jeanne d'Arc at the price of her own martyrdom in 1431.

Corbie could not have failed to suffer some repercussions of the appalling state of national affairs that was steadily worsening during Colette's adolescence. Robert's peace-loving heart must have quailed before the vision which the France of 1399 augured for the future, but he could only urge his daughter to renewed prayer and increased sacrifices for the salvation of her country.

Yet far worse than all this, because it struck directly at the heart of the Church, was the state of the papacy during Colette's youth. The fact that the popes had been absent from Rome during a great part of the fourteenth century, residing instead at Avignon with their independent powers steadily decreasing under pressure of the French thumb, had thrown the whole Catholic world into a state of agitation and discontent. Three years before Colette's birth, St. Catherine of Siena had finally prevailed upon the French pope, Gregory XI, to return to Rome: but her hard-won victory was short-lived. Pope Gregory found nothing but disorder and turmoil in Rome. Before long, he fell sick and died. And out of the conclave of cardinals which met to elect his successor was born the terrible Western Schism, which rent Christendom for half a century.

Outside the Vatican, the Romans were demanding a Roman pope —or, at the very least, an Italian—and demanding him with threats well calculated to strike terror into the hearts of the sixteen assembled cardinals. There seemed among them no Italian cardinal worthy of the papal honor; but the frightened electors seized upon the secretary of the late pope, the Archbishop of Bari, Bartolommeo Prignano. Although he had never worn a cardinal's hat, Archbishop Prignano was given the papal tiara; and henceforth he was known as Urban VI. He was a prelate of blameless life, given to personal austerities and respected for his piety. The Romans seemed satisfied. The cardinals breathed easily again. But not for long. It did not take Pope Urban VI much time to unsettle the hopes of the people. He launched at once into a program of fierce and violent reform which won him the fear of all and the hatred of many. "Accomplish your task with moderation," implored an anguished St. Catherine of Siena. "For the love of Christ crucified, curb these sudden impulses prompted by your nature." But Urban would not listen.

Before long, the French cardinals seceded in a body from their allegiance to the new pope, justifying their action on the grounds that his election was invalid because of the conclave's being intimidated by the Roman mob. Without further ado, they elected a new pope, Cardinal Count Robert of Geneva, a man better known for ruthless militarism than for sanctity, but of powerful royal connections. He chose the title of Clement VII, an oddly ironic name for one who had never been noted for clemency.

Colette Boellet was eight years old when Pope Urban died, breathing out his threats and his violence to the end. The small group of loyal cardinals elected Pietro Tomacelli, a man who seemed to possess no outstanding qualities for the supreme office in the Church, to succeed Urban as Pope Boniface IX. Five years later, when Colette was thirteen (and four years after she had received the revelations concerning the Franciscan Order), a Franciscan friar was elected by the dissident cardinals to succeed Clement VII. He was the Catalonian Cardinal Pedro de Luna, a man who seemed as well qualified for the papal honor as the true pope, Boniface IX, was ill qualified. Learned and virtuous, distinguished in bearing and affable in manner, Pedro de Luna appears to have been unquestionably sincere in believing himself a validly elected pope. However, as we shall see, his energy later on in defending his true apostolic succession was so fierce as to put a very heavy question mark on his detachment, if not on his integrity. He styled himself Benedict XIII; and with his accession, a double papal line was established, to the confusion and consternation of all Christendom.

From our comfortable vantage point of five and a half centuries later, it seems obvious enough that Pope Urban, whatever his tragic errors in governing, was the true pope, and that Boniface IX was his lawful successor. The question of the possible invalidity of Urban's election answers itself in the delayed protests of the seceding cardinals, and especially in their unwarranted and highly illegal summoning of a conclave which represented only the disgruntled section of the college of cardinals. Their seizure of power was unprecedented and wholly illicit. We find it difficult to understand how loyal

Catholics could have supported the "pope" of their choice, Clement VII, or his successor, Benedict XIII. Besides the perspective of centuries, however, we have also totally different systems of world government and communication. We of the twentieth century accept the boon of news releases within an hour of any and all events as a routine affair. World inter-communication is taken for granted. And the right to form our own opinions and to argue them unto exhaustion is one of our most prized rights.

In the fourteenth century, things were considerably different. News of conclave and counter-conclave was delivered by that most undependable of all mediums, word of mouth. Warring kings and petty nobility used the general confusion to their best personal advantage, rallying to the side of whichever papal throne seemed the likelier support for their own selfish ends. And in each kingdom or duchy, bewildered Catholics followed the lead of their overlords. Their unhappy lot was not bettered by the fact that their leaders often enough transferred their allegiance from one papal claimant to another, depending on which way the political wind blew, swearing a loud fealty to Boniface this month and undying loyalty to Benedict the next.

If we remember all this, we shall not be scandalized to discover the great St. Vincent Ferrer ardently championing the rights of the anti-pope. We shall not be hindered but helped in our love for Colette by finding her also among Pedro de Luna's adherents. Helped, because we see how human and fallible were the saints when not especially enlightened by God, how limited in their supernatural scope by the caprice of their earthly sovereigns. It appears that God designed with divine care that His greatest saints during the time of the great schism should be found in both papal camps.

Robert's long talks with his daughter on these dismal subjects, however, were always shot through with the rays of faith and hope. There was still a God, and His powers were not at all diminished. "I see no likelihood," said the priest-poet James Donohue of our times, "that the kingdom of God will be shaken." Neither did Robert Boellet in 1399. Together, the old man and the young girl faced a future that was fuller of God than of disaster.

When Boellet felt that his last days had surely come, he made a final trip to the abbey. This time he did not take Colette with him.

And when Abbot Raoul de Raye came down to the parlor to see him, the master-carpenter delivered to the Benedictine something far more precious than any handiwork of his long past service to the abbey. He gave him the care of his daughter.

5   *Attempts at Religious Life*

It is to the everlasting credit of Abbot Raoul that he separated himself from the ranks of many abbots of his day by accepting the guardianship of a carpenter's daughter with willingness and even devotedness. The abbot who had been so fascinated by the small girl of years past could not have failed to remark the change in Colette's appearance, her miraculous growth, the aura of her sanctity. He knew all about the preaching in the fields of Corbie and the fame it had brought her. He understood that he was taking upon himself the care of a predestined girl.

Whether it was her father or the abbot himself who afterward told Colette of how the request was made we do not know, but we have, from Sister Perrine, Colette's account of the interview. M. Boellet's appeal to Dom Raoul de Raye certainly shows him to be "the very sweet person" of his daughter's description. "Monseigneur," the old carpenter began, "in your goodness you have always loved me very much, and so I have loved you, too. I beg you for the love of God, and by the affection there has always been between us, that after my death you take charge of my only child whom I now give over to you and place under your protection. May it please you to take her as your own daughter." That such an appeal could be lodged with the lord abbot of Corbie is perhaps Dom Raoul's best praise.

It is pathetically characteristic, however, of this almost-great man that the plans his quick brain was already evolving for Colette's future leaned half to the supernatural side, half to the wholly natural side. While part of Abbot Raoul de Raye surely realized his profound need of divine guidance in directing the vocation of so extraordinary a young woman, the other side of his character had already disposed of her future. "I will find her a good, solid Catholic husband." But the abbot was warm in his assurances to Boellet, and the old man made his slow way back to the Rue de la Chaulcie comforted and at peace.

Quick to sense something unusual in her father's manner that day, Colette tells us she spent the whole time of his absence in prayer. When she heard his familiar slow step on the walk, she ran from her oratory to greet him, and clung to him for long moments. A few days later he died in her arms. It was 1399, and Colette was eighteen years old.

After the first lonely weeks had passed, the young orphan went to see Abbot Raoul. He looked at the girl before him, so completely alone in the world, and his voice was gentle as he explained his guardianship of her. He reminded her that she was now of an age to settle down into the life of a good Catholic wife, to establish a fine Christian family. He warmed to his subject as he went on, steadily refusing to let himself be disconcerted by Colette's complete silence. When he finally looked directly at her, he saw such determined resistance that he doubtless had to bolster himself with a deep breath and get a hard hold on his pectoral cross so as not to spoil the climax of his speech. With labored enthusiasm, he promised to select a husband for her himself. In fact, he already had just the right man in mind. He was a very worthy. . . . But Colette's voice severed his description of her future husband like a fine steel wire. "I shall not marry any man, your lordship. It is not God's will for me." There was something in Colette that made this man, long-accustomed to bending others to his will, understand that argument or persuasion was useless. "But if you do not marry, child, what *will* you do?" he finally asked. The answer was certainly not one to reassure her guardian. "I don't know," she replied.

One thing, though, Colette did know. She knew just what she intended to do with her inheritance (and we are told it was considerable). Yes, she had very definite plans for investing her funds. The house on the Rue de la Chaulcie was much too large for a lone girl.

She would dispose of it to advantage. Her new businesslike tone must have fallen like music on the ears of Abbot Raoul. Evidently the girl was less an impractical mystic than she appeared. Later on, he would get back to the subject of marriage.

The abbot went back to his room, by all appearances feeling much better. No one has recorded how he felt when he learned that Colette had literally given away every franc she owned. Her way of investing her funds was to give them all to the poor. The house on the Rue de la Chaulcie was indeed disposed of, but with material gain to the poor rather than to Colette. She accepted nothing for it. Relieved of the burden of any possessions, she now felt much more secure about her future, as she was later to tell Sister Perrine.

The guardianship Robert Boellet had delivered to Abbot Raoul was evidently a loose affair, more a matter of word-of-mouth promises and a general paternal protectiveness than of legal procedures, since Colette was left so free to dispose of her inheritance according to her own desires. But, although the abbot had no legal authority to prevent what he considered the height of improvidence, he could at least belabor his ward with reproaches; and he did. Abbot Raoul's loud protests, however, could not have been any more eloquent than those of Pietro di Bernardone two centuries earlier in Assisi when his young son, Francis, had equipped himself for the future in exactly the same manner.

Uncertain of everything except the love of God and his own vocation to the way of evangelical poverty, Francis set out singing into the unknown. In just such a spirit, Clare of Assisi eloped from her castle home in 1212 to become his first spiritual daughter. And in 1400, Colette of Corbie, rich with the heritage of Francis and Clare and poor in all else, set out for Amiens, a neighboring town to Corbie.

It is directly in keeping with Colette's ideals of renunciation, her ardent love of the poor, and her deep-seated attraction for the Franciscan way, that she should prepare herself for the future by disposing of every possession possible, much as another might look to his future by making sound financial investments and banking his ready money to gather interest. According to her Franciscan outlook, Colette was being eminently practical. For the kind of life to which she aspired, this was the only possible preparation. It is easy to picture the same St. Francis who gleefully assisted the wealthier of his first sons to distribute all their goods to the poor, leaning out of glory in his delight over the Franciscan business acumen of Colette Boellet. She was making investments that could not possibly fail. She banked her funds where neither the rust nor the moth could consume them. There is a noticeable ring of satisfaction in Sister Perrine's brief summation of the saint as a youthful financier. "After the death of her father and mother, she kept nothing at all, but gave everything to the poor."

Colette had decided to go to Amiens in order to seek counsel for her future from Father Jean Bassan, a Celestine priest, who was establishing a new house of his Order in Amiens just at this time. She had met this priest once on his visit to Corbie when she was twelve, and made her confession to him. From that day forward, although she had not seen him again, Colette had felt a strong bond with the holy Celestine. By now, Father Bassan's reputation for sanctity was well established, although he was apparently fairly young when Colette turned to him, as he did not die until forty years after this second meeting. As she walked toward Amiens, Colette knew nothing of God's plans for her future beyond her certainty that they involved utter evangelical poverty and perpetual virginity; but she hoped the Celestine would undertake her spiritual direction. He did.

In Father Jean Bassan's case, the reputation for holiness was richly deserved. A genuinely spiritual man, he recognized at once the worth of the young woman before him. They were two souls entirely given to God, and they understood each other perfectly. It must have been disappointing, then, when their several interviews terminated in Father Bassan's admitting that he was wholly unenlightened about Colette's future. He advised her to wait and to pray.

Colette's disappointment was softened by one concrete suggestion the priest had for the present. It was that she should make a vow of perpetual virginity. She was overjoyed at the idea, and after several days of prayer and preparation she made the loved vow before Father Bassan, giving her heart perpetually to God, as she later told Sister Perrine.

Shortly after this turning-point in her life, Colette returned to Corbie, still knowing nothing definite about her future, but with a seal set on her love. She was no longer alone in the world. She was espoused to Christ now. She had a Lover "more beautiful than all the sons of man." No wonder the townsfolk remarked that the young and penniless girl who came back to Corbie had the radiance of a new bride on her face.

It seems probable that Colette had supported herself in Amiens by doing needlework. We are never told of her having relatives there, and we do know that later on she did a great deal of fine needlework of the kind always in demand. It is easy to imagine this beautiful young stranger finding ready customers for the work of her gifted hands. It was the accepted procedure for widows and unmarried women to work at embroidery, fine sewing, and lace-making for a livelihood; and that would have been a second motive for Colette, who always wished to lose herself in the obscurity of the common-place.

On her return to Corbie, however, she felt constrained to do something more constructive spiritually. So, after consulting Dom Raoul de Raye, she resolved to ally herself to the company of the Béguines. These were a group of pious women, elderly for the most part, who lived a semi-religious life. They made no vows and usually did not live in community but in small separate dwellings called *béguinages* facing around an open court. They devoted their energies entirely to the care of the poor and the sick, nursing them in their homes and in the hospitals, and spending much of their remaining time in prayer. Unless they had means of their own, they depended for their maintenance on what they might be freely given in return for their services. Some of these groups are still active in Belgium today. Colette harbored no illusions as to this being a permanent way of life for herself, but Father Bassan had urged her to wait on God's will. She would wait in service to His very poor.

After a year of this apostolate, her soul became restive. The Béguines had their own labor of love, and Colette appreciated it; but, as she later confided to Sister Perrine, it was definitely not for her. She yearned increasingly for a regular religious life. And in 1401, on the suggestion of Dom Raoul ("to please him" is, in fact, the way she expressed it to Sister Perrine), she asked to be admitted to the Benedictine abbey of nuns near Corbie. It could scarcely have been to please the abbot, however, that she applied as a lay Sister; and the nuns must have been startled at the form of her petition, since her excellent knowledge of Latin, the artistic work to which she was accustomed, her great love for the Divine Office, and her whole general makeup seemed to indicate her aptitude for the life of a choir nun. But the abbess' suggestions were met by Colette's smiling refusal. Perhaps she realized that this, too, was to be more a novitiate for a yet unrevealed future than for the life of a professed Benedictine nun, and wished to serve, as she waited, in the humblest offices possible.

She was accepted, and in short order established herself solidly in the affection of the community. Her modesty and humility kept her unaware of the admiring eyes that watched her wheeling in barrows of apples from the orchard or scrubbing the kitchen floors with the grace of a genuflecting angel. The nuns reverenced their lay postulant, and very likely some of them stirred uneasily in their comforts.

A few months passed, and Colette experienced the same repugnance that had forced her to part company with the Béguines. She criticized none of the relaxations she saw in the abbey. She admired all that was praiseworthy. But she knew again that none of it was for her, though, with charming simplicity, she later told Perrine that the Benedictines had wanted "very strongly" to keep her. Sister Perrine relates that one day when Colette was dusting a statue of St. Francis in the abbey, it came alive, one arm commanding her, with a gesture towards the outside world, to depart.

With or without miraculous statuary, the attraction of St. Francis' and St. Clare's way of life was growing more irresistible, and Colette began to wonder whether her true vocation might not be with the Second Franciscan Order, the Poor Clares. Father Bassan was not available to give advice, nor was there anyone else in Corbie to whom she could confide her uncertainty. It would scarcely have been tactful to outline for the Benedictine abbot, Dom Raoul de Raye, the reasons she knew she could never find her spiritual fulfilment with the Benedictine nuns. So without any guide save the Holy Spirit, and quite sure that He was sufficient, Colette asked to be received by the Poor Clares at the monastery of Pont-Sainte-Maxence between Compiègne and Senlis. They took her readily enough, as a servant.

Whether this term "servant," used by both Sister Perrine and

Father Pierre de Vaux, meant literally a servant or whether it was used as a synonym for lay Sister, makes little difference, since both are equally incompatible with the primitive Poor Clare observance. St. Clare, whose concept of manual labor was that of "a grace," and who wished all her daughters to live entirely on alms and the work of their own hands, would have tolerated neither servants as such nor lay Sisters as such at San Damiano. St. Clare did have Sisters who went outside the enclosure to attend to things necessary, but they were certainly not designed to take the burden of manual work from the choir nuns. "The grace of working" was a blessing to be shared by all. However, the Poor Clares of Pont-Sainte-Maxence were Urbanists, following not the primitive Rule of St. Clare but the Rule of Pope Urban IV. Colette knew this, but she was not prepared for the wholesale changes from the original way of Francis and Clare which obtained at Pont-Sainte-Maxence, changes resulting not from the Urbanist modifications but from weak human nature's relaxations.

Her vision when she was nine of the decline of primitive Franciscanism had shown her the scandals and abuses rampant among so-called Observants who observed very little of what St. Francis had laid down. Evidently it had not given her to understand that some Urbanists were as relaxed in their separate observance as the Primitives were in the original. Pont-Sainte-Maxence's kind of divergence from the way of St. Francis was too much for Colette's Franciscan heart. "Our Lord," she was to tell Sister Perrine in future years, "made me understand He did not want me to stay there longer." She left the Poor Clare monastery and returned to Corbie, saddened but with undaunted faith that God would yet show her His Will.

This time, her return to her home town produced raised eyebrows and set gossiping tongues wagging. What an unstable girl that Colette Boellet was! She was a failure everywhere—with the Béguines, the Benedictines, the Poor Clares. It just proved what a stubborn piece she was to argue with a man as wise and as holy as Abbot Raoul. Everyone knew he wanted her to marry. Who did she think she was, to set her judgment up against his? Only a few of her old friends, like Jacquette Legrande and Guillemette Chrétien, remained unshakably loyal to her. These were very tense days for the lonely girl, but her faith was rewarded when Father Jéhan Pinet, guardian of the Franciscan Friary at Hesdin and custos of the entire province of Picardy, came to Corbie in the course of his canonical visitations of the different Franciscan houses.

Father Jéhan's name was familiar to nearly everyone in Picardy. He was a man of God and a true son of St. Francis. It was common knowledge that he sorrowed over the deterioration of the primitive Franciscan ideals, but his was no sterile melancholy. He worked with all the spiritual energy of his great soul to restore the original observance. And if he was not always obeyed, he was certainly always respected. Colette saw in his coming God's direct intervention in her life. She went to him at once and gave him her confidence. She could not have had a more sympathetic listener. He understood her, and knew himself understood in return.

Before he left Corbie, Father Jéhan assured his grateful young client of his faith in her Franciscan vocation. However, he could say little more. He knew that the kind of observance she had found at Pont-Sainte-Maxence was no worse than what she would find in other Poor Clare monasteries in the country. And he knew he could not send her to any of them. There was nothing for him to do but repeat Father Bassan's direction to pray and wait. But when he returned to Corbie a little later he had something much more definite to suggest.

If Colette could not be content in the neighboring Poor Clare monasteries, perhaps she could be happy as a Franciscan of the Third Order. This was the branch of the Franciscan family founded by St. Francis primarily for people living in the world, either married or single, who wished to observe the Franciscan Rule modified to suit their state of life. They were invested with the Franciscan cord, had a brief Office to recite and certain religious obligations to perform, could wear the Franciscan habit if they wished and were always buried in it. Their office was to be a leaven of spirituality in a materialistic world. They were called "Third Order Seculars," and their company had been graced with kings and queens as well as merchants and day-laborers. St. Elizabeth of Hungary was a tertiary, as the members of the Third Order were called. So was St. Louis of France. And besides these secular tertiaries, there were the so-called "Third Order Regulars," who wore the Franciscan habit continuously and lived a regular religious life bound by vows but followed a less austere rule than that of the Friars Minor or the Poor Clares.

The thought that she could yet be a member of the Franciscan household filled Colette with a delight so obvious that Father Jéhan must heartily have thanked the Holy Spirit for putting this idea in his mind. He himself invested Colette with the habit of the Third Franciscan Order at a Mass he offered for her. We wonder whether he was given any intimation that this simple ceremony was closely akin to the first Franciscan investiture of a woman, when St. Francis had thrown the rough garb of penance over St. Clare's satin gown in the chapel of St. Mary of the Angels outside Assisi two centuries earlier? Certainly the flame of Francis burned in the heart of Father Jéhan Pinet. The ideals of Clare lived again in the heart of Colette.

Like St. Francis, Father Jéhan had no definite plans for his spiritual daughter's future. But just as God never failed to work out all details for St. Francis, so did He do the planning for Father Jéhan. During the Mass of Colette's investiture, the Franciscan friar had an inspiration so strong and sure that he could not doubt its origin. Why should not this young religious who could never satisfy the longing of her soul in the world step out of the world as completely as it is given a human being to do? Why should she not be a recluse? Father Jéhan knew that such a life required the very rarest strength of soul. Looking down at the girl kneeling on the altar step in her rough brown habit, he decided that Colette had that kind of strength.

6   Dom Raoul vs. Colette

The word "recluse" falls on our ears like a sound from another world. The concept of a severance from society so total as was the life of the medieval anchorite or anchoress is perhaps more difficult for our twentieth-century-conditioned minds to grasp than the notion of separate humanities on other planets. However, during Colette's lifetime, this very ancient way of life was still followed by a considerable number of men and women, some of them professed religious attached to monasteries; others, layfolk who lived on the alms of the townspeople or of passersby if the anchorhold was situated outside a town. One of the sharpest contrasts between our way of thinking and the medieval outlook is in the attitude taken toward these recluses.

If one of our acquaintances expressed the desire to build himself a little lean-to against one of our big city churches, there to live and die in complete seclusion and utter dependence on the goodwill offerings of people going into the church, all the neighbors would probably agree that he should certainly be locked up. Perhaps his friends would hustle him off to a psychiatrist, who in his turn would be delighted at having so rare a specimen to study. It was not so in the Middle Ages. A recluse was the pride and glory of his town. Sometimes he was given a regular pension out of the town coffers, made annual gifts of clothing; altogether, he was highly respected as one singled out by God. The recluse became a symbol of God's protection over a city, and the people guarded their treasure jealously as a kind of spiritual lightning-rod. It is quite possible that there was a goodly admixture of superstition in this kind of veneration; but the basic spiritual outlook was there, too.

Some of those who embarked on this way of life were penitents who wished to wash out the stains of their own past swindling or lasciviousness, or what-have-you, with prayer and austerity. Others were individuals whose personal past was the lightest of burdens, but who wished to offer themselves as holocausts of reparation for the sins of the world or for particular sinners or classes of sinners. In still other cases, the motive of reparation was secondary to the simple desire to be as closely united to God as is humanly possible. These latter wanted nothing on earth except to be utterly alone with the Lord they loved, waiting on Him by day and by night, their lives uncluttered by any material interests, living in complete and happy detachment from all the things other men spend their lives and energies pursuing. Colette was one of these. Yet, Father Jéhan must have had more than one inward tremor about what he was proposing to this lovely young woman. He admitted that the vocation of a recluse was one beyond his own spiritual powers, and he tried to test Colette's motives by accenting its objective harshness. Relentlessly he pressed upon her imagination the concrete details of the life she was about to embrace.

She would be actually sealed into one or two tiny rooms. (The ritual for enclosing a recluse included an official sealing of the door.) Think what it would mean: Never to walk again in the fragrant fields of Corbie at twilight. Never again to feel the wind or sun against her cheeks. Never again to feel the warm pressure of a friend's hand, or to join in the laughter of Jacquette Legrande and Guillemette Chrétien over the wonder of being alive and young. She would be completely dependent on the charity of others: she would eat the food they might bring her; or nothing, if they forgot her.

Then, the austerity of the life itself, with all the pleasant distractions of the world removed: prayer and penance; the recitation of the Divine Office; assisting at Mass through a wicket opening into the church. And for relaxation—and as a possible means of support if alms failed—some needlework, perhaps.

When Father Jéhan had completed his word pictures, he swung his gaze back on the girl before him. If he expected to see indrawn lips, thoughtful eyes, and that slight forward thrust of the jaw which her biographers describe as the characteristic sign of Colette's moments of struggle, he was disappointed. She was smiling, and she had only one question to ask: "When may I begin? I am ready."

Father Jéhan did not at first reply. Probably he could not. But Colette repeated softly: "I am ready, Father." The priest finally stood up. "Yes," he said, "I believe you are." He blessed her and sent her away until he could make arrangements for carrying out their plan.

It is not clear from the ancient biographies where Colette was living these days, but very probably she stayed with Jacquette or Guillemette, her most loyal friends. We know that she told them of Father Jéhan's inspiration, and that they received her confidence with a great deal of awe and no small measure of sorrow. Both the older girls were convinced that Colette Boellet had the rare qualities of soul for the austere life of a recluse, but the thought of losing her was almost unbearable. Jacquette and Guillemette suddenly realized how Colette had entered into the very core of their own lives, steadying them. Now the ground was shifting under their feet. They cried.

Colette comforted her two friends, receiving the testimony of their affection quite simply. The greater the holiness, the greater the power to love and the capacity for being loved. The young girl who was so delighted at the prospect of being enclosed in a tiny hermitage for the rest of her life had in its perfection the first prerequisite of a recluse: a love for God and men so great that it could not express itself in any measure less than that of holocaust.

With all her bride's eagerness, Colette kept her businesslike sense of the importance of details. And the biggest and most formidable detail to be attended to was Dom Raoul de Raye. The spiritual aspect of his guardianship becomes fully apparent here. For although Colette had disposed of her earthly goods on her own initiative and with a free heart, she evidently felt that her entering upon the life of a recluse was a matter entirely within Dom Raoul's jurisdiction. Years later she confided to Sister Perrine her memories of that difficult time, and from what we know of the characters of Colette and Dom Raoul we can imagine what the encounters between the two might have been like.

One day in August, taking inward reassurance from the Franciscan habit she wore and the solid reality of the Franciscan cord knotted around her waist, Colette set out for the Abbey of Saint-Pierre to disclose her plan to the abbot and obtain his consent to it.

It was a familiar journey, and at every few paces she must have found some reminder of her childhood walks with her father. One can imagine her coming out of the sunlight into the coolness of the abbey parlor, sitting on the edge of one of the stiff chairs, listening, with prayerful anxiety, for the abbot's precise footfalls in the great flagged hall.

At last he came, looked speculatively at the brown habit and white cord—and perhaps more speculatively at something in Colette's eyes—and took his seat before her. In her usual direct way, she outlined Father Jéhan's suggestion for her future life, trying to compensate by her own enthusiasm for the total lack of response she saw in the abbot's face. Silence. She began again, with a rising inflection, asking his opinion on various points. Still not a word. And then she fell to her knees, as she had done when she was a small child, and said simply, "Will your Lordship permit me to be a recluse?"

At last Abbot Raoul de Raye spoke, and his words must have fallen like small hammer blows in the summer stillness: "I most certainly will not. This is nonsense. And I do not intend to betray the trust of your father by being a party to the wild scheme of Father —Jéhan—Pinet." Abbot Raoul's voice was a marvelous instrument. It dragged the Franciscan friar before the bar of justice on "Father," condemned him on "Jéhan," and sentenced him with "Pinet."

All her life, Colette had seen the great abbot at his best, with that odd mixture of reverence and indulgence he reserved for M. Boellet's daughter. Now, for the first time, she saw the forbidding countenance of an abbot whose mind was closed.

He rose, gesturing for her to rise too, and dismissed her: "I have a number of things to attend to, and I will ask you to excuse me. In any case, the subject is closed." He held out his hand, and Colette went on her knees again to kiss his ring. She glanced up at him, her eyes full of tears, and he softened a little. "Go along, child," he said. "You will see for yourself that this is all nonsense. Come back to see me next week."

Colette had been defeated in the first engagement, but there was another Party involved. She prayed that He would intervene.

Sister Perrine tells us that she went again and again to the abbey, and time after time Abbot Raoul heard her out impassively. And then one day when she was almost in despair of gaining his consent, with the lightning quickness of inspiration she fell prostrate at the abbot's feet, and the old man suddenly yielded. He stooped down and raised her to her feet. She looked up at him and heard his voice, more gentle than she had ever heard it before: "Go, child, go, and be a recluse." And then, after a pause, the unbelievable words: "I will help you."

In the days that followed, all Dom Raoul's best qualities of soul and heart, too often submerged in half measures, came swimming to the surface of his character. Once this powerful man determined to do something, he did it with despatch and thoroughness. This time, his efficiency was tempered with genuine love for the girl he knew was already greater than he would ever be; but he proceeded with an energy that must have forced Colette to hide a smile more than once.

Like the practical businessman he was, the abbot first announced to all the people of Corbie that they were to be blessed with a recluse of their own, and that the one who wished to place herself in spiritual bondage for their good was no other than his own ward, Colette Boellet. Dom Raoul de Raye, remember, was the reigning lord of Corbie. If the people's sense of pleasure at the notion of having a recluse in their midst needed any whetting, the immense force of the abbot's personality would supply it. The townspeople were not asked if they wished to support a recluse. They were told that they were to be privileged to do so and that a delegate of the abbot would shortly be calling on them to take up a collection for the erection of an anchorhold for his protégée.

The fact is, the people were genuinely happy and grateful to God for what their faith considered a rare gift to the town, but the identity of the recluse was a thunderbolt. A converted sinner, yes; maybe a strong man of middle years, or perhaps an aged widow on whom the world had no claims and for whom it held no attractions. But the most beautiful girl in their town! The one who could preach as well as the famous priests in Paris! The happy, innocent daughter of the Boellets! This was too much. They forgot all their grievances against Colette's supposed instability. Where they had criticized her for not following the abbot's advice in the past, they now blamed her for acting under his authority.

However, the men, women, and children of Corbie were tame opposition for the determination of Abbot Raoul de Raye. The affair was settled. The ceremony of Colette's enclosure in her anchorage would be held on Sunday, September 17 of that year, which was 1402. All were invited to attend the solemn rites, over which he himself would preside, in the abbey church. And now, please, a generous donation toward the little dwelling which was to be placed between two buttresses of the parish church of Notre Dame in Corbie.

It needed the intense drive of a Raoul de Raye to get the three-room anchorhold erected and finished in detail by September 17. Doubtless his enormous prestige, as well as her own personal admiration for Mlle. Boellet, inspired the widow of the town provost, Mme. Guillemette Gamalin, to give the entire sum necessary to construct the anchorhold, although the abbot continued to solicit other offerings for Colette's security. The complaints of workmen who objected to all this haste lodged sidewise in their throats when Dom Raoul came to inspect their progress. One just did not argue with this man. He directed that his own monks should supply the choir for the ceremony of Colette's enclosure, and that all the civil and ecclesiastical dignitaries should conduct her in procession to the abbey church. Surely it was a magnanimous gesture on the abbot's part to invite the Franciscan friar, Father Jéhan Pinet, to be present and to receive Colette's vow of perpetual enclosure before the high altar in the Benedictine church. But it was my lord abbot who would preside from his throne during the ceremony. Everyone was given to understand that this was no mere carpenter's daughter who was electing to follow the very ancient religious life of a recluse, but the gifted ward of Abbot Raoul de Raye, lord of Corbie. Colette doubtless continued to smile to herself over Dom Raoul's way of conducting the whole affair. Yet she loved her guardian and saw, perhaps more clearly than any other ever did, the seeds of greatness in his soul. She left him a free hand in arranging for her future as a recluse.

September 17 dawned bright and cloudless for the procession of Corbie's most distinguished persons conducting a young girl in a Franciscan habit into the abbey church of Saint-Pierre. The flawless Gregorian chant of the Benedictine monks swept worldly concerns out the back doors of the church, and there remained inside only the intense vitality of spiritual reality. Colette was incensed and asperged. She renewed her vow of perpetual virginity, and then Father Jéhan stood directly in front of her and received in the name of the Church her vow of perpetual enclosure. The abbot rose from his throne and signalled the procession to form again. He walked at the end, with Colette immediately in front of him, carrying in her hand the key to the anchorhold in token of her freedom of choice.

Throughout the long and impressive ceremony, Colette had remained serene in her quiet recollection, but when the procession at last parted ranks before the small anchorhold and she came face to face with it, emotion overcame her. She told Sister Perrine in later years how she knelt down and kissed the threshold. Then, in something of a transport of joy, she cried out: "Here is the place of my rest, and here I will dwell, for I have chosen it."

Women began to weep when Colette rose and smiled a last goodbye to her friends. Some in the procession instinctively knelt down. Even Abbot Raoul de Raye permitted himself some moments of silence after Colette disappeared into the tiny dwelling. Then, with his characteristic energy, he stepped quickly forward and placed his own great wax seal on the door. The ceremony was over. Corbie had a recluse. The next day, the door was secured with mortar, and Colette began to follow what she never doubted was her final vocation.

7   *The Anchorhold*

Abbot Raoul had gone to a great deal of trouble about the tiny dwelling in which Colette now set up housekeeping, although the three narrow partitions, more cubicles than rooms, offered little scope for his efforts. The ruins of the anchorhold can be seen in Corbie today, and the records of its construction and Colette's entrance into it on September 17, 1402, are preserved in the archives of Corbie.

Its first small room opened directly on the street with only a one-step rise to its entrance. It was large enough for three or four visitors if they were sufficiently stalwart to remain standing. The comfort of chairs was entirely ruled out by the exigencies of space. At the other end of this miniature parlor was the heavy door marked with the abbot's seal, and never to be opened. It had, however, a small barred wicket set into it which Colette could open to receive the food, water, and other necessary supplies which were brought to her by friends and benefactors, and through which she passed out the altar linens she made and the mending we are told she did for the poor. Judging from the masterpieces of darning and patching on her mantle, which is preserved even today at the monastery in Ghent, those were fortunate poor who had Colette to sew for them. This little open square which framed the face of their recluse became one of the real centers of the life of Corbie's people in a very short time.

Behind this sealed door with its wicket, ordinarily kept locked from the inside, was Colette's living apartment. The "furniture" accepted as necessary by the young recluse was so sparse that Dom Raoul's ingenuity must have been pressed to its last outposts as he attempted to make the place as attractive and comfortable as possible. The tiny room could not have admitted a bedstead even had Colette agreed to tolerate one. But that problem was simply solved. Colette's bed was a mat of straw laid on the floor against one wall and flanked by two logs. A small wooden block served her as a pillow. As she did a great deal of needlework and, later on, wrote extensively, we can presume that there was also a small table, and that a low bench was sometimes used as a variant for her ordinary sitting position, which was to settle back on her heels as St. Francis had been accustomed to sit. Her chinaware consisted of a drinking vessel and a couple of bowls, her "plate" of a spoon or two.

Dom Raoul had insisted on a small stove for warmth in winter, and its little chimney was thrust through the roof like an impudent finger.

The small window set high in one wall had been placed there at his command, too. No one could look through this high-set window, nor could Colette look out; but the sunlight found it and so did the birds. The hygienic facilities of the little dwelling were meager, but not more so than those of any ordinary dwellings in town; and Colette's love for cleanliness and order kept the elfin quarters always scrupulously swept and shining. Over the "bed" hung a small picture of our Lady.

Beyond this combination bedroom-livingroom-kitchen-and-diningroom was the last of the three cubicles, Colette's oratory. It held a prie-dieu, a little shelf for her books and breviary, and a crucifix. And in one wall was set another small wicket. This one opened into the interior of the church of Notre Dame, and Abbot

Raoul had arranged it with the greatest care so that Colette had a direct view of the high altar and still remained unseen by those in the church. The wicket was set between the main altar and the communion rail. It became the focal-point of Colette's new life. There she received Holy Communion. There also she confessed her sins, closing the shutter of the wicket at these times. There she recited the Divine Office, now as an official sharer in the tremendous work of praise and intercession which had thrilled her heart as a small girl. And there at the wicket Colette spent many hours of the night, pouring the fullness of her love out into the dark emptiness of the big church and into the listening heart of the One who dwelt there. This little barred wicket is preserved by the Poor Clare nuns in Bruges.

The joy of Corbie's new recluse during the first months of what many would call her interment bordered on the ecstatic. If she was buried, there certainly was never a gayer corpse. The sweetness which God almost invariably lends to the beginnings of religious life was hers in full measure. Having given God everything then in her power to give, she received from Him His own abundance.

Those early months in the anchorhold witnessed a kind of contest between the Almighty and Colette. In the gladness of her gratitude to have actualized at last the deepest desire of her heart, the young anchoress offered God every sacrifice she could fasten on. Love stands tallest when it suffers; it is proved in sacrifice. Colette's love added many a cubit to its stature during those solitary months. She curtailed her hours of "repose" on the straw mat to two or three, that she might pray longer. She scourged her bare shoulders several times a day. She ate so little even of the frugal meals Jacquette and Guillemette brought daily to the outer wicket that they went to deliver anxious reports to Abbot Raoul, not daring themselves to expostulate with the one they so reverenced. But when Dom Raoul came to see his ward, prepared to reproach her sharply for such imprudences, he saw the young face at the wicket so obviously alight with health despite the ivory paleness, that his admonitions must have caught in his throat, for there is no record of his delivering them.

Now, Abbot Raoul de Raye was not a man subject to lumps in the throat. He distrusted emotion and prided himself on his purely

intellectual approach to life and all its problems. The glowing face
of his young charge must have discovered rather disconcertingly to
Dom Raoul that he had a heart as well as a mind, for it appears that
he simply stared at her in silence. No one but an idiot would claim
that this clear-eyed girl with animation flickering on her lips was
wasting away from her austerities. Colette's vitality after penances
calculated to wilt a giant could have only one explanation.

Obviously, there *was* a contest under way in the little anchorhold.
Obviously, too, the Lord was winning, hands down. The less sleep
Colette allowed herself, the more energy and endurance God supplied to her. The more she curtailed her poor meals, the more God
nourished her without need of food. If she lashed her shoulders in
reparation for the sins of the world and in union with His scourging,
the Lord laid His caresses on her soul. Probably Dom Raoul said
as much; and with her customary candor and simplicity, Colette
told her guardian that he was right. Things went just like that. "Blood
for blood, sorrow for sorrow" was Colette's cryptic description of
her way of life. Yet even the "blood and sorrow" one gave to God
was first a gift from Himself. And the returning to Him of what
was already His brought new gifts in reward.

The abbot must have listened to this as a man listens to the
songs of a native land quitted many years ago. It was the kind of
music a man of affairs could not afford to hear very often. Abbot
Raoul had long since judged it prudent to secure himself on the
decks of the world with the chains of ambition and vanity. He had
taken care that the songs of the Divine Siren should not lure him into
the spiritual deeps. So now he bade his ward farewell. He blessed
her. He asked her, humbly enough, to pray for him. And Colette
watched the great man turn away, as he had turned away before. He
closed the low door behind him, and after a few moments Colette
could hear the wheels of his carriage protesting against the uneven
cobblestones. She closed the outer wicket and went to the inner one
opening into the church. Perhaps Abbot Raoul felt her prayers
pulling at his elbow as he rode back to the abbey.

Father Jéhan came often, too, to visit his protégée; and rejoiced
as he saw the unmistakable evidence that his inspiration for the
young tertiary's future had indeed been wrought by the Holy Spirit.
Sometimes there was the joy of a letter from Father Jean Bassan,

now in Naples as superior general of his Order. Then, after a few months, Colette's occasional visitors, old friends of her parents and her own girlhood chums at first, began to swell in numbers and in kind. Before long there was a daily line of people of all stations in life waiting to talk to their recluse. There is an ancient fascination in true joy. Since the fatal day in the Garden of Eden when joy took exit from the hearts of Adam and Eve, men have striven to recapture it. Their very sinning is a perverted seeking after joy. And when they see it as triumphantly regained as they saw it in the face of this young anchoress, men invariably react strongly. The virtuous claim kinship. The struggling reach out for the vision. The fallen plead for rescue. And those become totally impervious to grace hate.

For all who came to seek her advice in their problems or to warm themselves at the fire of her love and compassion, Colette had a wide heart and an untiring ear. Even for the merely curious who were a sore trial to her, she could preserve a courteous and smiling face. But the unending stream of callers played havoc with the schedule Father Jéhan had written out for her. Days could no longer be divided between the canonical Hours, work, and silent prayer. If she knelt at the wicket to recite Sext and None, the loud knocker would summon her to listen to a wife's recital of her husband's trespasses. When she sat down to eat a few mouthfuls, the knocker would herald the arrival of a young girl in tears over the prospect of an unwanted marriage. As soon as she prostrated herself before the crucifix in her oratory, the knocker would be raised by a priest wanting her advice on a case of conscience.

Colette's prodigious infused knowledge drew many priests and scholars to her wicket; and Father Jean Guyot, parish priest of Notre Dame and her confessor in her girlhood, even sent his young brother, Jacques, to be tutored by her in matters of religion.

We are amused but not surprised to learn that fifteen-year-old Jacques was far from enchanted with the idea of being tutored by a recluse and a nun. He went off to his curious schoolroom, which was the little extern parlor of the anchorage, grudgingly, kicking at the gravel as he went and promising to flatten the nose of any of his young friends who would taunt him about his forced visits to the anchoress. Colette looked out from her wicket at the gangling youngster before her, his lower lip thrust out belligerently and his expression daring her to teach him anything. She forced her lips not to smile and calmly began the lessons. They were based on the psalms, whose depths she had plumbed in silent hours.

After a while, Jacques' lower lip receded to its normal position. And not too many weeks had passed before the gravel kicked on his way to the anchorhold was only accidentally displaced by his running so fast to get to his teacher. This boy lived to a very advanced age and testified at the beatification of Colette when he was a stooped old man with a flock of shining memories of a young nun-teacher who had accomplished the astounding feat of making a fifteen-year-old boy forget fist-fighting for the glory of the psalms. Colette might be an apt patron for the modern religious teachers of teen-agers.

Father Jéhan could not fail to see the good Colette was accomplishing for all manner of persons, but he also saw her strain and fatigue. He talked the matter over with Dom Raoul, and the two determined to put a stop to the unregulated visiting. They appointed two hours in the day when people might come to the anchorhold. Callers at other hours, no matter what their station or their business, would not be admitted. Abbot Raoul asked whether everyone understood this clearly. Everyone did.

So Colette turned back to her loved schedule of prayer and silence and work with gratitude. She was wise enough to know that she could benefit the people of Corbie even more by her prayers and her penances than by her words to them. Only one caller remained unimpressed by Father Jéhan's and Abbot Raoul's announcements. He came more and more often and stayed longer and longer. His name was Satan.

Until this beginning of the infernal visitations, Father Pierre de Vaux and Sister Perrine, both always primarily concerned with Colette's miracles and the coming work of her restoration, give only the sketchiest details of her life in the anchorhold. Secondary sources, such as the works of Sylvère d'Abbéville, Thonon, Abbé Douillet, and others, supply the lack. While their writings do not have the indisputable authority of the first two biographers, centuries-old traditions as well as the actual material relics from the anchorhold support their testimony. It seems safe to believe that what they say of Colette's reclusion is accurate.

It has been said that the devil's greatest victory is that he is not taken seriously. St. Peter cautioned the early Christians that the devil "goes about like a roaring lion, seeking whom he may devour." Those who chant the Divine Office repeat the warning each evening at Compline. Yet it is all too easy to let the awful words become as casual as a remark about the weather. We realize this when we contrast what our reaction would certainly be to the sight of a roaring lion in our front hall with the nonchalance with which we remain in the company of the father of lies while he fans our temptations into flames.

Now, some may be apt to turn away from the regimen of Colette's life as a recluse with offended sensibilities. How really revolting and sadistic—this young woman scourging herself, starving herself, squandering her sleep on endless prayer! And the Freudians will be sure to rush forward with dark suggestions of masochism. They are so much more balanced, these people. If they live on crackers and parsley, it is for the very sensible reason of preserving their figures and not for some nonsense about self-abnegation for the love of God. They may swarm like sycophants on those higher in the social scale, but for a really great reward like being mentioned in the newspaper as among the guests at Mrs. Dives Lorgnette's New Year's tea. To curry God's favor is outside the limits of such a triumph. Their feverish, killing activity brings them, after all, the tangible recompense of an extra zero in their yearly income. If they get heart attacks—well, a man must take the risk for that extra zero.

Doing voluntary penance for the love of God so that souls who do no penance may perhaps yet be saved has, of course, no ponderable results. It is foolish. It seems rather disgusting. So argues many a man and a woman. The one who was the most beautiful of the archangels is wiser. Lucifer lost his throne in heaven, but he did not lose his archangelic intelligence. He knew the young tertiary was a threat to his kingdom of lost souls so terrible that no time must be lost. He determined to call on Colette personally.

The period of divine consolations had lasted well over a year, and now the young anchoress was beginning to experience the dryness of spirit and aridity in prayer which Father Jéhan had warned her would inevitably come. For every soul, there are seasons of joy and seasons of sorrow, alternated by God with divine artistry, that the soul may be strengthened by suffering to bear loftier joys and supported by joy to endure more profound suffering. The holier the soul, the more refined are both its joys and its sufferings. Colette was to experience the exquisiteness of both.

It is the ordinary strategy of the devil to strike at a soul when it is most vulnerable. And, as does any cad, he stabs from the back. Into the desert of the young recluse's spirit, from which all the oases of enthusiasm and gladness seemed to have vanished like mirages, came the silken sympathy of Satan. "It is too much to bear, this living death. And to what purpose is it, my dear? No wonder your heart is full of sadness and weariness. No one can go on like this very long. Admit you have made a mistake. It is not too late."

Colette recognized the voice of "l'ennemi d'homme," "the enemy of man," as she preferred to call Satan. And she ignored him, throwing up against her sense of discouragement and lethargy the iron defenses of faith. The devil (who cannot see into our minds) apparently mistook her silence for his gain and, appearing to her in visible form, pressed his sympathy further. "How will you be able to stand this life in your prison for twenty, thirty, or perhaps sixty years?" He had taken Colette's intelligence into his reckonings, but not her wit. She wheeled on him in contempt. "And you? How will you be able to endure the torments of hell—not for twenty or thirty or sixty years, but for all eternity?" The young tertiary's words must have smitten Satan like an echo of God's answering curse to his own defiant, "I will not serve!" He left Colette for a time.

When he returned to the attack, he brought a numerous company of demons with him. They taunted her, abused her, threatened to tear her to pieces. Colette surveyed them with faint amusement. "You must be very brave indeed to come in such numbers against one poor little creature like myself." The demons replied with howls of rage. But if they thought to intimidate their young adversary, they were mistaken. She gave them another dose of truth. "He who has cast you out of paradise will not permit you to harm one hair of my head." Victorious in faith, Colette terminated the visit. She gestured toward the church. "God's Presence is here. Get out!" They knew It was. They got out.

The demons' retaliation, however, for this triumph of hers came in a form calculated to make any woman, and perhaps a French woman particularly, take to her heels; or, in the event of her being a recluse behind a sealed door, at least to give out some really fortissimo screams. Loathsome reptiles appeared crawling across the little floor she kept so spotlessly clean. They undulated their ugly lengths across her straw mat. Some rose up and poised themselves to strike at her. Hideous vulture-like birds appeared from nowhere and flapped their black wings against her head. Apparently this was the one of Satan's attacks that affected Colette most, for there is no record of her giving any witty replies this time.

She who could snap her fingers at the threat of being torn to pieces fell to her knees and prayed God to take away the snakes. The horrible creatures were everywhere. Three centuries earlier, St. Clare had moved the heart of God with her touching woman's plea in the face of the invasion of her monastery by the Saracens: "Lord, don't deliver over to beasts Your little handmaids who trust in You." And she held up the pyx containing the Blessed Sacrament, her weapon against the barbarians. They were vanquished in a moment. Colette went for a weapon, too. She snatched her crucifix from the wall and held it high against the writhing, slimy serpents, too frightened to manage any prayer beyond "Oh, dear Lord!" He heard it. The snakes all disappeared. Chivalry is not usually listed among the Divine Attributes, but one cannot fail to remark it in the Lord.

The devil's final siege at this period was laid against the anchoress' reputation. One night he broke down the wall of her room which gave onto the street. Evidently he accomplished the demolition from inside the anchorhold, as Colette has left us the detail that "he came down the chimney," a circumstance which would be amusing out of context. The breach he made was quite large enough for a person to step through, as the saint later described it to Sister Perrine. Viewed by the townspeople in the morning, it would mean the end of her good name. She would be seen as no recluse at all, but a hypocrite and deceiver, very likely a low woman. The anchoress surveyed the huge gap giving into the darkness of Corbie's midnight. Something had to be done, and quickly. She could not replace the stones, for they had all mysteriously disappeared. Anyway, the rent was so jagged it could never be concealed. To try to explain the destruction as diabolic would be useless. Scandal is always so much more credible than Satan is.

So Colette simply shifted the responsibility to shoulders stronger than her own. Sister Perrine has recorded how the saint took her little picture of our Lady down from the wall and placed it against the broken outer wall, face on. The image of Mary must have been almost lost to sight in the enormous gap, but Colette did not waver in her confidence. After a last prayer, she lay down on the straw mat to get a little sleep. It would not be like our Lady to resist such trust. When Colette awakened, the wall was repaired. No trace of the demolition could be seen.

Satan had apparently exhausted his bag of tricks for the present. But instead of entering upon a season of undisturbed solitude after these harrowing encounters, Colette was led deeper into the mystery of her vocation by a series of visions. She was now brought by God to the home of her tormentors; and from the threshold of hell, she watched souls plunging themselves into the eternal agonies. Above the pool of flame, as she described it, she saw other souls swirling, "as thickly as autumn leaves," ready to be sucked into the frightful fire. She saw the world in great panoramic visions which revealed to her all the estates of the Church and of secular governments. She knew the sins committed by the rulers and subjects of both. God then placed hell again before the eyes of her soul, and she saw more and more souls dropping into its torments.

Years later, she told her confessor, Father Pierre de Vaux, and her confidante, Sister Perrine, how terrified she had been that she would "slip and fall in." A very human reaction to a dreadful spiritual reality! She took very human precautions, too, against the danger, clasping with all the force she could muster the bars set into the little wicket in the door. They were the strongest thing she could find to hold on to during this ordeal. It continued at intervals for seven days; and when the eighth day finally brought surcease, Colette found herself quite unable to relax her desperate grip on the bars. When she at last regained control of her hands, she managed to calm herself. In later years she declared that the terrible things she had seen would remain engraved on her soul until her death. She began to pray with more fervor than ever before for the salvation of souls, and that the evils in Church and state might be uprooted.

However, Colette had not yet understood the full malice of sin. The Friday following these seven days of terror brought her an entirely different experience. Having seen the hell into which sin plunges men, she now saw to what a state the burden of sin He took upon Himself had reduced our Redeemer. Our Lord appeared to her as He had looked at the time of His crucifixion. "Our Lord Himself," she said simply to Sister Perrine years later, "permitted me to see and hear all the sufferings which He had endured for the love of men." She added that it was only by the miracle of His sustaining strength that she had not immediately died of the sight. Something of death, however, did enter into her soul at the vision; for Father Pierre de Vaux tells us that until the end of her life Colette would become frozen and insensible with grief at any mention of the sufferings of our Lord in His Passion and crucifixion.

After this visitation, which caused her far deeper anguish than had the visions of hell, God consoled Colette, giving her to understand that there would be a reform in the Church and in society, and that it would come in large measure from the restoration of primitive observance and fervor in the Franciscan Orders. She tells us that she received this revelation with boundless joy. Her unswerving devotedness to St. Francis and St. Clare increased her happiness at learning that their religious children were to do so much to repair the insults to God's honor. From her little anchorhold, as a member of the Franciscan family, she would share by prayer and penance in all that was to be accomplished. But then came the climactic vision.

One day Colette beheld her beloved St. Francis himself on his knees before Christ. Behind him, half-hidden in a kind of mist, stood a woman in a religious habit very like Francis' own. With one pierced hand, St. Francis drew her forward. The other hand he stretched out, open-palmed, to Christ, in the manner of one asking an alms. Colette heard the voice of the little Poor Man begging the Lord to regenerate his religious family. He prayed that the woman beside him should be given to the Franciscan Order to be the leader and chief in its reform. Christ manifested His willingness, and the anchoress watched St. Francis prostrate himself in thanksgiving. Then the nun in the vision moved forward, and Colette began to tremble. For the nun chosen by St. Francis and appointed by Christ for the reform of the Franciscan Order looked at her, and Colette saw that it was herself.

For days she could not eat or sleep. She protested to God with arguments that touch the heart both by their human urgency and by the intimacy with our Lord which they reveal. "No, no, Lord!" she kept repeating, following this outright refusal with reasoning which, as she later told Sister Perrine, seemed to her enormously convincing if only because it was so obvious. "How can an ignorant girl and a miserable sinner like me even think of undertaking such a work?" In her naïveté, it seems, Colette expected Divine Wisdom to reply: "You're right. I have made a mistake." But there came no further word or vision from heaven, only her vast uneasiness, which could not be dispelled either by prayer or by reasoning.

Desperate, she produced her trump card: her vow of enclosure. Years later, Colette told Father Pierre how, with an ingenuousness that must surely have stirred the mirth of God, she objected: "Now, Lord, how can I run about the world and work for You on the outside, when it is through Your own doing that I am enclosed within these walls forever?" But even this delightful bit of remonstrance with the divine plan brought no direct reply from God. His only defense of His own will came in a very curious form which the saint has described for us.

Miraculously, a golden tree sprang up in the little anchorhold. Then, quickly, and rooted only in air, numerous tiny golden trees appeared clustering around the large one. Colette admitted later to Perrine that she had sensed what this meant, yet she refused the interpretation, thrusting it from her mind with an energy worthy of a better cause. She caught hold of the lovely little trees and flung them from the small window of her room. (She must have had to climb up onto her table and possibly even place her little bench on top of that to accomplish this feat. The picture of her scrambling up and down this improvised ladder with handfuls of golden trees and tossing them out the window as though they were dead mice is surely one to treasure.)

"This is all the work of the devil," Colette kept assuring herself, rather in the manner of a small boy whistling in the dark. But after each clearance, new little trees would spring up around the immovable large one. Finally, Colette could no longer resist the voice within her soul which told her that this tall tree was herself and the tiny gold forest around it was the company of those who would follow her in the work of the reform. With something of desperation, and after many hesitancies, she finally confided all this to Father Jéhan, still half-hoping to be told that it was a deceit of the devil. Far from fulfilling her hope, Father Jéhan dashed it by confiding to her in turn that he himself had been granted a vision. (The account of it is preserved by Sister Perrine.) He had seen a young girl working most laboriously in a tangled, weed-ridden vineyard. With untiring patience, the girl uprooted weed after weed, pulled each shrivelled leaf off the vines, and tied up the young plants with the most painstaking tenderness. He had been told that the vineyard was the religious life and the girl was Colette.

The Franciscan friar's voice was very gentle as he humbly related this vision of his. With love and sympathy he showed her how it accorded with her own vision of the miraculous trees. He was kind but unshakably insistent when he told her that she must accept God's will. He reminded her that God's grace would always outmeasure His demands. He promised to help her in every way possible. Colette clung to Father Jéhan's reassurances. She determined to leave the whole matter in his hands. But then Father Jéhan did a most unco-operative and even inconsiderate thing. He died.

Oddly enough, instead of throwing her back into a state of spiritual turmoil, this untimely death seemed to confirm Colette for a time in her new serenity. The whole affair was so utterly impossible, to her way of thinking, and this new development sealed its incredibility. If it was as fantastic as *that* from human perspective, perhaps, after all, it *was* the divine will. The reflection established her in a temporary measure of peace that left her wholly unprepared for the fresh tide of revolt that suddenly shook her soul.

This time God took dramatic action against her objections. The revolt which she justified to herself on the grounds of her own unfitness for the enterprise was shown to her by God as containing as much of human obstinacy as of humility. To impress this on her, He struck her dumb. For three days, she remained mute, appearing at the wicket only to refuse with a shake of her head the little supper brought her each evening by her friends. Jacquette and Guillemette, and Marie Sénéchal who often joined them now, wept at the sight of Colette's pinched white face and the pathetic pantomime by which she showed them what had happened. They wept even more when, on the fourth day, the wicket was opened by the clumsy hand of a blind girl. To muteness, God added the trial of blindness when Colette still refused to submit.

Those were six days of pure anguish, but Colette emerged from the martyrdom with a splendid prize. She had learned complete obedience. Her heart framed at last the words her lips could not: "Dear Lord, I am Your handmaid." That was all, but immediately she could see. Her tongue was loosed in an instant, and she repeated aloud: "Dear Lord, I am Your handmaid." The Lord ever afterward kept the anniversary of this submission which had cost her more than life, by referring to her always as "My little handmaid," as though it were her name. Father Pierre almost constantly describes the saint, throughout his long biography, as "la petite ancelle."

There was nothing to do now but wait. She had given herself entirely to the divine will at last. When and how it would be manifested further was outside her sphere of action. She prayed and waited, spending her free hours in filling page after page in her brisk French script with detailed memoranda of her revelations and the work she had been given to accomplish. She added the last article to the little sheaf of manuscripts one day early in July, in the year 1406. She had been enclosed for well over three years now, and every detail of the anchorhold was dear as life to her. She looked around the familiar room with affectionate satisfaction, and then tilted her head up to the high-set window where one of the miraculous golden trees was still "growing." Then she heard the hard fall of the knocker on the outside wicket. She went over and opened it, prepared to hear of some townswoman's newest difficulty. She stepped back in surprise when she saw instead an elderly woman, obviously an aristocrat, with two servants flanking her like bodyguards and eyeing the small parlor with some displeasure. But the tired face of the woman under her rich hood was gentle and kind.

Behind her stood a Franciscan friar, dusty and travel-stained, and Father Jean Guyot. Colette greeted them in the name of God and wished them peace. Then Father Guyot stepped forward. "These friends have travelled many miles to speak to you, my child." He turned slightly to one side, crowding the disgruntled servants still more, and bowed to the lady. "Madame, my Lady, I present to you our recluse, Colette Boellet." And turning to the surprised anchoress, he said: "This is her Ladyship, the Baroness of Brissay. And this" —a nod toward the friar—"is Father Henri de la Baume."

8 *The End of Reclusion*

In 1405, the confusion over who was the true pope was fast worsening. The ineffectual Boniface IX, successor to the violent Urban VI, had died the year before; and the conclave had elected Innocent VII as the new pope. Innocent was well-intentioned enough, and the hope of perplexed Christians for an end to the schism began to revive. However, Innocent was to live only two years after his election, and he never managed to cut any sort of clear path through the jungle of politics and intrigue in which the papal claimants seemed now hopelessly lost. Pope Innocent held the precarious loyalty of most of Italy, while Pedro de Luna, styled Benedict XIII since his election by the dissident cardinals as successor to Clement VII in 1394, was again supported by France, though that country had for a time withdrawn her allegiance to Benedict and stoutly refused to recognize any pope at all.

Time was ripening for the election of a third "pope" by the unwieldy and illegal council of Pisa, and many of the most learned and brilliant churchmen of the time admitted themselves at a loss to untangle the skeins of claim and counterclaim. Innocent VII sat on his throne, unhappy but convinced of his true apostolic succession. Benedict XIII travelled indefatigably from city to city, encouraged by the return of France to his side to seek the allegiance of the north of Italy and finally to "take" Rome. The fact that the clergy of France had been summoned to discuss the authenticity of the double papal claims no less than four times since the accession of Boniface IX gives a clear enough idea of how complex the issue had grown.

Among the intellectuals of the French clergy who could reach no satisfying conclusion was a Franciscan friar of the monastery of Chambéry, Père Henri de la Baume, Pierre de Vaux, who was his close friend, describes him as "a man of great perfection, loving and fearing God from his youth, ignorant of transitory and temporal things but wise and prudent in spiritual affairs." Perhaps Father Pierre's enthusiasm for his friend's spiritual genius led him to point it up with this facile contrast. Actually, the diplomacy with which Henri de la Baume approached such formidable nobles as John the Fearless of Burgundy and the energy with which he later stood his ground for the cause of the reform, even to the extent of engaging lawyers to defend Colette's interest, indicate that Father Henri was far from ignorant of temporal affairs and their expeditious handling. That such things were distasteful to a man more inclined to prayer than to argument is witnessed throughout the friar's life by all who knew him well. That is probably all that Father Pierre de Vaux intended to convey to us.

The Chambéry friar had a reputation for great holiness as well as mental acumen, and many of the laity turned to him for advice on the burning question of the papal claimants. Father Henri listened to their perplexities with something of fright as well as sympathy. Himself unsure, how could he advise the troubled laymen, and priests too, who sought him out? In 1405, he could bear such a responsibility no longer. After months of study and prayer for light, he decided to ask his superior for permission to make a pilgrimage to the Holy Land. He felt he must get free of the stale air of confusion in which he was suffocating in France. And he had a deep confidence that personal contact with the most sacred spots in Christendom would bring him not only spiritual graces but enlightenment on the tragic state of the papacy. Permission was given to him; and in 1406, Father Henri began his journey toward Jerusalem. The pilgrimage he was undertaking would probably involve his absence from France for two or three years. Surely there was reason to hope that the issues at stake in the Church might be less obscure by then.

Father Henri was forty years old when he set out along the banks of the Rhone, and the spirit of the Poverello was strong in him. This true son of St. Francis had no intention of cushioning his pilgrimage with the wealth and prestige of his family (probably a junior branch of the ancient and powerful house of de la Baume which branched from the Dukes of Savoy whom it served, and at all events "one of the foremost of the country," as the earliest chroniclers assure us). He begged his bread as he went along, and never met a refusal. Father Henri, we are told, was a handsome man possessed of great natural charm. People were intrigued at the sight of this friar of such noble bearing whose luggage consisted only of a bag and a stick, humbly asking an alms of them; they felt honored to give it to him. The cares and anxieties of secular and ecclesiastical affairs steadily receded as he strode along under bright Provençal skies, and Father Henri started to sing. His plan was to walk to Marseilles and then take ship for Syria. However, his arrival at Avignon marked the end of his proposed pilgrimage to the Holy Land and the beginning of his life's great work.

Avignon had a recluse of its own, Marie Amante, who was much respected for her holiness and insight. As nearly all pilgrims passing through Avignon did, Father Henri determined to call on her and ask her prayers. He was startled when Marie Amante looked at him through the little wicket for a long time without uttering a word. Finally she spoke, and the friar's amazement was complete. "Sir pilgrim, it is not to Jerusalem you are to go. God has other designs in view for you. That path is not the right one to take." Father Henri would have liked to smile this advice away, but Marie Amante was said to receive frequent communications from heaven. She asked him to return the next day and told him she would spend the entire night in prayer for him. Very likely Father Henri spent it the same way. He could have had little inclination to sleep in the face of this intimation that his escape was to be blocked.

When he returned the next day, Marie Amante shattered any doubts the friar might have had about her reliability as bearer of God's plans by quietly reminding him of a number of facts in his past life unknown to anyone but himself. Father Henri's jaw dropped, and he stood silent, waiting to be set in another direction. He was told it was Picardy.

Marie explained to the priest that there was a young recluse in Corbie of Picardy. The girl was called Colette, she said, and had been entrusted by God with a great undertaking, one she could not carry out alone. She was to restore the Franciscan Order to primitive observance. And it was God's will that Henri de la Baume should go quickly and help her, and that he should try to procure the necessary support for such an undertaking on his way.

It was certainly quite a task to impose on one who had been fleeing responsibility. But Marie Amante only smiled as sweetly and calmly as though she had asked him to fetch her a bunch of wildflowers. "Turn to the north," she said, "there is the right road." She asked for his blessing, and he traced over her the sign of the cross like a man in a dream. She rose again and looked at the friar's face, and apparently felt a sudden wave of compassion for him. "May God assist you," she added gently. "I will pray for you." She closed the wicket and Father Henri turned out into the strong sunlight of the Avignon morning.

Now, whether Marie Amante's knowledge of Colette and her mission was entirely supernatural, as the old historian Sylvère d'Abbéville insists it was, or whether she had been told of the strange happenings in the Corbie anchorhold by travelling Franciscan visitators or pilgrims (to whom Colette might easily have confided her mission, and her perplexity about carrying it out, in the hope of receiving the friars' advice and prayers) is for each one's free decision. The saint herself has not informed us. God's hand is certainly evident throughout Colette's life, but it would be a mistake to insist that every event in it was supernatural. There has been all too much of this in past accounts, with the result that Colette has become increasingly remote, a kind of super-being quite beyond our human horizons. It seems very probable that Colette would humbly send word by travelling priests to her sister-recluse in Avignon, asking for her prayers and perhaps inquiring whether Marie Amante might have been enlightened in any way as to how Colette was to set about the tremendous enterprise God had entrusted to her.

Gradually the full impact of Marie Amante's words broke through Father Henri's sense of shock. Although his conviction of his own complete unworthiness for any such task as the Avignon recluse had outlined grew rather than diminished, he later admitted that he could not shake off a strange feeling of joy even in his perplexity and fear. For the dissension within France and the schism in Christendom were not the only sources of Father Henri's agony of soul. His own Franciscan Order paralleled Church and country in its state of confusion, division, and conflict.

Himself fiercely dedicated to the ideals of St. Francis and to primitive observance "without gloss," he had suffered all his religious life from irreconcilable ideal and practice. A man of de la Baume's spiritual proportions was unable to follow the reasoning of those who argued that the Franciscan ideal was no longer practicable. To Father Henri, this was to maintain that the Gospel no longer provided working principles for life and sanctity. With his innate horror of dispute and wrangling, he kept aloof from the quarrels between the zealots and the mitigants, only trying to govern his own life as far as possible by the first ideals of the founder and praying unceasingly that his Order might somehow be restored to its original lines.

The idea that he himself should be co-agent in this restoration was too preposterous ever to have occurred to Father Henri. The notion that he was to work for this end in company with a young girl of whom he knew nothing—whom he had never even seen!—put the finishing touch on the fantastic outlines of the whole affair. It was simply inconceivable. Marie Amante was deluded. But he was a sensible man. He would go on to Jerusalem as he had planned.

All this made sense with the bright sunlight and the small clatter of ordinary living about him in Avignon. But the face of Marie Amante looked out at him from every turn in his path. Her level gaze met his when he opened his breviary or fingered his rosary. And the joy of her message grew stronger. The reform of the Franciscan Order! The distillation of his own hopes and dreams! Could he refuse? Had God any real need of a worthy worker? Did He perhaps will to be the more glorified by attaining His divine ends through a fool like himself—like Henri de la Baume who had preferred flight to combat? Finally, he gave in, afraid, as he said, to disregard the recluse's counsel. He retraced his steps to Savoy and went to call on his great friend, Countess Blanche of Geneva.

Blanche de Genève had been widowed since 1390, and now lived alone, a woman of immense wealth, limitless prestige, and—unusual complement to these—boundless benevolence. She was the sister of Count Robert of Geneva, the first anti-pope who had been known as Clement VII. Blanche never for a moment doubted that her brother had been the true pope, and she exerted immense influence on the thinking of those about her. Rather despotic, and greatly attached to her position and her dignity, the old countess was nevertheless an entirely good woman, one who could always be reached on the spiritual plane. The fact that she listened to Father Henri's strange tale of his interrupted pilgrimage with such acute interest and determined at once to help him is proof enough of this.

The countess had the greatest esteem for Father Henri's learning and sanctity, and she now declared herself ready to put her resources at his disposal. The first thing she gave him was a letter of introduction to her friend the Baroness de Brissay, Isabeau de Rochechouart, a very wealthy and childless widow who lived at Besançon and devoted her time and her riches to works of charity.

Obediently, Father Henri set out for Besançon. He had full permission from his superior to act as circumstances would indicate; either because the superior believed God's hand was in the affair, or because he had no intention of crossing the wishes of the redoubtable Blanche de Genève.

The Baroness de Brissay was likewise moved by Father Henri's story, and with her usual energy made immediate plans for the journey to Corbie, which would take about twenty days. She appointed a small train of attendants for herself, as befitted her position, and appointed Father Henri as chaplain of the group. It was a strange little party that set out that June morning in 1406. The ageing baroness sat back in her rich carriage with servants facing her and flanking her on either side in anticipation of her every want. A second carriage held more servants and supplies. A few lowlier attendants walked on foot, in their midst an aristocratic-looking Franciscan friar who had stoutly refused a place in the carriage. And the goal of their difficult journey under a summer sun was a tiny anchorhold set against the church of Notre Dame in Corbie, where a twenty-four-year-old girl of lowly birth and very little education held in trust one of the greatest and most difficult enterprises ever entrusted to a woman.

It was July when they arrived in Corbie. They went at once to the parish priest of Notre Dame, Father Jean Guyot, and were heartened to hear his high praises of the young recluse. The priest took it for granted that this important party was just one more of those who wished to satisfy their piety, and very likely their curiosity too, by a visit to Colette. The patient man led them to the door of the anchorhold, doubtless with a surge of civic pride that a great personage like the Baroness de Brissay should come to little Corbie, and a sense of satisfaction in having this hermitage for a place of pilgrimage.

As Colette looked into the face of Father Henri, she was suddenly caught up by an inspiration she could not resist. She ordered the servants of the baroness to throw down the door of her hermitage! They moved to obey her without a word.

Somewhat dazedly, the friar and the baroness stepped inside Colette's little retreat. Isabeau de Brissay looked around at the sparse furnishings, the little mat of straw on the floor, the immaculate cleanliness of the poor place. And she began to weep. Father Henri and Colette seemed unaware of her. Under a common impulse, they had begun to praise God, facing each other, and apparently overcome by the intuition that they represented two great choirs, the First and Second Franciscan Orders. Their extemporaneous chant rose and fell, while the baroness looked on, tears splashing on the film of dust that covered her thin velvet mantle.

After a while, Colette disappeared into her oratory without a word, although no kind of normal human greeting had yet been interchanged. No one seemed to feel it necessary. Outside, people were gathering around the broken door of the anchorhold, and Father Jean Guyot was in a ferment of anxiety. Had Colette gone mad? And how was it that the servants of the baroness had been able to get the heavy stones around the door loose in a matter of moments? The distinguished visitors seemed to make nothing strange of what she had done; and he retained sufficient mental clarity to know he dare not remonstrate with the baroness for entering the hermitage, or even with Colette while the great lady was present.

In her oratory, Colette was on her knees at the inner wicket, with thought for no one but the One in the tabernacle, at whose golden doors her eyes were straining. Sister Perrine has left us the text of the saint's prayer at this epochal hour: "I dedicate myself," Colette whispered into the shadows of the church, "in health, in illness, in my life, in my death, in all my desires, in all my deeds, so that I may never work henceforth except for Your glory, for the salvation of souls, and towards the reform for which You have chosen me. From this moment on, dearest Lord, there is nothing which I am not prepared to undertake for love of You." The young anchoress certainly meant this dedication with its full profundity, however little she was able to plumb it at that moment. The Lord took her at her word.

At last she rose from her knees and came back to the little room where Father Henri and the Baroness de Brissay awaited her in respectful silence. Suddenly she seemed to see the broken door for the first time. She stepped over to it, and with a serene smile assured Father Jean Guyot that everything was quite all right. She would explain to him later why she had ordered the door to be thrown down. The harassed priest was somewhat reassured at the calmness of her voice and turned to the people, waving them back with some return of authority. They were slow to obey, but Colette's gentle voice accomplished what Father Guyot's vehement gestures could not. "Please leave me now," she asked them. "I have been ordered by higher Authority to break this door, but I have no authority to come out. I will explain more to you later when our guests have departed."

This tactful reminder to the small knot of townspeople that there was a very distinguished person present to whom every courtesy must be shown had its effect. They began drifting away under Father Guyot's encouragement, and Colette turned back to her visitors. She saw them gazing at the high window where a glint of gold on one of the stones just under the opening had caught their eyes. It was the last of the tiny golden trees. She had evidently kept at the work of uprooting with dogged perseverance, for Sister Perrine writes that the little tree seen by Father Henri and Isabeau was "the one that had until then resisted the efforts of the humble anchoress."

Doubtless "the humble anchoress" had to explain its origin to her new friends, and with some chagrin, since she made a point of telling the incident to Perrine so many years later. Still, chagrin was surely less the mood of the hour than a kind of foretaste of the nostalgia she would later feel for this beloved place where she had spent nearly four happy years of solitude and prayer. Now they were ending. The servants of the baroness were throwing down some more loose stones from the door. Across five centuries we can hear the poignant symbolism of their falling.

9 *The Abbess-General*

Carried out of herself at the first encounter with the Franciscan friar who she understood was to be her helpmeet in the work of the reform, Colette had shown herself the true mystic, substituting the praises of God for small etiquette. But when the moment of intuition had passed, she set about making plans for the immediate future with a practicality that amazed the baroness and greatly pleased Father Henri. All her life Colette combined a disarming feminine gentleness with the forcefulness of a general who could not comprehend defeat. Demolishing the entrance of her anchorhold under divine inspiration was one thing. Stepping out of the small enclosure was another. She was bound by a solemn vow, and the first thing she needed was to be dispensed from it.

She sat at her table and wrote in her clear, swift hand the reasons why she now asked the pope to dispense her from her vow of enclosure. Father Henri saw her blink tears out of her eyes from time to time. "If you did not love the enclosure, madame, you would not be strong enough to live outside it," he said. She remembered these words and repeated them years later. This was only the first of hundreds of times when Father Henri was to reveal the curious bond between his soul and Colette's which made him intuitively perceptive of her needs. She could appreciate the "madame," too. To the friar, she was the spouse of God. She was Madame Colette.

At last her flying pen halted, and she held the long page out to the baroness. "As soon as the dispensation is granted, we must go directly to the Holy Father and lay everything before him. It seems to me the best thing that your ladyship and Father Henri should take this document straight to Cardinal de Chalant yourselves. We will get much quicker action if your ladyship is there in person."

Isabeau must have accepted this shrewd observation with some amusement. She read quickly through the document. Accustomed always to making whatever arrangements needed making and to giving all orders requiring to be given, the Baroness de Brissay accepted Colette's leadership with entire good grace. In the short space since their arrival at Corbie, the elderly women had already developed an affection for the young recluse. She was only surprised that one so evidently the mystic should be as evidently the cool-headed businesswoman. One is reminded of another Poor Clare, St. Veronica Giuliani, whose life astonishes us at nearly every hour with its extraordinary mystical phenomena but who designed and installed in her monastery a system of plumbing which was the wonder of the town.

Like an obedient ambassadress of the queen, Baroness Isabeau set out for Paris with Father Henri and her train of servants. The Apostolic Nuncio, Cardinal Jean de Chalant, showed himself a true son of eternal Rome by brushing away the talk of haste with a deprecating smile. "We do not grant dispensations from a solemn vow overnight, your ladyship." Isabeau de Brissay set her aristocratic jaw and went to work. She brought all the forces of her own eloquence and her high position to bear upon the cardinal. She reminded him that the whole affair was supernatural and that even a cardinal might have reason to tremble under his ermine if God were not obeyed.

She also was at pains to have him recall that this great spiritual enterprise which necessarily involved Colette's leaving her enclosure was sponsored by the sister of the late Pope Clement VII (God rest his soul), Countess Blanche de Genève. If Cardinal de Chalant was not entirely convinced of God's part in it all, he became very clear in his mind about the part Blanche de Genève had in it. He allowed himself to be persuaded to write to the Bishop of Amiens and ask that prelate to send one of his vicars to Corbie to interrogate Colette and examine into the reasons for the dispensation.

The report came back in short order, and it was favorable. Baroness de Brissay was long accustomed to getting her own will without delay, but this time she admitted that she had had to argue and plead like a commoner. Relating the events of these days in Paris to Colette afterward, the old baroness confided with somewhat ruffled dignity: "My dear, I have *worked*. I have *labored*. Really, it has been an ordeal!" Colette must have struggled against a smile as she sympathized with the great Isabeau de Brissay so misused by the Holy Roman Catholic Church as to have been obliged to work.

But Isabeau did succeed. With unheard of speed, the dispensation was signed on the first of August and published in the town of Corbie on the third. The objections in Paris had been to the haste on which Isabeau insisted. In Corbie, the promulgation of the dispensation raised hot objections to the action itself.

The people were incensed at the idea of having their now famous recluse taken from them. Dom Raoul de Raye was indignant at having been thrust into the background in the affair, and Colette tried in vain to appease her guardian with reminders of God's will and explanations of the supernatural turn of events which had taken the initiative out of her hands. Abbot Raoul was not to be mollified. The personal slight he felt he had suffered as well as the loss to the fame of his monastery and town which would certainly be sustained after Colette's departure cut the old man's pride to its core. He never again came to Colette's aid, even though she was to need it sorely in the trials that lay ahead of her. If she, of all who knew Dom Raoul, had seen him oftenest at his best, she now saw him at his very worst—implacably proud, betrayed by material considerations and human respect. She kept her grief and her disappointment to herself, however, telling Father Henri only much later in her life what these first days of estrangement from the abbot cost her. Determinedly, she set about organizing the long journey from Corbie to Nice, where Pope Benedict XIII was at that time residing in the course of his peregrinations in search of added support for his claims to the chair of Peter.

The past year had been an exhausting one for the thin Spanish friar who styled himself Pope Benedict XIII. When the Duke of

Savoy, for the moment his staunch supporter, had given Pedro de Luna his castle at Nice, the pope had promptly gone there, spending the first months of 1405 in calculations, negotiations, and endless interviews with the worldly great designed to further his cause with northern Italy. When these careful preparations were completed, Benedict chartered six galleys and sailed toward Genoa with every possible show of pomp and magnificence. It was his intention to overawe the Italians with his gorgeous display; and, in a measure, he succeeded. He received the full homage due to the pope at Monaco and Albenga; and when he finally arrived at Genoa, he was given one of those wildly enthusiastic welcomes at which the Italians are the world's masters. The great cries of "Viva il papa" were soothing music to the ears of Benedict XIII. However, all that followed was not so utopian.

For one thing, the unsanitary conditions in Genoa horrified the fastidious Spaniard. One of those vague medieval pestilences was wandering over Italy at the time, and he had no intention of getting in its path. Moreover, his reception by a number of princes in Italy was many degrees cooler than the vociferous welcomes when he landed. The restless, driven Pedro de Luna decided that the hour was not yet ripe for taking Rome, so he returned to Nice and began a fresh series of calculations for his meeting with Pope Gregory XII. Pope Gregory, formerly known as Angelo Corrario, had just been elected on the death of Innocent VII. Before his election, all the cardinals of the first obedience—that is, those supporting the successors of Pope Urban VI—had agreed that the one of their number chosen to be pope should do all in his power to end the schism, should meet with Benedict XIII, and even be willing to renounce his own authentic claim to the papal throne should Benedict likewise agree to resign. In that event, a new election could be held and the double succession ended. All of Christendom, therefore, hoped and prayed for some beneficial and lasting effects from this meeting; but it came to nothing. The canny Spaniard and the worried Italian merely sparred with words, parted with every observance of the social amenities, and returned to their respective thrones, each as convinced of his own claims as before, each unwilling to concede an inch to the other.

And now, into this charged atmosphere of intrigue and confusion, came the strange little party from Corbie. Those who prefer to paint Pedro de Luna all black are hard put to explain his readiness to listen to an unknown young Franciscan tertiary from insignificant Corbie. Surely this uneducated girl of low station could be of no possible aid to the pope's interests. Those, on the other hand, who are convinced of Benedict's sincerity point to his reception of Colette as proof of his unworldliness, his genuine zeal for the glory of God. The first meeting between the humble recluse from Corbie and the aristocratic pope from Catalonia does certainly draw into sharp focus the fundamental conflict in the character of Pedro de Luna.

Baroness Isabeau had taken care that this journey toward Nice should be used to Colette's advantage in every possible way. They set out one August morning in 1406, the baroness installed in one of the carriages, Colette insisting on walking with Father Henri and the servants, though later occasionally consenting to ride for a while on the one mule the party possessed. The whole of the town of Corbie turned out for the recluse's departure, with much muttering and some threats. Many of the women wept to see her go. Dom Raoul was conspicuously absent. And certainly no one was pleased.

Her friends later recalled that Colette's white face looked paler than they had ever seen it as she turned toward them that morning. The August sunlight picked out her tears, and for a moment the people stopped their murmuring, knowing themselves loved by this girl who was leaving them. But then a fresh sense of their loss bore down upon them, and the harsh, complaining farewells grew to new volume. Colette made a desperate sign to the baroness to order the coachman forward. Isabeau did, and the little party began to move, the baroness leaning back on her cushions, Father Henri and Colette walking quickly forward. She did not look back again at her people or her little anchorhold.

Baroness Isabeau had informed her friend Countess Blanche de Genève of how things were progressing, and that great lady had despatched a train of her own attendants and ladies of the court to meet Colette and her party at Dijon and escort them to Nice. Blanche had no uncertainties about the power of her name to provide an entree anywhere, and she named one of the ladies of the court to act as her personal ambassadress in this affair. She chose one on whose discretion she had relied in certain other instances and gave her a

detailed message to Benedict XIII in which she expressed her un-
qualified faith in the young recluse who was coming to lay before
him a plan assuredly divine. With careful intent, the old countess
ended her message by expressing the hope that his Holiness would
warmly receive this saintly girl as her own dear brother, Pope
Clement VII of beloved memory, would certainly have done.

All seemed in order, and Blanche de Genève settled back after the
departure of the party headed by her ambassadress with a sense of
satisfaction. She had reckoned on everything. Except the devil.

Still smarting from his recent defeats in the anchorhold of Corbie,
Satan contrived a revenge sufficient to abort Colette's plans and
hopes forever. He trained his diabolic batteries on the soul of
Countess Blanche's ambassadress. Without any warning, as her party
approached Nice, that high-born and prudent lady suddenly went
completely mad. Or so it appeared. Raving and incoherent, she ran
ahead of her impressive entourage and demanded to see the pope.
One can easily imagine the distaste with which Pedro de Luna's
elegant attendants viewed the hysterical woman. See the pope?
Never! Benedict XIII was not accustomed to grant interviews to
lunatics. But the woman persisted. There seemed only one clear
thought in the muddle of her madness: she *must* see the pope.

Here again, Pedro de Luna's curious greatness shows itself. His
servants despised the ranting woman. Her own companions were
horrified and revolted. Colette and Father Henri stood by, helpless.
Baroness Isabeau was on the verge of hysteria herself, and understandably; for both Father Pierre and Sister Perrine include in their
accounts of this weird incident the gross detail that the deranged
ambassadress would "tear off all her clothes, without any shame."
Yet, when the whole bizarre story was brought to Benedict XIII, he
was moved by charity to receive the woman. Aghast at his decision
and not a little disgusted, the servants grudgingly admitted this
woman, whose name has not come down to us but who is one of the
strangest figures in the life of St. Colette.

The ambassadress, behaving quite as insanely as on the preceding
days but at least this time fully clothed, entered the papal presence
and stared wildly about until her eyes found the spare figure of the
pope. At that moment the power of God broke Satan's hold on her,
and she went calmly forward to kiss Benedict's foot, explain her

mission, and deliver into his hands the documents written by Blanche de Genève. She seemed wholly unaware that anything unusual had been happening before the interview.

It would not have needed as sensitive a man as Pedro de Luna to be impressed by this extraordinary turn of events. He questioned the woman at length, and she answered him with the dignity and intelligence that had always distinguished her. Benedict did not try to conceal his interest. He appointed an audience for Colette the next day. He sent his warm personal greetings to Countess Blanche, with assurances that he hoped to show himself a worthy successor to her late illustrious brother in handling this unusual affair. The countess' proxy bowed herself out with her normal grace and elegance. The dazed servants of the pope were not the last to be overwhelmed by the happenings of these days. The cardinals who had escorted Benedict XIII to Nice were next in turn.

The following day, the pope sat on his throne, magnificent in apparel and imposing of manner, set like a small dark jewel in a scarlet mounting of cardinals. Something he probably could not have explained even to himself had prompted Benedict to receive the young recluse from Corbie as he would receive the greatest prince in Europe. This had baffled the cardinals sufficiently. But worse (or better!) was to come.

As Colette and her friends entered the pope's presence, the attendants' experienced eyes took in the impressive Baroness de Brissay and the distinguished-looking friar. They could not see much of the face of the barefooted young girl in the patched Franciscan habit. We have Father Henri's account, through Sister Perrine, of how Colette walked with downcast eyes until Isabeau urged her forward. She carried a kind of wallet in which were folded all the accounts she had written of her revelations and her formal request for the pope's authorization of the Franciscan reform. As she came to the step of the throne, she lifted her eyes to the pope for a moment as she was about to fall on her knees. But he was before her.

As though a giant hand had been laid on him, Benedict XIII rose from his throne and fell on his knees before Colette. (Father Pierre says, precisely, that "he fell," not that "he knelt down.") Years later Colette recalled to Sister Perrine the consternation with which she stood staring down at his ermined figure. The baroness and the friar drew back in alarm. But no one dared to touch the pope. It was he himself who finally broke the spell. He raised his head and held out his ringed hand to the nearest cardinal, who sprang forward to help him rise.

Benedict reseated himself on his throne and received Colette's obeisance as calmly as though this was the kind of reception he was accustomed to give visitors. He accepted the wallet and glanced quickly through its papers. Pedro de Luna had at one time been professor of Canon Law at the University of Montpelier. His practised legal eye sorted out the revelations and petitions with despatch. He was being asked for no niggardly authorization, though Colette's petition read like simplicity itself. She asked:

(1) to follow the apostolic and evangelical state according to the primitive Rule of St. Francis by entering his Second Order;

(2) to be authorized to undertake the restoration and reformation of the Orders which Sir St. Francis had instituted.

If he was inwardly shaken by the events of the past few days, the pope retained his native shrewdness. He knew that the opposition of the cardinals to these amazing requests was going to be vigorous, even outraged. He also knew that his own decision was already made, and by Whom. Until he could reconcile his cardinals and his own convictions, there was no purpose in keeping Colette. He dismissed her and her companions with promises to see them again after he had considered all these matters.

The pope's surmise about cardinalatial resistance was all too accurate. They stormed with protest. Strange as it may seem, they were almost as much opposed to Colette's first request as to her second. There had been so many sporadic and ephemeral attempts to live the first strict Franciscan Rule again. Experience had proved that it was all merely a romantic ideal, quite unsuitable for human beings. Men had failed. Could this frail-looking girl with the satiny pale face succeed? This was just the kind of misguided zeal which would occasion all manner of unfavorable reactions against the pope if he gave her his approval. And it was a time when Benedict could not afford to multiply his enemies, as the cardinals were careful to remind him. As if this were not enough, the girl talked of reforming the whole Order of St. Francis! No, the Orders! She would direct the friars as well as the Poor Clares, it seemed. It was assuredly the most preposterous scheme ever laid before any pope.

Benedict XIII listened to all these arguments. Probably the Franciscan friar under the papal robes listened to some memories, too. The first Franciscan Rule! The first ideals of the Poverello, his father! Once these things had been the term of his own ambition. The full Spanish lips set determinedly. And because the cardinals could see that the pope had made his decision, they argued the more passionately out of their desperation.

The pope wished to avoid open veto of his cardinals' recommendations, for he needed their support acutely. So he cast about for a way to convince them, meanwhile granting Colette several other interviews at which his admiration and respect for her grew prodigiously. He was amazed and delighted at the girl's intelligence and marvelous learning. And to think he had been told she was uneducated! Most of all, he was won by her humility. He gave her the unofficial assurance of his support, and asked her to pray that he could shortly make it official. With no hope of reaping any personal rewards from Colette's incredible undertaking except hostility and disdain, the Spanish friar-pope cast his resources down at her feet. Whether in his inmost heart he did sincerely believe in his true claim to the papacy, he knew that this girl—yes, this saint!—certainly believed in it. He was humbled by the knowledge. It made him at least momentarily great.

One day, Colette and the near-half of Christendom that clung to him would be completely disillusioned about Pedro de Luna's rights to the throne of Peter. But the reformer of the Franciscan Order was never to forget her debt to Benedict XIII. She was to perpetuate her gratitude in a poignant custom. To this day, each of her daughters is given the same penance before she makes her solemn vows. At the chapter of her reception, a young nun kneels before her abbess to hear her say: "And as a penance in preparation for your holy profession, you may recite the Office of the Dead for the pope who received the vows of our Mother St. Colette." Year after year, in all the monasteries of the world sprung from her reform, Colette's young daughters send up this plea for mercy for Benedict XIII, who certainly acted as a true and worthy pope toward their Mother-

Reformer. God would not be likely to forget what Colette and her daughters have remembered.

But this has been to anticipate. Deposition and death were far from the pope's mind in September of 1406. His immediate preoccupation was the winning over of his cardinals to Colette's enterprise. The plague came to his assistance. The murderous fever which had frightened him and his court out of Genoa now visited Nice, and with terrifying discrimination quickly snuffed the lives of the cardinals who led the opposition to Colette. Whether the other cardinals fell prey to a superstitious fear at this so sudden stroke of death or whether it really elevated them to a more supernatural way of thinking is God's secret. We only know that they did capitulate. Within a few days, Benedict XIII was able to summon Colette and her companions before him once more, this time to deliver to her his official approbation and receive her into the Second Order of St. Francis.

The pope made a solemn public ceremony of her investiture and profession as a Poor Clare. He invited the greatest ecclesiastical and secular personages among his supporters, and himself preached the sermon. The former recluse had now worn the Franciscan habit for several years. Pope Benedict personally placed the black veil on her head, dispensing her from the customary year of probation as a novice in the Second Order.

Relating these things to some of the nuns many years later, Father Henri told of the reverence with which Benedict handed Colette the Rule of St. Clare, gently exhorting one whom he held as a saint to live as "a very good and prudent religious" and to observe minutely all she had just solemnly vowed in his own hands. He renewed his promise to help her in all things and gave her a breviary, which is preserved at the monastery of Besançon.

It was Baroness de Brissay who told the rest, how the pope had then turned to Father Henri and solemnly delivered Colette into the friar's protection, telling him never to leave her. Father Henri never did. And, in a gesture worthy of St. Francis whose son he was, Benedict kissed Father Henri's shoulder, adding as if by inspiration: "Happy these shoulders which will carry the bread she will eat!" He turned to the noble assemblage and addressed all present: "Would to God that I was worthy to seek for and buy bread for this young girl to live on!" He had a word for the baroness, too, asking her to bring Colette "gently and peaceably back to her own country," where the reform was to begin. Lastly, he declared Sister Colette to be the abbess and mother of all who would accept her reform. These verbal authorizations were quickly reinforced in the following months by papal bulls.

Sister Colette heard all these words, it seems, as from a great distance; for afterwards she was surprised and grieved when the members of her little company insisted on addressing her as "Mother Abbess." When they reminded her that the pope had spoken, she announced that she would appeal to him against the honor. Like St. Clare before her, she was to continue to refuse the abbatial title for years. Even in their biographies written after the saint's death, Father Pierre de Vaux and Sister Perrine give evidence both of how stoutly Collette had resisted any title beyond "Sister" and of how equally determined her subjects were that she should be called "Mother." "Our glorious Mother, Sister Colette" is the compromise reached in their chronicles.

Actually, she was a pathetic enough abbess from all outward signs. She had no monastery, no community, not a single follower. And the extreme emotional strain of the past weeks began to take its toll of her. Weary physically and mentally, she was suddenly overcome by repugnance for all that lay before her.

In these leaden hours, the young abbess and the experienced friar exchanged places. Father Henri became the leader and mentor, reminding Sister Colette of God's love and solicitude for her in the past; patiently retracing for her, as one does for a frightened child, the outline of God's plan for her future. All that he had heard from the lips of a young recluse in Corbie who had seemed unshakable in her convictions, the friar now repeated to a fearful and exhausted abbess as though the revelations were his own. Gradually, her strength and determination returned.

Baroness Isabeau, shaken to see the indomitable Colette so suddenly wavering, must have watched with relief as animation returned to the young nun's words and gestures. All the depleted physical forces, however, were not to be so quickly rallied. Colette collapsed under the onslaught of a high fever and had to be nursed by Isabeau for long days and nights while Father Henri prayed at her side and tirelessly repeated words of encouragement and consolation.

At last she was well enough to go on, and the little party moved slowly forward again over the bad roads until it came to the castle of Countess Blanche de Genève at Roumilly. The old lady was delighted to see her protégée again and listened with relish to the full account of Pope Benedict's warm reception of her plan. She went over the documents given Sister Colette by the pope and remarked with satisfaction that her august brother apparently had a worthy successor. Blanche would have preferred to keep the new abbess-general with her longer, but Sister Colette was eager to get back to her loved Corbie and begin in earnest the work of the reform.

When the travellers came to Bourge-en-Bresse, there was another painful parting. There seemed no reason for the tired Baroness de Brissay to return again to Corbie, so Sister Colette and Father Henri left her. As Isabeau embraced her friend, she unexpectedly began to weep. Perhaps she had an intuition that she would never see this extraordinary young nun again on earth. If she did, it was a true one. The doughty baroness had found and already accomplished her life's great work. She had helped launch the Franciscan Reform. She never saw its first abbess again.

There was a last stop in Savoy, where young Count Amadeus offered Sister Colette a large part of his castle for a first monastery. His gift was refused with that blend of sweetness and determination which was Colette's particular charm. She had to begin in Corbie, her own city. The people there had wept to see her go. They would so rejoice now to have her return. They would take it for granted that the first monastery of the reform must be in their own town. The Count of Savoy understood. And so Sister Colette and Father Henri set out on the last lap of their return journey.

Sister Colette must have thought with joy of the welcome awaiting her in Corbie. Outside her native town there seemed nothing but increasing confusion. With the death of Pope Innocent VII and the accession of Pope Gregory XII, much had been expected and nothing obtained. Benedict XIII sat immovable on the second papal throne, watching the succession of popes occupying the first throne with something of pity and a little of disgust. Cardinals of both obediences were growing more and more restive. Some of them were already discussing the general council of Pisa, which was to eventuate in 1408 and burden the Church with a third "pope."

For the past two years, John the Fearless, young Duke of Burgundy, had been promising to surpass his dead father in cunning and fierce ambition. Already his followers were planning the murder of his rival, Duke Louis of Orleans. And the King of England was casting speculative eyes on the political ferment in France in 1406.

But these things slipped for a few hours into unreality for Sister Colette as she watched the contours of Corbie take shape before her. Her city! Her friends! Father Henri saw her happy anticipation. Whether by revelation or by intuition, he did not share it.

10 *The Reform Begins: the Community at Balme*

To the constant, fickleness must remain a mystery. It could never have occurred to Sister Colette that the tearful faces of the friends who watched her leave her anchorhold three months earlier could be transformed into those of the steely-eyed people who now looked at her in hostile silence. She and Father Henri went from house to house among her old friends and saw cold-faced strangers. Father Jean Guyot wanted to be kind, but the pressure of public opinion was too much for him. He told his callers nervously that there was considerable feeling against Colette in Corbie. He spoke of the old accusations of instability. He muttered about things like pride and vainglory. And he rumbled over the really shameful accusations against her which he could not quite bring himself to utter coherently under the gaze of the clear black eyes fixed on his face.

Sister Colette quietly thanked Father Guyot, and in silence she and Father Henri set out for the Abbey of Saint-Pierre.

Dom Raoul, they were told, was not in. Nor would he be in, was the clear implication of the porter's words. We can hope that he had the good grace at least to look away when Sister Colette thanked him and asked him to tell the Father Abbot she was sorry she always seemed to miss him, but that she prayed for him. Father Henri and the ward of Dom Raoul de Raye turned back to the town.

It became clear that there was no home in Corbie for Colette Boellet, who had given away her own home to its poor. Father Henri inquired and pleaded and argued to no avail. Finally, he brought her to an abandoned quarry just outside the town and told her simply that it was the only place he could find to shelter her. He would make shift for himself in the town until they decided what to do and where to turn. Sister Colette looked about her, and Father Henri puzzled over the many facets of her character. The nun who had visibly suffered in the abbey parlor had wholly recovered her equanimity; she was sizing up the quarry without a tear or a tremor. She assured him that it would do nicely. Then, suddenly aware, perhaps, of his distress that he could provide nothing better for her, she added, as we learn from Perrine: "Holy Father Francis is teaching us poverty, don't you see?" Much reassured, Father Henri left Colette in the quarry and went back into town to see what might be done.

Neither Sister Perrine nor Father Pierre de Vaux makes any mention of Colette's having a companion at this time. Yet it is inconceivable that after the parting with Baroness Isabeau and her entourage the friar journeyed on alone with the young nun. Furthermore, we know that Sister Colette spent at least several days and nights in the abandoned quarry. Father Henri certainly did not remain with her, but it is equally fantastic to suppose he left the beautiful twenty-four-year-old nun there alone. If it is only supposition that one or two maidservants of the Baroness de Brissay remained with Colette for the time being, it is at least supposition with the flavor of probability. The prudent old baroness would scarcely have waved a fond farewell to her protégée with no thought for safeguarding Colette's reputation. Nor could Father Henri, always so quick to protect his God-given companion in the work of the reform, have been such a fool as to suppose that the Corbians who had already slandered Colette with pure fabrications would overlook some really good material for their detractions.

However it may have been, this particular concern for Sister Colette was lifted from Father Henri soon enough, and by the first two postulants of the reform.

Marie Sénéchal and Guillemette Chrétien were not the only two persons in Corbie who regretted the calumnies and slanders bruited against Sister Colette, but they were apparently the only two courageous enough to stand out against public opinion and human respect. Her two girlhood friends had been watching Colette's reactions to the reception she had received in Corbie. The silence and serenity with which she had accepted all the abuse and slander furnished the impetus needed to set the wheels of their own vocations in motion.

"We want to join you," Marie and Guillemette told Sister Colette in the quarry-monastery. "We want to enter your reform." The two girls must have rehearsed the moment of their application more than once, for Father Pierre de Vaux has left us the charming picture Colette described for him of Marie and Guillemette reciting together the words of Ruth to Naomi in the the Old Testament. "Wherever you will turn your steps, we will turn ours; the place where you will establish your abode, we will establish ours; your family will be our family; and the land which will take you to its heart will take us, too."

Colette was authorized to begin the reform in Picardy. Corbie had failed her, so she told Marie and Guillemette she would attempt the establishment of a monastery of primitive observance first in Amiens and then in Noyon. Even better than that, she hoped to re-establish the primitive observance in the monasteries of Poor Clares already founded in those two cities. Accordingly, the three set out with Father Henri for Amiens, but they discovered soon enough that this was certainly not "the land that would take them to its heart."

Vicious gossip had preceded Sister Colette there, and she was treated with open contempt. Moreover, the Poor Clares at both Amiens and Noyon in 1407 were well content with the kind of life they were leading. They sought many privileges, but the privilege of poverty was not one of them. The austerities of the primitive Rule had gradually been abandoned as too demanding. When Sister Colette arrived at their monasteries, exhorting them to return to a strict observance of the primitive Rule, they found it convenient to

join with the townspeople in dismissing her as a fanatic and an innovator. So she left them and returned to the old quarry just outside
Corbie. It was a pleasanter place than the monasteries where nuns
who were neither poor nor daughters of St. Clare masqueraded as
Poor Clares.

Through the years, the ugly epithets fastened to Colette's name
at the turn of the fifteenth century have been replaced by terms of
reverence. The comparatively mild blame of "innovator" alone
has clung to her for five hundred years and defaced her true greatness.
Some still insist that she "put a new face on the Rule of St. Clare."
She is charged with superimposing her own austerities on the primitive Franciscan way, of forcing the joyous ideals of the saints of
Assisi into a narrow mold of harsh penances. No one has ever
adduced any least proof of this. Yet, without testimony or witness,
the lie endures.

What Sister Colette was commissioned by God Himself to do
was to restore, not destroy. It requires an almost incredible naïveté
to suppose that St. Francis and St. Clare besought the Almighty to
give them Colette to deface and deform their Orders. Still, apparently, a considerable number of persons are naïve in just that
measure. If the little anchoress of Corbie had been asked to establish
a new Order in the Church, her task would have been child's play
compared with what she actually was commanded by God to do.
"The reform of an Order is a harder task than to straighten an old
oak," observes Père Hilarin de Nolay. When St. Francis and St. Clare
had reinvigorated sensual and covetous thirteenth-century Italy with
their penance and their poverty, their glorious enterprise had the
freshness of a spring wind about it. Colette's arduous task was
the summoning of a second spring, not upon winter's bleakness, but
upon a dull and far-spent summer. In brief, she was asked by God
to do the humanly impossible: restore a lost ideal.

It is important to remember, however, that the Franciscan ideal
was by no means entirely submerged under the dark waters of 1407.
There were monasteries of the Poor Clares in Italy and elsewhere in
which fervor had never diminished; their communities clung with
joyous tenacity to the primitive way of Franciscan life. Sister Colette
had no business with such as these except to admire them and to
thank God for their fidelity. It was to the lost sheep of the house of

Clare that she was sent. And it was back to the sheepfold of Clare
that she wished to lead them, not to some separate pen of her own.

The history of those unhappy Franciscan times indicates that there
were lost sheep enough for her to lead. The breviary is painfully
accurate in its description of what kind of mission St. Colette had,
and to whom: "Tum se ad restaurandam sanctae Clarae Monialium
collapsam in locis pluribus disciplinam, a Deo variis modis admonita,
destinari cognovit." ("Then, admonished by God in various ways, she
knew herself destined for restoring the discipline of the nuns of St.
Clare, discipline collapsed in many places.")

No English translation quite achieves the thud of the Latin "collapsam" on our ears. How must the reality which it describes have
fallen on the heart of the young nun from Corbie! She stood among
ruins. And she knew it. It is worth pausing to note the "restaurandam," too. Her vocation was to restore, not to begin nor to alter.
She never described herself as other than the humble servant of
"Sir St. Francis and Madame St. Clare," as she loved to call them;
and her only aim and ideal was to restore without any change of
spiritual architecture what they had built. This is plain enough from
everything the saint said or did during her life. The greatest injustice
that could be done St. Colette of Corbie would be to pretend she
was a foundress. She was a reformer in the basic and beautiful sense
of that term; that is, she was a restorer.

In our times, the late Pope Pius XII showed his sensitivity for the
harsh connotations that have defaced the word "reform" when he
proposed to the faithful the Holy Week liturgy as we are now ob-
serving it. "We are not reforming the liturgy of Holy Week," the
Pontiff insisted, "we are restoring it." The dictionary may assure us
that reform means "to restore to a former good state," but our
minds cling stubbornly to the odious connotation that such men as
Martin Luther have given the word. Granting the power of continual
misapplication, we do St. Colette a genuine service, therefore, by describing her as the restorer of the primitive Rule of St. Clare where
it needed restoring.

Equally mistaken is the notion that she established a separate
branch of the Second Franciscan Order. The Colettine Poor Clares
live by the primitive Rule of St. Clare without the change of a comma.
What the saint of Corbie did was to write Constitutions which clarify

the Rule, throw up a bulwark of defense around it, and protect it from any of those "glosses," which St. Francis always feared. St. Colette has deservedly been called a mirror of St. Clare.

This has been another anticipation, but it is important that we launch out after Sister Colette and her first two followers with compass in hand. Otherwise, we shall steer off her course before we have sailed half a mile.

When the disillusioned quartet returned from Amiens and Noyon to Corbie, Sister Colette turned to Father Henri for advice. He had some ready. When he had seen the reception given her in Picardy, the friar had secretly despatched a message to Pope Benedict XIII, asking permission to begin the reform in another district of France, and a second message to his brother Alard in Savoy, asking hospitality for Sister Colette and her two companions in the de la Baume castle until he could make some different plans for their future. Alard was devoted to his younger brother and quickly sent a brief message back to Father Henri, inviting him warmly to come and bring his strange little trio along. Alard de la Baume had heard of the former anchoress of Corbie and was curious to meet her. His message was brief only because of a pressing personal grief. His wife, nearing the end of her pregnancy, was so ill that the household was in a state of high alarm.

Sister Colette acceded to Father Henri's suggestions readily enough. They could start their journey without delay, for there was certainly a minimum of packing to do. No parental objections from the Sénéchals or the Chrétiens to the apparently quixotic plans of their daughters are recorded; but it may be that both girls, now close to thirty, were orphaned by this time. While Marie and Guillemette busied themselves with closing their affairs, and Father Henri set out on a begging tour which finally rewarded him with a mule, Sister Colette walked alone to the top of a hill overlooking her native city. Without bitterness for the anguish it had given her, she made her private farewells to the place on earth she loved most; but she admitted later that something like a sword of prophetic foreboding had turned in her heart as she looked. "Oh, Corbie! Corbie!" she said aloud. She sat down on a piece of log and blotted out the vision of the city with her hands. She was still sitting there, weeping, when Father Henri came looking for her.

Typically, the friar said nothing. He led her gently down the hill; and when her tears finally stopped, he launched into a description of the mule he had just annexed, dwelling proudly on its strength, beauty, endurance, and other sterling qualities until Colette was smiling again. The two postulants were waiting for her, and Marie and Guillemette must have rejoiced to see their young abbess looking so lighthearted. Father Henri kept a very different picture pressed in deep folds of his memory. For, in his old age, he told Sister Perrine that he had never afterward seen a picture of Christ weeping over Jerusalem without remembering Sister Colette's tears for Corbie.

The three young women took turns riding the mule on the journey to Frontenay, the hilly market town where Alard de la Baume made his home. Some of the time, all four went on foot, each carrying the small bag which held all the material possessions considered necessary for the initiation of the reform. They followed the winding road along the foot of the Jura Mountains and stopped in each of the little towns and villages that lay between Corbie and Frontenay to hear Mass and receive Holy Communion. The friar begged their food as they went along.

At Dijon, Father Henri hired a carriage to take the three women the rest of the journey. Very likely, Alard had sent on a sum of money to Dijon at his brother's request for just this purpose. For if Father Henri had a profound feeling for penance, he also had a driving sense of chivalry which rebelled at too great hardships for young women. It was easy enough to hire a carriage. Dijon held the ducal palace of the house of Burgundy, and was at that time one of the most colorful cities in Europe. Father Henri himself continued on foot for the entire way, walking behind or beside the slow-moving carriage. The four often prayed together, not forgetting the need of Mme. de la Baume, and finally reached Frontenay, dusty and weary but full of joyous anticipation.

Their smiles disappeared when Alard came to greet them. "My wife is dying," he said with terrible simplicity.

Instinctively, the friar and the two girls looked at Sister Colette. After a moment, Alard de la Baume looked at her, too; and, without a further word to his brother, he said to her: "Will you come to my wife? Will you come and pray?" Her compassionate eyes were surely all the answer he needed.

Alard turned quickly down the hall. Sister Colette followed him swiftly, the three others coming after. He sped up the wide stairway, Colette on his heels, and led her into the large bedroom where his two older daughters knelt weeping beside their mother. Perhaps the servants standing around forgot their sorrow for a moment in the shock of seeing their master burst into the dying woman's room. And who was this with him? A nun! And a young nun. A nun with bare feet, and patched robes covered with dust. They watched the stranger go to kneel beside their mistress.

Mme. de la Baume's face was a death-mask. Sister Colette took one of the woman's hands into her own left hand. She ran her right hand lightly across Mme. de la Baume's forehead and traced there a small sign of the cross.

Odile and Mathilde de la Baume looked at the travel-stained nun who had come and knelt beside them so unselfconsciously, and whose dark eyes were fixed on their mother's face with the sympathy of another daughter. Unknowingly, they stumbled on the mystery at the heart of the contemplative vocation. They would understand more fully later on that Sister Colette did grieve for their dying mother as they themselves grieved, and that wherever there is suffering in the world the contemplative nun has her mission.

In this case, God permitted Sister Colette to be more than friend and consoler. She was inspired to ask Him for a miracle for this brother of the friar who had already sacrificed so much on her account. She asked it, and she received it. Odile and Mathilde watched Sister Colette run her fingers once more over Mme. de la Baume's forehead and then stand up. The dying woman's eyes fluttered open. Mathilde said sharply, "Papa, look at her!" Alard had never ceased looking at his wife. But now he fell on his knees.

A touch of color was returning to Mme. de la Baume's lips. She closed her eyes again. Sister Colette moved toward the door, piloting Marie and Guillemette before her. Alard seemed not to hear her ask where the chapel was, and Father Henri spoke to his nieces. Full of awe, Odile and Mathilde led their four visitors to the small chapel at the front of the house. Sister Colette prostrated herself before the Blessed Sacrament and remained there, unmoving. The friar's elegantly garbed nieces stood staring at the huddle of dusty veil and mended robe that was Colette. Then they knelt down beside their uncle.

An hour later the castle shook off its mourning. Evening was near, and Alard ordered every room to be lighted. He had a child! A beautiful, perfectly formed little daughter. And Mme. de la Baume lay back on her pillows, spent but very decidedly alive. Servants were despatched to draw the best wine. There were Savoyard songs coming up out of the kitchen where other servants were preparing a great feast. And Odile and Mathilde smiled into the wrinkled face of the little sister they were told would be called Petronilla.

This miracle was the origin of the cult of St. Colette as patron of expectant mothers which grew steadily and has endured to our own time. There is a special aura of tenderness over the invoking of a cloistered nun to aid mothers in childbirth, or to intercede for childless couples that they may be blessed with a family. The little girl born to aged parents in Corbie and grown to womanhood as a consecrated virgin continues to show her compassion and solicitude for those called to a very different way of life.

To this day, the nuns of her monastery in Ghent preserve a veil the saint wore in her lifetime. Expectant mothers flock to the monastery for the privilege of having the veil of St. Colette placed over their heads. They leave feeling secure in her protection. In our own country, there is at least one nun whose mother felt the comforting folds of St. Colette's veil around her when her future Poor Clare daughter was a small stirring beneath her heart. The daughter is now a young professed nun in the monastery in Cleveland, Ohio.

The details of Petronilla's birth and Mme. de la Baume's miraculous recovery at the prayer of Colette are not given in the two first biographies of the saint. However, the other biographers are agreed on all the circumstances here described. Abbé Douillet, honorary canon of the Cathedral of Amiens and curé-doyen of Corbie, one of the most reliable of the later biographers, and the most painstaking in his efforts to credit only what is indisputable in the saint's life, gives the story in full. It seems probable that the account appeared in the manuscript of Father Henri de la Baume previously referred to, which had freely circulated among Colette's daughters and others before the saint herself got hold of it and threw it into the fire.

This is the only disagreement Sister Colette and Father Henri seem ever to have had, and the abbess took such high-handed action only because she was aghast at the praises of herself and her miracles which she found in the writing. Sister Perrine records that Colette spoke to the friar "sharply enough for writing in praise of her, whereas she was a great sinner, full of defects and worthy of all reproaches." Father Henri was her confessor at the time, and Perrine adds that she said to him: "Sir, I do not wish anything more than that you should know my faults and sins, and if it will please you to do me any service, then grant me the pardon and remission of them."

At any rate, the story of Petronilla's dramatic entrance into the world is one of the most venerable traditions of the Franciscan Order. And such a scholar as Douillet, so careful to weigh his evidence, sets down the affair as true beyond question.

Petronilla de la Baume grew into charming young girlhood and became, quite understandably, the particular pet of her parents. The affectionate diminutive "Perrine" came to be a permanent substitute for her baptismal name. As Sister Perrine she was to become one of the most outstanding figures in the reform, the trusted intimate of Sister Colette, and the saint's faithful secretary whose writings we have already quoted so freely.

But, to return to our story: Seigneur de la Baume's gratitude for the preservation of his wife's life and the safe delivery of his child was overwhelming. He begged as a favor that Sister Colette and her companions should accept his castle as a gift and use it as a monastery, at least temporarily. He would move himself and his family out of their home at that very hour if Sister Colette wished it. However, she did not wish it. She told him that she and her two postulants would be forever indebted to him for the temporary use of one wing of his mansion until she could make a definite foundation in Savoy under the direction of the Holy Father.

De la Baume assured her that she had only to select the part of his home she preferred, and it would be closed to his household and reserved for her on the instant. As he might have anticipated, she chose the least luxurious and most inconvenient wing, stripping it of its most comfortable furnishings and putting as monastic a face on it as she could. She drew up an order of the day for her postulants and set about instructing them in the fundamentals of religious life according to the spirit of St. Clare.

As it turned out, the "monastery wing" of Alard's home did not long remain closed to all of his household. Both Odile and Mathilde came begging their father to let them join Sister Colette in religion. When he consented, his pretty daughters took off their rings and their earrings. They never put them on again. Both became postulants in their own home, living in complete seclusion from their parents and the rest of the household.

Both Sister Perrine herself and Father Pierre de Vaux write these details of Colette's being given part of Alard's castle, and also of Mathilde de la Baume's becoming a postulant there. Père Ubald d'Alençon, editor of the original manuscripts of the two first biographers, thinks it curious that they do not likewise mention the entrance of Odile, since this is certain from other records.

Sister Colette taught her four postulants to chant the psalms; and after a few weeks the servants, as well as their master and mistress, had learned at what times one could slip behind a half-closed door of some room adjoining the chapel and hear the four unsure young voices stumbling along the ancient Office chants after the voice of their abbess. Those stouthearted enough to rise at midnight could hear them then, too, spreading the benediction of their chants over the sleeping household and the countryside.

In less than two months, several other girls came asking to be admitted to the quaint novitiate. One of them was Jacquette Legrande, the third of Sister Colette's trio of girlhood friends. It is not clear why Jacquette did not join her two friends when they made application at the old quarry outside Corbie, but the fact that she lost so little time in following them seems to indicate that she had been deterred only by some commitment of time or some duty at home.

By now, news of the miracle of Perrine's birth and Mme. de la Baume's recovery had traveled with the swiftness of a forest fire, and Savoy was full of wonder and curiosity. More important, the fragrance of the Franciscan second spring was drifting past Frontenay's borders and into the whole countryside. It became clear that Sister Colette and her fast-growing novitiate must have a real monastery.

The new abbess spoke to Father Henri of appealing to the pope again. But Countess Blanche de Genève was before her. The old lady had conceived a holy envy of the de la Baumes. She longed to have her protégée establish a monastery in her own ancestral castle. And so sure was the lovable old despot that Sister Colette would fall in with her plan to take over the big rambling castle at Roumilly, that Blanche obtained all necessary permissions from the pope on her own initiative and simply presented the affair to the abbess as a *fait accompli*. Blanche de Genève was the first, but far from the last, of the French nobility to discover, however, that Sister Colette had a mind of her own.

Roumilly was an unfortified town offering none of the protection cloistered nuns would need in a country constantly in a state of war. With her characteristic practicality, Sister Colette disposed of the place as entirely unsuitable; but she explained her reasons to the old countess with such simplicity and humility that the great lady, so long accustomed to having her desires received as laws, graciously yielded. She even came forward with a substitute offer. Would the abbess consider another castle of hers, that of Balme-en-Génévois? She would, and she did. The town of Balme presented no such dangers to the young community as did Roumilly; and Sister Colette, with Father Henri's encouragement, accepted this offer most gratefully.

Alard and his wife both wept when the little band left their home. And Mme. de la Baume embraced Sister Colette with as much tenderness as she did Odile and Mathilde. Father Henri had at least ten young women to shepherd on this journey. The divine plan was obviously unfolding.

Along with his permission for the nuns to establish a monastic life at Balme, Pope Benedict XIII turned over to them the old Poor Clare monastery at Besançon. The nuns there followed a mitigated Rule, and no new subjects had come to join their way of life for so long that the community now consisted of only two elderly nuns. With the single provision that these two should be provided for in perpetuity and that they should not be obliged to follow the austerities of the primitive Rule unless they themselves desired it, the pope, in a bull dated January 27, 1408, deeded over this ancient monastery to the reform. His solicitude for the two nuns grown old in a manner of life far less austere than the one Sister Colette proposed to her followers is surely another credit on Pedro de Luna's record.

It is not certain why Sister Colette did not accept the governance of this monastery at once, but it was probably because the papal schism was at this time reaching a high point of turmoil and confusion. The Council of Pisa was forming. Benedict XIII's adherents were dropping off alarmingly. And Sister Colette herself admitted that she was beginning to doubt the authenticity of his claims to the papacy. In such an anguish of uncertainty, she and Father Henri thought it best to settle at Balme and wait on God's hour. As it turned out, they were to remain there for three years.

More and more young girls came asking to embrace the primitive Rule of St. Clare. And in her joy at their generosity, Sister Colette could forget for glad hours her doubts about the pope who had endorsed the reform. These years at Balme correspond to the days of St. Francis and his first friars at Rivo Torto, to the idyllic first years of St. Clare and her nuns at San Damiano. They were golden years, when the lost ideals of the saints of Assisi were rediscovered to eager young hearts by the abbess who also acted as novice mistress.

The primitive Rule of St. Clare was re-established in all details. The community at Balme kept a continual Lenten fast except on Christmas day. They observed perpetual abstinence from meat and slept on mats of straw. The nuns wore coarse veils and rough habits. They kept silence except for the daily hour of recreation when the old castle of Balme-en-Génévois certainly shook with more laughter than it had heard for scores of years, since the early biographers love to linger on Colette's contagious joyousness. The Divine Office was chanted day and night. And poverty came out of her ignominious exile and was again the honored "lady poverty" of St. Francis.

11   *The Community at*
Besançon

The peace and happiness of the Poor Clares at Balme were anything
but symbolic of the general state of France and all of Europe at the
end of 1408. Angered at the stubbornness of Gregory XII and Benedict XIII in holding fast to their personal claims at the expense of
the unity of Christendom, and nearing a state of despair over the
chaos in the Church, cardinals of both lines to the number of twenty-
four took it upon themselves to convoke a general council at Pisa.
The usually ineffectual Gregory was not slow to take alarm at the
proposed usurpation of his authority, and he promptly excommunicated those of his cardinals who had subscribed to the idea that
a general council could be convened without the sanction of the
pope and had power to act independently of him.

In this, unhappy Gregory was certainly right. The schismatical
Council of Pisa sowed the seeds of the so-called "conciliar movement" whose dangerous tenets threatened papal authority for many
years afterward. If ultimate power in the Church were to lie with a
general council, the successor of St. Peter and vicar of Christ on
earth would be reduced to the status of a mere executive or adminis-
trator. Gregory XII was well along in his eighties when the Council
of Pisa convened, and the poor old man fought desperately to maintain his dignity against his mutinous cardinals.

Benedict XIII had at least this much in common with Gregory.
The Spaniard equally foresaw the threat such a council laid against
the very structure of the Church. He also strove to forestall such a
schismatical action by his cardinals; and when the Avignon princes
refused his pleas and warnings with the same obduracy as the
Romans, Benedict followed Gregory's example and issued a sweep-
ing excommunication against them.

It must be remembered, however, that these twenty-four excommunicated cardinals were no ordinary mutineers. They were men of high principle whose desire for the end of terrible schism had reached the last outpost of desperation. It is easy enough to sit in judgment against them from our vantage point of five centuries later. In 1408–09, the affairs of the papacy were wrapped in such a thick fog of claim and counter-claim, ambition and political intrigue on the part of secular princes (and, unhappily, a number of ecclesiastical princes as well), that scarcely any issue stood out clearly. Cardinals aspiring to end a papal schism by a schismatical council loom as pathetic figures indeed on our horizons. In 1409, most of Christendom hailed them as liberators and crusaders. The hope of Europe looked to the Council of Pisa. One hundred and eighty-two bishops and hundreds of other churchmen joined the cardinals in council, and so sure were these misguided prelates of the authority of their gathering that they dared to summon both Gregory and Benedict to appear before them. Naturally, both refused. When they did, the council replied with a cool sentence of deposition against both "popes" on the grounds of heresy and schism.

In the mind of the council, the papal throne was now empty. The councillors proceeded to fill it with Alexander V, who had been the Greek cardinal and Franciscan friar, Peter Philargos. Thus the gift of the Council of Pisa to Christendom was a third "pope." Confusion now reached its peak. With truth so obscured, the worthiest and most learned prelates aligned themselves in fairly equal numbers behind whichever of the three cardinals they regarded as the true pope. What is most difficult to understand now is that the third "pope," whose claims seem to us obviously the weakest, commanded a greater following than the other two. In fact, most of the Franciscan family joined the company of some of the saintliest prelates of the fifteenth-century Church and rallied to Alexander V. This first Pisan pope lived only ten months after his ominous election, but it was long enough for him to confirm the bulls and decrees of Benedict XIII, authorizing the reform of Sister Colette.

The abbess confessed to her nuns that the plight of Pedro de Luna caused her increasing anguish. The tragic Spanish pope now set himself so furiously against any talk of conciliation, clung to his perilous position with such fierce obstinacy, that even his staunchest adher-

ents were dismayed and ashamed. Yet, she owed to Benedict XIII
more favors than could ever be repaid. Daily at Balme, her community was urged to pray for its most distinguished benefactor,
even while it now acknowledged Alexander V as the Supreme Pontiff.

Alexander's following grew steadily larger, and false calm descended on the Church. Six months after his election, under shelter
of this deceptive peace, Sister Colette decided to move her nuns into
the monastery at Besançon. Countess Blanche de Genève was unhappy to see them leave her castle, but the old lady realized that such
a makeshift monastery could not be a permanent dwelling. Magnanimously, she herself wrote to the Archbishop of Besançon, Thibault
de Rougemont, presenting the papal decrees and praising the sanctity
of Sister Colette and her nuns in terms calculated to whet the prelate's eagerness for the foundation in his archdiocese. Douillet writes
that de Rougemont was "well instructed by the countess."

Archbishop de Rougemont had, in fact, already heard a great
deal of the new Poor Clare abbess, all of it testifying to her holiness
and her miraculous powers. Moreover, the two old nuns living alone
in the monastery of Besançon had been a worry to him for years past.
He was glad enough to hand this problem over to Sister Colette, and
jubilant to have his archdiocese graced by her presence.

In his enthusiasm (doubtless fanned by loyal Countess Blanche),
he went so far as to declare a holiday for the city on March 14 when
Sister Colette and the first seven novices of her community arrived in
a covered wagon to prepare the monastery for the arrival of the rest
of her nuns. Indeed, he and his clergy, along with the magistrates
of the city and a sizable procession of layfolk, went three miles outside Besançon to meet her at the village of Beure and give her a royal
escort into the city, as Abbé Douillet relates in detail.

Countess Blanche, accompanied by her niece, Countess Maude,
and Father Henri, came in advance of the covered wagon. The
shrewd old countess knew well enough that her presence would give
unlimited prestige to the coming of the Poor Clares. It very decidedly
did. The people were awed by the great ladies and impressed by the
fine-featured friar in such a poor habit. Their excitement grew
steadily; and when the swaying covered wagon came into view, they
broke into wild shouts of welcome.

Although Sister Colette wanted nothing more than to escape outbursts of admiration, could she have avoided contrasting the welcoming cries of the Besançonites with the sneers and insults of her own Corbians four years earlier? Surely there was a tide of painful memories to force back as she climbed down from the wagon, followed by her novices, to receive the episcopal blessing. She remarked to the archbishop how dear old Isabeau de Brissay would have rejoiced to see this day of their coming to her own Besançon, but the baroness had died more than a year earlier.

Archbishop de Rougemont insisted that Sister Colette ride the rest of the journey in his own coach, and installed her between the two countesses, to the satisfaction of Blanche de Genève and the delight of young Countess Maude, who was overjoyed to have this chance to observe her aunt's saintly protégée at such close range.

The archbishop evidently had a flair for drama. When the entourage reached the city gate of Notre Dame, he ordered all to alight and form in procession. He vested in pontifical robes then and there, and led the way to the monastery while his clergy sang psalms and canticles. After some prayers in the chapel, the archbishop and his assistants, along with the city magistrates, led the eight nuns into the chapter room where the two Urbanist Poor Clares who had lived in this monastery so long were waiting.

It is not hard to imagine the fears great and small that besieged Sister Simonette and her companion, who had the same name as Alard's daughter, Odile. They had heard much of the young abbess-reformer, and the exaggerated tales of her austerities had not reassured them. The old pair stood in the chapter room like souls awaiting the hour of doom. When Archbishop de Rougemont led in the eight nuns, Sister Simonette and Sister Odile searched one happy young face after another, and looked again toward the door. Evidently Sister Colette had not come yet. But then the archbishop extended his ringed hand toward one nun in the group, and with his other hand motioned the two old Poor Clares to come forward. "This is your abbess, Sisters," he announced. "This is Mother Colette."

Sister Simonette and Sister Odile stood silent and motionless before the smiling young abbess. She looked at the two lined faces before her and stepped forward quickly to enfold Sister Odile in her arms. "May the Lord give you His peace," she greeted the old nun.

She turned to Sister Simonette and embraced her just as warmly. "You are so good to let us come here," she said.

Sister Colette beckoned her other nuns to come forward and embrace the two old Poor Clares, and Archbishop de Rougemont, satisfied that all was going well, led Sister Colette to the abbess' chair under the large crucifix and handed her the documents which gave her possession of the monastery. He urged the magistrates to encourage the people of Besançon to aid the new community as much as possible. And, after a final blessing for all, he and his retinue departed.

As it turned out, the love of the people of Besançon for Sister Colette's first community went much deeper than emotional outcries. They could see the extreme disrepair into which the monastery had fallen under the pathetic administration of the two old nuns living alone in it. They gave very generous alms (doubtless with some encouragement from Countess Blanche) for its repair. And they never, in all the years ahead, wavered in their loyalty to and esteem for this first monastery of the reform.

Poor Clare community life could now be followed in a real monastery, and makeshifts discarded. There was an immense amount of work to be done on the old place, and its finances needed Franciscan ordering; but Colette's first thought was for the two old nuns into whose home she and her young community had so colorfully moved.

Abbé Douillet tells us that the abbess-general addressed herself to the two aged Sisters "with respect and love." He adds that she repeated to them words she had uttered before and was to insist on again and again. They are likewise recorded by Sister Perrine: "My Sisters, I tell you that this way of religious life is not the way of Sister Colette nor of Father Henri, but of our Lord Jesus Christ, because He has come in Person to restore it again." She showed a tender understanding of the difficulties two nuns grown old in a very different way of life might have in embracing the primitive Rule of St. Clare in their last years. And she assured them that if they preferred to keep to their former manner of life, she would see that they were safely conducted to another monastery of the mitigated Rule and well supplied with everything they might need.

She also told them, however, that if they wished to make trial of the primitive way, she would welcome them with all her heart into her community. "If you do feel called to our way of life," she said, "I shall not look upon you as my daughters, but as my mothers in religion to whom I owe all filial respect." The poor old pair were completely conquered.

In the end, however, Sister Odile decided that the primitive Rule was beyond her power to observe. She chose to enter a community of Bernardines (a branch of the Benedictines) in Besançon. Until Odile's death, Sister Colette showed the most loving solicitude for her, sending her messages and inquiring for her health and happiness with genuine devotedness.

Sister Simonette came to a very different decision. Probably a little frightened of her own choice, she asked the abbess to let her attempt to keep the primitive Rule with the others. God was not slow to reward Simonette's heroic resolve. Almost miraculously, she fell in with the new observance and found to her own amazement that she could keep the first Rule of St. Clare not only without physical detriment to herself, but with such a sense of peace that something of her youthful vigor seemed renewed. Sister Simonette lived in the restored monastery at Besançon for a number of years after this, a joy to all the nuns by her perfect observance of the primitive Rule and her fervor in practising virtue.

No one was happier over the success of Sister Simonette's brave attempt than her abbess. Perhaps it was the sight of the old veteran faithfully following every least prescription of the Rule which inspired Sister Colette with some of her exhortations to her community at chapter. "My very dear Sisters, I most humbly entreat you, in the name of our sweet and amiable Savior Jesus Christ, and of His loyal spouse, our Holy Mother the Church, to cherish your vocation! For our Savior says: 'No one can come to Me except My Father draw him.' "

It is not difficult to suppose that the aged nun's eager practice of the strictest poverty underscored these words of the abbess: "Be well satisfied with the poor habit allowed by our holy Rule, and consider it pernicious to possess anything as your own. Content yourself with what is strictly necessary, and be careful not to fasten your affections even on that, that you may by means of your vow of poverty the more easily obtain possession of the true riches of the heavenly kingdom. By this poverty, I mean the continual abstinence from meat, the daily fast, bare feet, the hardness of your bed, and continual mental and bodily labor." The nun who had awaited the arrival of the Poor Clares of primitive observance with such apprehension died a blessed and peaceful death at Besançon in the arms of her abbess; and Colette thanked God for the triumph of His grace which was Sister Simonette.

There remained a staggering amount of work to be done on the old monastery, and the question of its finances now had to be settled. Sister Colette took care of the latter with despatch. There were various revenues attached to the monastery. All these rents and other sources of income the abbess promptly deeded over to the papal legate in Burgundy, Peter de Thuray. That great prelate was struck with admiration for such sincere detachment and used some of the funds to establish a permanent chaplaincy at the monastery. Three secular priests were consequently appointed by Archbishop de Rougemont in an ordinance dated October 24, 1410, to offer daily Mass in the Poor Clares' chapel and to celebrate other desired services during the year. The abbess accepted this arrangement, stipulating only that she wished the confessor of the nuns to be always a son of St. Francis. What money remained, she asked the papal legate to distribute among the poor of the city and its hospitals.

A heavy burden was lifted from Sister Colette's shoulders when she disposed of all means of regular income for her community. Shortly before his death, St. Francis had called money "the chief cause of corruption to our profession and perfection." Now the chief cause of corruption was removed from her first community and, by force of precedent and example, from all others. She had no worries about the heavy taxation which might have been laid on the old place, thanks to the intervention of one of the most powerful ladies in Europe. This was Duchess Margaret of Burgundy, the intimate friend of Countess Blanche de Genève. Her first brief meeting with the Poor Clare abbess, an encounter most carefully engineered by the tireless Blanche, had made a deep impression on the pious duchess. She prevailed on her husband, the famous John the Fearless, to issue a bill of tax exemption for the monastery. This act of kindness proved to be only the first in a long list. Margaret of Burgundy and her formidable husband were to figure largely in the abbess' life from that day forward.

Around this time, just when there were so many temporalities to be attended to, Sister Colette fell into a sustained ecstasy, of which we have Father Pierre's account. Nothing could rouse her, and she continued for days in this state while the half-admiring, half-frightened community looked on. Now, ecstasies are most marvelous spiritual phenomena; but any community will agree that it becomes increasingly inconvenient for the nuns when their abbess is unavailable for days at a time, however exalted the spiritual state which occasions her absence. With a practicality they had learned from her, they appealed to Father Henri to do something. What? They didn't know. They thought he should. The friar thought the matter over and decided on a very simple expedient. "Sister Colette," he loudly commanded, "return to us! The community needs you." And return she did, obedient as always. The nuns probably filed away in memory for possible future reference this method of retrieving their abbess!

At the end of the first year in Besançon, the new community found itself already overflowing the old monastery. Yet the amazing increase in subjects was by no means due to their being accepted with little discrimination. Colette sorted out applicants with unerring judgment. There were three classes of prospective postulants for whom she had a particular disinclination, Sister Perrine declares. The first among these were widows, who, the abbess thought, would find the adjustment to a life of primitive observance beyond them. Doubtless there were some exceptions, for St. Clare herself had sometimes accepted young widows, though with caution and discernment; but most often such applicants received a negative reply.

Especially unwelcome at the monastery of Besançon were the frivolous and worldly, those whom the abbess drily described as "having a large flow of talk." It often happens that a life so completely unlike their lives in the world exercises a strange fascination for the superficial. However, Sister Colette knew only too well that vocations are not built on the principle of the attraction of opposites, and that the cloistered life loses its fascination for the frivolous in very short order. Prayer and penance may dazzle *à longe*. But once embraced as a permanent way of life, they reveal themselves for what they are: avenues to the Light Eternal—narrow avenues.

The third class on which the abbess turned a discouraging eye was, strange as it may seem to some, the "pious." Although still young in religious life herself, Colette had observed the unshakable tenacity with which those entrenched in their own modes of spirituality cling to the pleasant regimen they have worked out for themselves. (Pleasant, because it is self-elected and self-satisfying.) Such souls, the abbess had noted, are about as pliable to obedience as the rock sidings in the old quarry outside Corbie.

Yet, when all discernment had been exercised, there still remained so many deserving postulants that it was obvious a second foundation would have to be established soon.

Sister Colette continued, at great inconvenience to herself, to act as novice mistress, since none of her young subjects was as yet sufficiently trained to be entrusted with so vital an office; and she watched over each of her fledgling Poor Clares with absolute devotedness. Nothing escaped her, were it only the drooping mouth of a homesick postulant or the dragging step of an over-tired novice.

She was particularly on the watch for signs of discouragement, knowing it to be the most useful of Satan's tools in his efforts to unhinge a vocation. Once she saw all the signs of the devil's success beginning to appear in one of the novices. Thoroughly discouraged, the young girl was tempted to leave the monastery but could not bring herself to declare her feelings to her superior. She had no need. The abbess sent for the child and spoke to her of the temptation to discouragement which is the particular lot of cloistered nuns who never see the results of their missionary apostolate and who must live entirely by faith. She told the novice it was the true vocations against which Satan levelled his fiercest attacks, whereas he relished nothing so much as smoothing the path for a girl who lacked a vocation.

The novice stared at her mistress as the loving voice went on, outlining the young Sister's trials with unerring accuracy. At last she fell on her knees and acknowledged the truth of it all. "But I am so weak," she complained. "And it gets so hard. How can I persevere?" Sister Colette traced the familiar small sign of the cross on the novice's forehead. "You will make your profession," she assured her young daughter. She added simply: "God has told me." Years later, the former novice told all this to Sister Perrine; and that faithful scribe set the story down for others to cherish and remember.

Sister Perrine also left accounts of two others who joined the community at Besançon in its first years. One was gay and pretty Etiennette Hennéquin, daughter of a very wealthy merchant of the city. It took all Etiennette's eloquent pleading to wheedle her doting father's permission to enter the Poor Clare Monastery. She finally triumphed, but it proved to be a short-lived victory. Once the engaging pleader was out of his sight behind the enclosure walls, M. Hennéquin lent a ready ear to the shocked reproaches of his friends. Such a way of life was all well enough for ordinary girls, and no one denied the piety and good fame of the monastery; but it was no life for a belle like his Etiennette!

Properly bolstered by his relatives and friends, M. Hennéquin appeared at the parlor grate of the monastery, demanding the return of his daughter. The abbess tried to calm him. She reasoned with him. She even ventured to remind him that he had given his formal permission for his daughter to enter religious life, and that if it was considered dishonorable to break one's pledged word to another man, it was certainly a heinous thing to violate a promise made to God.

M. Hennéquin remained entirely unmoved by all this, his only reply being the repeated demand for his daughter. Etiennette was summoned to the grate, and the young postulant wept and pleaded with her father to leave her in the cloister. But nothing would do but that M. Hennéquin should carry her off. So the enclosure doors opened again for Etiennette. "Our Mother gave her up to him," wrote Sister Perrine years later on the testimony of those present at the time, "but she did so with great sorrow, and went off to pray, weeping over the loss of her daughter." It was evidently no mere sense of responsibility Sister Colette felt for her nuns, but the warm and tender love of a mother.

Exultant at his success, M. Hennéquin went on a purchasing spree for his pretty daughter. Etiennette's wardrobe bulged with new gowns; her jewel cases multiplied. He and his wife thrust their unhappy child into a whirl of social diversions and pretended not to see the sadness in her eyes. One day, the determined father had Etiennette deck herself out in her newest ensemble, and ensconced her in his carriage to be carried off to a special festivity. We do not know what prayers were framed by the young heart under the shimmering satin, nor what penances a loving abbess in her cloister may have offered for her lost child that day; but M. Hennéquin did not, after all, escort his daughter to that particular festivity.

The carriage had gone only a little way when the horse sat down in the middle of the road, with an air of finality whose ludicrousness was quite lost on Hennéquin. He climbed down from the carriage and switched the horse till the poor animal gave him a reproachful look and struggled to its feet. Hennéquin beamed. But before he could reach out to give the horse a pat of forgiveness, the beast sat down again. "It's just no go," the horse's mournful eyes tried to tell its master. But he only set to switching the horse again.

The animal made one more gallant attempt to show M. Hennéquin the uselessness of it all. It stood up, and immediately collapsed again. This time its body stiffened. Etiennette, springing down from the carriage, ran over and took the horse's head in her lap. "Papa, you've killed him!" she said. She added, on a sudden inspiration: "If you keep on forcing me to go where I don't want to go, maybe I'll die, too."

The vehemence of this threat was too much for M. Hennéquin, and he sat down weakly on the step of the carriage. Etiennette went to him and put an arm around his neck. "Papa, let me be a Poor Clare! Take me to the monastery." Her father nodded. A passing carriage was hailed, and the bewildered Hennéquin and his jubilant daughter presented themselves at the doors of the cloister an hour later. Her father punctuated Etiennette's excited story with a phonographic repetition: "Wouldn't move. Just sat there in the middle of the road." That Sister Colette did not laugh is witness enough of her heroic self-control. She only remarked that it was certainly strange.

The distraught merchant was still shaking his head and repeating: "Like a dead horse," when Etiennette kissed him on his perspiring forehead and disappeared into the cloister. She never came out again. And the horse, to Hennéquin's further amazement, made an immediate return to health and vigor. "From that day," Sister Perrine sweetly comments, "M. Hennéquin began to lead a truly Christian life and was regularly seen at church." In fact, he was so mellowed by this strange event that he even let himself be persuaded by Sister Colette to stop doing business on Sundays, a departure which reduced his income considerably but surely enlarged his soul.

Marie Chevalier was the second novice of this period whose life

Sister Perrine took special pains to record; but the circumstances of her vocation were as lofty as Etiennette's were droll. The Chevaliers were of the cream of Besançon society, and they were of the spiritual elite as well. Their daughter, Marie, had been singled out by God in so marvelous a manner as to compare with that of Colette herself. The young girl had been favored with a vision in which the heavens opened to reveal a splendid palace. She saw several princesses moving through it, smiling and gorgeously attired. While she was marveling over the sight, she heard a voice saying: "This palace is the dwelling of the religious of Sister Colette." In all simplicity, Marie went to the monastery and told the abbess what she had seen and heard.

Sister Colette was impressed by the girl's story because of the charming candor with which Marie told it, but the mystic of Corbie was far too practical-minded ever to accept subjects on the strength of their supposed visions or revelations. In fact, she was inclined to dismiss "visionaries." She examined Marie's motives for wishing to enter with even greater thoroughness than she would have those of a more usual applicant, and put the girl off to try her spirit. She questioned her time and time again. In the end, she discovered in Marie nothing save a profound humility and an intense desire to serve God in the obscurity of the cloister. She finally admitted Mlle. Chevalier as a postulant, and every subsequent day of her life had reason to rejoice that she had.

Marie's gifts of soul were accompanied by brilliance of mind. She wrote two books, one of which, *The Treasure of the Soul,* gave a striking synthesis of the disorders Lutheranism was destined to cause throughout the Church. The other book was *The Life of Jesus,* to which the Lord gave His own imprimatur, appearing to the Sister as the Divine Child in the arms of His Mother, praising her for her work, but warning her that she must not yet expect the reward of His kingdom. "It is not yet time!" A charming additional word indicates that the Holy Child anticipated a Maternal intervention in favor of Sister Marie's being taken to heaven at one. "No, she must work a little longer for love of Us," He insisted.

Under the special guidance of her abbess, Sister Marie Chevalier rose to heights of sanctity. Years later, she was made abbess of the

Poor Clare monastery at Vevey in Switzerland, then at Chambéry
(the place from which Father Henri de la Baume had set out to
make his pilgrimage to the Holy Land in 1406), where the citizens
esteemed her as a saint. She lived to a very great age, dying on January 4, 1470. When her body was exhumed in 1609, it was still fragrant, as it had been in death.

While life in the monastery of Besançon was flowing on like a
peaceful river, affairs in the Church, however, remained as muddled
as ever. When the "pope" of the Council of Pisa died in 1410, the
schismatic cardinals, erstwhile supporters of both the true pope,
Gregory XII, and the first pretender, Benedict XIII, hastened to
elect the Cardinal Legate of Bologna, Balthazar Cossa, to succeed
him. Cossa styled himself John XXIII, and to him belongs the
tragic distinction of bringing the affairs of Christendom to their very
worst stage. He was a thoroughly worldly man, and Pastor has written
that the election of Cardinal Cossa was "the worst of all the miserable
consequences of the disastrous Council of Pisa."

Engrossed with political affairs, and absorbed in feeding his in-
satiable ambition, John XXIII seems never to have troubled himself
with any such spiritual enterprise as the Franciscan reform until
he was put under pressure by the Duke and Duchess of Burgundy.
Father Henri brought tragic accounts of the actions of the third
"pope" to the community at Besançon, and the abbess wept to hear
them. Yet, in the midst of the four-year reign of the unscrupulous
and worldly-minded Cossa, she made her second foundation. It was
simply a necessity no longer to be avoided, and Father Henri advised her to trust in God and go ahead.

After three years at Besançon, Sister Colette had a nucleus of well-
trained and zealous religious living according to the primitive Rule
of St. Clare. She could easily leave one of them in charge while she
went on to supervise the founding of a new house. And she had already determined who the abbess of the second monastery should
be. It was young Sister Agnes de Vaux, niece of the Franciscan Pierre
de Vaux who was later the saint's confessor and biographer, already
so frequently quoted here. Sister Agnes was a warmhearted and
compassionate religious, a natural leader and an accessible model
of virtue. The choice of her was an easy one for the abbess to make.

The choice of the site for the second monastery of the reform was much less so. The Duchess of Burgundy had a place all selected, and Sister Colette had to nerve herself for the ordeal of informing that great lady that she had no intention whatever of going to Dijon.

12 *Dôle*

Margaret of Bavaria, Duchess of Burgundy by reason of her marriage to John, son of the handsome old Duke of Burgundy who had died in 1404, seemed a strange type of woman to enlist the affections of the man who was styled *sans peur* but who certainly was not *sans reproche*. However, unscrupulous John did deeply cherish his gentle and spiritual-minded wife. Margaret, on her part, had a genuine love for her blustering husband.

Even physically, the two were remarkably unlike. The portrait of the duchess in the Dijon museum shows us a sweetly serene, almost childlike face of delicate modelling. Margaret's aristocratic features and noble carriage were in striking contrast to the features and bearing of her ugly little husband—short and thickset, with an enormous head. His face was coarse, even repulsive. His voice was harsh, and its normal volume seemed to be set at "roar." He had a talent for intimidating the strongest men, and for a time he held the greater part of the power in France. Yet, though Margaret had constant fear for the duke, she had no fear whatever of him. She could bend this rough man to her will in many things. When she set herself to win his patronage for a new monastery of Poor Clares to be founded by Sister Colette, her motive in aiding the spread of the reform was secondary. Her first motive was the salvation of her husband's soul. The Dijon portrait shows her, significantly, with hands folded in prayer.

As we have seen, John's partisans had early taken care to secure his position after the death of the old Duke of Burgundy by murdering his chief rival, the powerful Duke of Orleans. Louis of Orleans was the lover of King Charles VI's ill-famed queen, Isabeau; and his chief political strength lay in the queen's infatuation. Although the hand of Duke John of Burgundy was not the one that murdered the Duke of Orleans, Duchess Margaret knew well enough that her husband had been party to the crime. What sickened her even more was the exquisite malice with which the murder had been planned. Louis of Orleans was struck down just as he was leaving the apartments of his royal mistress one grey morning in 1407. Worse than Shakespeare's king facing death "unhousel'd, disappointed, unaneled" was the plight of Louis, murdered in the vestibule of his adultery.

The memory of this infamous crime was Margaret's torture day and night. She grasped at every opportunity that offered to make reparation for her husband's sin. In the erection of a monastery for nuns dedicated to a life of prayer and penance, the agonized duchess thought she saw such an opportunity.

Spiritually, as in every other way, John the Fearless was a man of contradictions. Consumed with ambition, even near-mad for power, he had none of the affectations of most men of his ilk. He wore coarse and ill-fitting clothes. Most of the time they were patched besides, for he would seldom consent to a new uniform if the old could be made to hold together. He showed himself capable of annihilating anyone, however powerful, who crossed him. Still, he was easy prey for the solicitations of his soft-spoken wife. Murder apparently weighed lightly on his soul. Yet he carried with him at all times, even into battle, a handsome breviary, and faithfully recited the canonical hours whenever possible! One scarcely knows whether to laugh or weep at the picture of this ill-formed, murderous, ruthless man pacing up and down, breviary in hand, before some historic battle.

When Duchess Margaret seized upon the foundation of a Poor Clare monastery at Dijon, the capital of Burgundy, as a likely way of appeasing the wrath of the Almighty against her husband, it simply never occurred to her that the abbess at Besançon would be anything but charmed with the idea. If she was gentle and pious, Margaret was also accustomed to being obeyed. She despatched her chamberlain, Guillaume de Vienne, to place the magnanimous offer of Dijon before Sister Colette as a piece of finished business.

From the abbess' point of view, Dijon was even more undesirable a place for a cloistered monastery than Roumilly, the choice of Countess Blanche. The presence of the court of Burgundy made Dijon one of the greatest centers of worldliness in the kingdom, and the saint had no desire to dwell in the shadow of the ducal palace. Small, fortified towns were what she wanted. She explained all this as humbly as she could to Guillaume de Vienne. If she rejoiced that the great man, a noble of the Orders of St. George and of the Holy Cross, and founder of the Confraternity of St. George, seemed to appreciate her point of view, her relief vanished when de Vienne came forward with a plan of his own. He offered the abbess his castle at Gray, which she likewise considered entirely unsuitable.

To complicate matters further, Countess Blanche felt inspired at this time to renew her offer of her castle at Roumilly. Sister Colette now found herself cornered, with three aristocrats to be at once refused and appeased.

After the peaceful years in the cloister at Besançon, the abbess was anything but inclined to make even a temporary excursion back into the world outside. However, the establishment of a new foundation involving the house of Burgundy and other assorted aristocrats, whose well-meant blundering could easily halt the reform, demanded her presence. On Father Henri's advice, and with permission from Archbishop de Rougemont acting for the pope, she left the enclosure of Besançon to visit the Duchess of Burgundy at Dijon.

We are not told the identity of the nun who accompanied her, but very likely it was the one already chosen to be the next abbess, Sister Agnes de Vaux. Father Henri and another friar, Pierre Psalmon, went with them. For months past, Father Henri had been travelling about the country looking for the most suitable site for the second monastery of the reform. In Auxonne, a small fortified town on the borders of the Burgundian dominions, he thought he had found an ideal spot. Sister Colette agreed with him. It remained to propose this alternative to Margaret of Burgundy without giving that noble lady offense.

Detached as she was from earthly grandeur, the abbess must surely have experienced a natural sense of excitement as Father

Henri and Father Pierre Psalmon led the way up the magnificent marble steps of the ducal palace at Dijon. Although the detail is not recorded by Father Pierre de Vaux or Sister Perrine (and understandably enough, since their interests invariably lie in the spiritual and miraculous), later biographers tell how the soldiers presented arms as the strange little party approached. As she walked between men-at-arms, Sister Colette could see attendants in gorgeous attire milling around the entrance. Priceless tapestries hung on the walls, and former lords of Burgundy looked down on her from great portraits. The four barefoot Franciscans, their patched robes dusty and rumpled from the hard journey, could only have freckled the face of all this splendor; but the servants received them with utmost deference. Duchess Margaret had prepared her household well for the coming of these extraordinary visitors; and the young abbess' reputation for holiness had preceded her, too.

There had been a number of striking miracles worked in those quiet years at Besançon, the most impressive being the raising of a dead infant to life. Dijon was still ablaze with enthusiasm over the Prucet miracle when the wonder-working abbess arrived there. The story has been recorded by both Father Pierre and Sister Perrine.

M. and Mme. Prucet had been heartbroken when their little daughter was born to them dead. In fact, the distraught father simply refused to believe it, and seizing the lifeless body, he ran off to the parish church with it, insisting that it should be baptized. There was no doubt, however, as to the baby's being quite dead; and the father had to return home with his pathetic burden. His friends and neighbors, perhaps in genuine faith but probably also out of a desire to ease the young father's desperation with action, encouraged him to take the dead infant to the monastery and ask the prayers of the abbess. Willing to snatch at any hope, he ran off to the Poor Clares and begged to see their superior.

Sister Colette, when she was told the story, went at once to the grate, where M. Prucet fell on his knees before her and held out the small bundle of his dead child in mute appeal. The abbess sank to her knees, too, and began to pray. Prucet's friends and relatives, who had come crowding into the parlor behind him, fell silent at the sight of the father and the abbess both on their knees. One after another, they followed suit, the men pulling off their caps as though in church.

After a time, Colette rose and stepped back from the grate. She took off her veil and had it given out to the father. "Wrap the child up in it," she directed, "and take her back to the church to be baptized." Prucet did not answer a word, but obeyed like one of the community's novices. When he and his friends arrived at the parish church and Prucet once more asked Baptism for his little girl, the sympathetic priest cast about for suitable words of comfort for a father he felt was taking leave of his senses. The next moment, the good curé wondered whether he was perhaps taking leave of his own. For the unmistakable cry of an infant very much alive came from the folds of the black veil.

When M. Prucet could speak, he stammered out his story. The priest, fearing that the child's return to life might be momentary, decided to baptize her at once. "What name?" he inquired abruptly. "What will you have the child called?" Prucet had no need to consider. "Colette," he said.

The priest's fears that Colette Prucet's return to life was only for a brief time proved groundless. She grew into sturdy girlhood and entered the monastery at Besançon when still very young. Eventually she made her solemn vows there, and later became abbess of the Poor Clare monastery at Pont-à-Mousson in Lorraine. Sister Perrine writes that "Colette Prucet herself told me all this." The Prucets had undoubtedly repeated the story to their daughter countless times.

Raising the dead to life has always been considered the greatest of miracles, and a power seldom granted to a woman. St. Colette is credited with many such miracles, four of which figured in her beatification. The restoring of Colette Prucet to life greatly increased the developing cult of the abbess as intercessor not only for expectant mothers and childless couples, but also for infants mortally ill.

It is easy to imagine the frenzy of enthusiasm in Besançon over this miracle. Nor could the memory of it grow stale with little Colette Prucet for a living reminder. People with every kind of malady began flocking to the monastery. The abbess prayed for them all, but such was her horror of being credited with working wonders that she employed every device and stratagem to turn attention from herself. "Miracles are worked by God in reward for your faith," she would insist to the people. And when such a miracle as that of little Mlle. Prucet aroused demonstrations in her honor, Perrine tells us that the abbess would hide herself in her cell for days at a time, as though making reparation for some crime.

Similarly, she could not have missed the obvious deference shown her by the servants of Margaret of Burgundy; but there was no place to hide herself in the palace. When the two friars had respectfully greeted the duchess, they departed for their friary at Dôle, where Sister Agnes de Vaux's uncle, Father Pierre, was eagerly awaiting them. Father Pierre de Vaux had been following the work of the Poor Clare reform with intense interest and with the hope of its being extended to the First Order. He knew that the abbess had papal authority for doing just that; and he wished to discuss the matter at length with his great friend, Henri de la Baume.

Duchess Margaret gave Colette an enthusiastic account of her plans. The new monastery could be built right next to the palace, as far as she was concerned. The abbess must have groaned inwardly at the very thought of this, but she did not voice any objection. At last Margaret finished and settled back to receive the expected out-pourings of grateful acceptance. Instead, the abbess began to sketch out her own ideas as to where cloistered monasteries should be erected.

Her guest spoke with such sweetness and deference, and expressed such gratitude, that the Duchess of Burgundy did not at first realize that her offer was being refused. When the fact finally struck home, she was sufficiently anesthetized by Sister Colette's gracious reason-ableness to accept her views with a minimum of disapproval. She did attempt further arguments in favor of Dijon; but, however much she was accustomed to having her own way, Margaret had now met another woman who, like herself, had a gentle manner and a strong will.

Only a little grudgingly, the duchess finally asked: "Well—where, then?" "Auxonne," the saint replied. The duchess had a long list of objections to little Auxonne; but Sister Colette struck them off, one after another, with a logic that Margaret had to applaud. In the end, she was so completely won over that she declared Auxonne to be her own choice after Dijon. After all, her favorite château of Rouvres, where her son Philip had been born, was situated midway between Auxonne and Dijon. She could often go on to Auxonne from Rouvres. (Surely the abbess received this news with mixed emotions!) As things turned out, however, the Duchess of Burgundy interfered very little in the affairs of the Poor Clares. And she was to the end of her life their staunch friend and benefactor.

As soon as the affair was settled with Margaret, Sister Colette was eager to go at once to Auxonne and make preparations. Countess Blanche and her Roumilly, and Guillaume de Vienne and his Gray could be dealt with later. The Duchess of Burgundy, however, had to remind the abbess that formal permission from the duke was required. Margaret had no doubt about getting her husband's permission, but she feared there might be a little difficulty over the site Father Henri had selected and described to the abbess. It was a little hill near the Saône, and it had two houses. The second was merely an appanage of the first, but Margaret explained that the first house occupied a central position in the duke's affections. His father, Philip the Bold, used to mint counterfeit money there! Some historians claim that John himself continued this lucrative Burgundian hobby. It is known for certain that John's son, Philip the Good, took it up later with a sense of dedication. In fact, so well known was this craft of the house of Burgundy that the building at Auxonne was quite openly referred to as "la maison des sous."

Duchess Margaret insisted on keeping Sister Colette and her companion at the Dijon palace for several days. During that time, the two friars returned from Dôle, and Father Henri was commissioned to go to Paris and present the duchess' proposal to John the Fearless.

Affairs between the Orleanists (whose cause the powerful Armagnacs had espoused after the marriage of the young Duke Charles of Orleans to the daughter of Count d'Armagnac) and the Burgundians were at continual boiling-point these days. The Duke of Burgundy had attempted to cover up the evil odor of the old Duke of Orleans' murder by paying a handsome sum to a dubious doctor of theology, Father Jean Petit, to deliver a discourse at the Hôtel St. Pol before a carefully selected and representative audience of clergy, nobility and soldiery, defending the crime as an act of high patriotism. Evidently this "doctor of theology" so open to hire was "petit" in more than name.

John the Fearless had also made a number of overtures to the children of the dead Louis, even indulging his sense of the melodramatic by riding on a mule with the son of the murdered d'Orleans in token of the reconciliation of the two powerful houses. Neither these nor other extravagances, however, succeeded in dispelling the foulness of the crime. And, though John the Fearless was at this time reigning like a king over Paris, idolized by the citizens and the universities, the Armagnacs formed a full circle around the capital city, ready to seize any opportunity for revenge. It would not have been prudent or even safe for the Duchess of Burgundy to send her normal envoy, Guillaume de Vienne, one of John's best soldiers, there. Father Henri, protected by his religious garb, would also be respected for it. The important commission was given to him, and he set out for Paris. It was early August, 1412, just six years since he had set out another August morning to escort a tearful ex-anchoress to the papal court at Nice.

As the duchess had anticipated, Father Henri's religious habit opened the Armagnac lines around Paris for him. He entered the city and went directly to the headquarters of the Duke of Burgundy. John the Fearless received him with courtesy, and even with as much reverence as his coarse nature was capable of. He fell in whole-heartedly with the plans of his duchess for the erection of a Poor Clare monastery at Auxonne, and to Father Henri's vast relief did not even demur when the site chosen by the friar and the abbess was put before him. It would have been very like this strange little man to have found the idea of penitential nuns minting spiritual coin for Burgundy an appealing one. It is certainly true that Duke John rarely showed a more open hand than on that third of August in 1412.

With the nervous energy peculiar to him, he at once dictated several letters patent, sealed them with his great seal in green wax hung with a silken cord, and signed them with his own hand. The letters were addressed to the Chamber of Accounts at Dijon and to his treasurers and receivers. The grant itself was worded this way:

We bestow, with full knowledge and as a special favor by these presents, for God and as a charitable gift, our rights, share and portion in this place and grounds, no matter of what kind. For we will and desire that our cousin, Guillaume de Vienne, or his representatives shall found for the praise, reverence and honor of God and of His divine service, a monastery of the Franciscan nuns of the Order of St. Clare; and that our most dear and most beloved consort the duchess, and our heirs and successors, shall participate in the Masses, intercessions, prayers, and other works of charity and benevolence which will take place within the said monastery. We charge our trusty accountants that they hold and confirm the religious of the said monastery free and discharged from all payments.

Thus the all-important tax-exemption was given in advance also.

Father Henri could not have hoped for more. His only remaining care was to get the proper authorization from the second Pisan "pope," John XXIII, then at the peak of his popularity and little inclined to give his attention to anything so materially unprofitable as the Franciscan reform. The friar explained his anxiety to the duke in very cautious terms, but John the Fearless caught the overtones easily enough. However strange an admixture of contrasting character traits he himself was, the powerful duke could take the measure of other men unerringly. He knew that the worldly and ambitious John needed only a nudge from the house of Burgundy to develop a most benevolent interest in a Poor Clare monastery at Auxonne. On September 25th, Pope John XXIII, duly nudged, was to despatch his papal bull authorizing the erection of the new monastery. After the most respectful expression of thanks, which the rough soldier-duke brushed aside with something like impatience, Father Henri returned at once to the palace at Dijon to deliver all this good news to the abbess awaiting him there.

Sister Colette had not been idle during the friar's absence. It had taken all her persuasive powers to wean Guillaume de Vienne away from his cherished plan for a monastery adjacent to his castle at Gray. De Vienne had a free enough hand for charity when he was in the mood for it, but he also had a great fondness for the sound of the trumpet. A monastery of the reform established in his name and in the shadow of his own dwelling was a project which recommended itself strongly to his heart. To be merely a helper in the erection of a monastery at Auxonne under the patronage of the house of Burgundy was decidedly less appealing. However, in the end, the gentle-voiced abbess was able to win his support, even to the extent of Guillaume's pledging to Auxonne the full amount he had planned to spend on a monastery at Gray.

In placating Countess Blanche, Sister Colette had the assistance of Duchess Margaret. The two noblewomen were not equal in rank, but had long been intimate, both of them sincerely devoted to God and the spread of His kingdom. Then, too, each had at present a more mundane concern to cement their interests. Duchess Margaret had fastened upon Blanche's niece, Countess Maude, as the right kind of wife for her young nephew, Duke Louis of Bavaria. Although yet a little uncertain about the worthiness of Louis for her precious niece, Countess Blanche was anything but unaware of the honors involved; and she was flattered by the duchess' choice of her Maude. Too, Blanche had the deepest affection for Sister Colette and had bowed her aristocratic head to the abbess' wishes on several occasions before this. She capitulated again, and good-naturedly promised to donate to the monastery at Auxonne all she had proposed to spend on remodelling her castle at Roumilly into a monastery.

The friar and the abbess exchanged their stores of good news. Duchess Margaret reviewed with satisfaction the grants given by her husband. And, after a regretful farewell, she let her visitors return to Besançon to complete their plans and select the full number of nuns for the new foundation. The duchess had developed a sincere affection for Colette and would have liked nothing better than to keep her at the palace for weeks more. Sister Colette returned Margaret's affection, but she was eager to escape from these rich surroundings and slip back into the obscurity of the cloister.

Back at Besançon, she set about selecting the foundresses for Auxonne as soon as the papal bull of authorization arrived in late September. Besides Sister Agnes de Vaux, she chose two sisters by birth, Sisters Marguerite and Marie Estocquette, young Sister Agnes Tinquerie, three nuns whose names we do not know, from Franche-Comté, and two from Picardy. Those remaining at Besançon had the comfort, in this second parting from their abbess, of her promise to return to them as soon as everything was well established at Auxonne.

News of the proposed foundation had spread through Besançon by this time; and the people, supposing that Colette was leaving them permanently, were in an uproar. They descended upon the monastery, indignant and reproachful. That Auxonne should take from Besançon its abbess was regarded by the townspeople in much the same light as the theft of a public monument. Sister Colette could rejoice that the reform had become so much a part of Besançon's life that its citizens did not hesitate to scold the abbess when they thought it proper. It must have required effort not to laugh aloud, however, when these simple people finally told her they would allow her to go only on condition that she return very soon; but she thanked the city magistrates with disarming gravity.

A covered wagon was again the chosen vehicle for the pioneers; and before they set out, the votive Mass of the Three Kings was said, as Father Pierre records had become customary before Sister Colette set out on any of her journeys. Sometimes the abbess rode inside the wagon; sometimes she made more room for the nuns by riding on a mule next to it, despite the protests of the others. Father Henri led the mule, and Father Pierre Psalmon walked beside him.

They were scarcely outside the borders of Besançon when the abbess, on the mule, went into an ecstasy. Her face became so radiant that the two friars were bathed in the light streaming from it. People stopped their work in the fields and came clustering around the party. Quite overcome with the wonder of what they saw, many of them knelt down in the road. Some timidly reached out to touch her mantle and then quickly blessed themselves. When they saw that she was completely unaware of their overtures, they were emboldened to touch her hands and her feet. Still she remained insensible of them; and the two friars, speechless before such a marvel, walked steadily on. It must have been Father Henri who later gave all these details to Father Pierre de Vaux and Sister Perrine. Strangely, the people did not try to halt the party. Perhaps they were too overcome with awe and a certain sense of fear. It was sufficient for them to see her and to touch her quiet hands or her poor mantle. After a little while, the wonder became known to the nuns in the covered wagon, but they had no reason to fear. They had seen these things before. Colette in ecstasy on the way to Dôle, admiring peasants around her, has always been a favorite subject for artists.

She remained still insensible when they arrived at Dôle. Something had to be done now, for Father Henri knew Sister Colette had urgent business with the friars of the Dôle community. So he stopped the mule and commanded its ecstatic rider: "Madame, come back to us. We are at Dôle." The abbess opened her eyes at once. She looked at Father Henri and smiled, as though he had only called her from her spinning.

There was a little unoccupied cottage just across the road from the Franciscan friary of Dôle, and Father Pierre de Vaux had made arrangements with the owners for the nuns to use it during their brief stopover. As soon as Sister Colette had established her little band of nuns in it, she crossed the road to the friary in the company of Father Henri and Father Pierre Psalmon. She needed no rest, she assured them. She felt very well. And they had to admit that she looked fresh and rested after the long ride. After all, she had not made the journey in any ordinary fashion! As she left them, she told her nuns to take some rest and refreshment and then to pray without ceasing until she returned. She had no need to explain what she meant. They all knew how much hinged on this visit to Dôle. It might mean the beginning of the Franciscan reform in France among the friars. Or it might mean ignominious defeat for her and Father Henri's hopes.

A number of the friars across the road had been busy with their prayers all these days, too. There were several besides Father Pierre de Vaux who longed to see the friary of Dôle restored to primitive observance. Father Pierre had, in fact, spent several years in a friary of the primitive Rule in the environs of Poitiers, where the Italian reform movement of the great St. Bernadine of Siena had penetrated. After those golden years, he could not reconcile himself to the mitigated observance of Dôle. Father François Claret was another who pleaded for a return to the primitive Rule. And some others, less courageously outspoken but not the less eager, were watching for the arrival of Sister Colette and Father Henri. In fact, the whole community was watching for their coming, though many of them waited more to see the miracle-working abbess than the reformer. The guardian of the friary, Father Jean Foucault, despatched some of his community to meet the visitors and take them into the church. As she was entering it, the abbess again fell into an ecstasy. One might expect Father Pierre to have noted the admiration of the friars for this spectacle. Instead, he tells us that "this somewhat distressed the community"! His account hastily adds:

"For they had hoped to converse with her and hear her speak."

God apparently took pity on the distressed community, for the abbess returned to her senses shortly. So delighted were the friars over this, that they prevailed upon their superior to take her into their chapter room. Father Jean Foucault hesitated at first. Women may never be admitted within the enclosure of the friars. But the community insisted that Colette was not a woman but a saint. And Father Pierre de Vaux reminded the superior that the dying St. Francis had declared that the rule against the entrance of women into the friars' quarters was not made "for our Brother Jacoba" (St. Francis' affectionate tag for the Lady Giacoma Settesoli). Father Jean could not resist this superb reasoning. Sister Colette was conducted into the chapter room.

The friars, about fifty in number, sat on benches along the sides of the room. The abbess sat on a low stool out in the center. Father Henri and Father Pierre and those of like mind with them told how they sent prayer after prayer up to heaven that God would give her words to move the hearts of all present to return to primitive Franciscan observance. She began to speak at last, and they could stop praying. To listen to this woman of God was itself a prayer.

She spoke very simply of the beauty of the religious life and of their Franciscan vocation. She outlined for these men, most of them far older than she and all of them priests, their obligations to our Lord; and not one of them seemed offended at being instructed by her. Then, Sister Perrine writes, she began to speak of Franciscan poverty, of the primitive Rule, and of Franciscan joy in Franciscan austerity. Her eloquence held them all. At the end, she herself was again caught up into some spiritual realm where they could not follow her. The same light that had brought the peasants outside Besançon running from their fields poured from her face in the chapter room. One after another, the friars fell on their knees. For the time at least, Sister Colette had completely won the community at Dôle.

13 The Monastery at Auxonne

It was a joyous party that left Dôle to complete the journey to Auxonne. Sister Colette was not so inexperienced as to suppose that the community's first reaction to her words would bring about a permanent change of viewpoint for all the friars at Dôle. But surely it augured well for the reform that men so entrenched in the comforts of life should show such a willingness to forego them and return to the primitive way. If she suspected that many of the friars she had left on their knees would probably return to their former views as soon as they got back on their feet, she knew that those were by no means obdurate hearts that could be so moved, if only for a few hours. She said so, and rejoiced.

The abbess was prevailed upon to ride inside the wagon for the rest of the journey. Very likely Father Henri reinforced the Sisters' pleas with the shrewd advice that, if God were again to favor her with an ecstasy, it would be better that she were hidden from public view inside the wagon.

Sister Agnes de Vaux was particularly delighted with this arrangement, for she had been meditating on a little plan of her own ever since she had seen the marvels on the way to Dôle. If the holy Mother were rapt out of herself again, Sister Agnes would take her in her arms, so that she could cherish for the rest of her life the memory of having held a saint in ecstasy. After all, she knew that Colette would not remain long with the new community at Auxonne. Perhaps she would never see her Mother on earth again. Sister Agnes intended to compensate herself in advance for the years of separation.

All went just as Sister Agnes had hoped. She managed to get the place next to the abbess in the wagon. The other nuns were too much occupied with their prayers and with the business of keeping themselves secure on the benches inside the swaying wagon to notice with what extraordinary intentness their future superior was praying. Only the Lord read Sister Agnes' moving lips and her heart besides. "Dearest Lord, please let our Mother fall into an ecstasy right away, won't You?" He would. She did. And jubilant Sister Agnes de Vaux tenderly enfolded the abbess in her arms. In the years to come, the first nuns of Auxonne loved to tell this incident to the community's new members. Sister Agnes herself always declared it was the greatest deed of her life. "I held a saint to my heart," she said.

Sister Perrine de la Baume has left us this vignette on the testimony of Guillemette Chrétien, adding that the ecstasy was also witnessed by Sister Agnes Tinquerie and Sisters Marie and Marguerite Estocquette. This would seem to indicate that Sister Guillemette was one of the "two from Picardy" included in the founding group for Auxonne. Very likely the other was Jacquette Legrande or Marie Sénéchal, and the Picardy nuns are not named simply because Colette's old friends were so much taken for granted.

The abbess returned to earth as the party reached Auxonne, and Sister Agnes, whose sense of enterprise had a strong mixture of prudence in it, promptly released her hold on her superior. She was absorbed in her breviary when the abbess opened her eyes and smiled around at her daughters.

The monastery at Auxonne was not yet built, but this was no surprise to the abbess. She had, in fact, given orders that the construction should not be begun until she herself was there to supervise it. The foundresses arrived at Auxonne on October 28, 1412, and were welcomed with almost as much pageantry as at Besançon. The mayor, the aldermen, the parish priest, Father Pierre Esserces, and several of his assistants, a considerable detachment of soldiers captained by Guillaume de Vienne, and a very large crowd of the townspeople were waiting at the city limits. As soon as she saw them, Sister Colette left the wagon and rode into the city on the mule. She intended to look what she felt she was—the servant attendant on the other nuns. For all that such public demonstrations cost her, the abbess always took into account the genuine devotedness to the cause of God which had at least some part in them. So she showed herself to the people gracious and smiling. "You are the people of God," she said. She and her nuns took up temporary residence in a house near the parish church of Notre Dame, but the abbess left it early each morning to supervise the work on the new monastery.

If the workmen had supposed that being directed by a famed mystic and ecstatic was going to be a lark, and that they would be free to do what they liked, at their own pace, they had a rude awakening the very first day. They found that this nun gave orders with the precision of a construction boss. She apparently had several pairs of eyes that missed nothing. She never raised her voice, but her words carried more emphasis than any they had previously heard from men who underscored every command with an oath. She measured and marked off and rearranged. And if the construction crew deviated ever so little from her instructions during her absences, they regretted it. "Tear it down," Sister Perrine tells us was her terse comment on their attempts to bypass her orders. This was the first monastery the abbess had built, and she wanted it to be a model for future foundations in every detail. It was to be small and poor, as St. Francis and St. Clare had always wanted their dwellings to be. And so true was the reality to her ideals that outsiders remarked that the nuns' cells looked like "dwelling places for bees, rather than for women," as Colette amusedly recalled years later to Sister Perrine.

When the workmen finished the day's construction, they went home to wives who were burning with curiosity. "Does she pray all the time?" "They say she is often raised off the ground into the air!" "She doesn't know what is going on around her, does she?" But a tired Jean or François or Jacques could only reply: "Ha! She sees *everything!* If anyone is going up in the air before this job is done, I'm the one!" The wonder-working abbess of Besançon came to be admired and respected by the workmen of Auxonne as the best construction boss in the business.

At last the monastery was finished, and Duchess Margaret came with her retinue from Dijon to be present at the dedication. No less a notable than the Benedictine Dom Guillaume de Bussel came to bless the new building. Abbot Guillaume de Bussel was lord of the ancient abbey of Luxeuil, from which the Abbey at Corbie had been founded. His presence must have been a painful reminder that all these years had brought no word from Dom Raoul de Raye. Sister Colette's many letters to him had never won her the least reply.

Duchess Margaret, far from being charmed with the results of the abbess' construction, declared to all and sundry that the place was preposterously small. She would enlarge and improve it; she would build an entirely new chapel. As always, Colette knew how to placate her high-born benefactors without conceding principle. She could not permit any alterations on the poor little monastery, but she would consider it a great favor to God and religion if the duchess wished to build a permanent chapel onto the monastery. It would be a perpetual memorial to the house of Burgundy and surely draw down abundant blessings from heaven on the duchess' husband. Any reminder of John's need of blessings was enough to throw Margaret into a fever of activity. Nor did the abbess try to restrain her. If she wanted the poorest living quarters for her daughters, she wanted the most beautiful for her Divine Spouse.

In a very short time, an exquisite little chapel was joined to the abbess' humble building. The completed building was called the Poor Clare Monastery and Chapel of Ave Maria, and it flourished from the beginning. Subjects flocked to it, and the reform put down deep roots in Franche-Comté.

Sister Colette remained for some time to advise the young abbess, Agnes de Vaux, and help her train the new subjects. That the nuns profited from her teaching and example is evident in many incidents of these first weeks at Auxonne which Sister Perrine has written down for us. Here is one.

Sister Jeanne Roberdelle had been appointed portress, an office which also gave her charge of the community's supply of wine—a very important commodity in a land where wine was the common beverage taken with meals. Sister Jeanne was busily drawing out the day's supply from a keg donated by a benefactor in Auxonne when she heard the foundress ring the call-bell with what seemed like unusual urgency.

Fearing there had been some accident, Sister Jeanne ran off to answer the bell with such haste that she forgot to turn off the spigot. She found that Sister Colette was perfectly well and had only needed an errand done without delay. The portress did it and then returned to the wine keg. It was quite empty. The floor around it bore fragrant witness to Sister Jeanne's haste and forgetfulness. This was a domestic tragedy for the poor little community, and the portress burst into.

tears. She went back to the abbess and told what she had done. "It's empty," she wailed. "It's all gone, every drop!"

The abbess smiled at her. "I don't think so. Surely there is some left. Go back and see." She paused a moment, and her face grew very serious. "Go in the name of the Lord, and have confidence." Sister Jeanne did not hesitate or ask a single question. She ran back to the cellar, picking up the skirt of her habit so as not to trail it through the spilled wine. But the floor was dry. She went to the keg and found it full. And at recreation after dinner that day, the nuns, like the chief steward at Cana, remarked that today's was the best wine they had ever had. The portress was not slow to share her secret with them. "It was the prayer of our mother," she told them wonderingly. The story, of course, came back to Colette. "It was the obedience of Sister Jeanne," she insisted.

If the new monastery was flourishing, however, the foundress' health was not. During all the stress of building time, God seemed to have supported the indefatigable abbess with loans from His omnipotence. Now, as she and one companion prepared to return to Besançon with Father Henri and Father Pierre Psalmon, she experienced the full weight of her infirmities. The flesh around her waist had still not healed since one day at Besançon when she had obeyed Father Henri in a matter of penance.

There is very little that enclosed nuns do not know about one another's doings. How some of the nuns at Besançon had learned that their mother wore an iron chain fastened very tightly around her waist, we do not know for certain; but they had. Perhaps Sister Jacquette Legrande or Sister Guillemette Chrétien, who knew all about their lifelong friend's use of penitential instruments, had told the others of the chain she wore even as a child, and gave it as their opinion that she wore it yet. In any case, some of the community became alarmed lest this torture should be undermining their abbess' health. They lost no time in telling Father Henri of their fears, and he shared them.

When he asked if she had an iron chain fastened around her waist, Colette admitted that she had. "Take it off, then," Father Henri commanded. Obedience is better than sacrifice, he reminded her, and the abbess smiled. "I am not attached to the chain, Father. If you wish, I will take it off." Father Henri reported his quick success to the worried nuns, but most of them never knew what this obedience cost their mother. If her will was not attached to the chain, the abbess discovered that her body certainly was. (Afterwards she wrily confided to one of the nuns that obedience is always more painful to the spirit than instruments of penance, but sometimes more painful to the body as well.)

Over a period of years, the links had grown into her flesh. She tugged and tugged, giving little outcries of pain with her efforts. When she found that she could not dislodge the links with her hands, she grimly tied one of the ends of the chain, which hung down at the point of fastening, to a peg in the wall of her cell. Then she set her teeth and spun herself away from the peg. The chain was wrenched free, but the flesh in which it was imbedded came with it. Her waist was literally torn to ribbons. The sores which resulted caused her so much more pain than the chain had, that Sister Colette later told the story as quite a good joke between herself and the Lord. Father Henri was obviously so pleased with her obedience and with his own prudent care for her health!

There were other maladies, too. She suffered almost constantly from severe neuralgia. She was subject to sudden chills and high fevers. Often she could not sleep even during the few hours she allotted herself. Sometimes her beautiful face was so distorted with pain and her body was so bent that she was scarcely recognizable. The fact that she bore all these infirmities with unruffled patience, and even casualness, makes us sigh. The restorer of the primitive Rule of St. Clare must be made of different clay from ours, we are inclined to think. Then we find a chink in this armor of fortitude and endurance, and we want to cheer! She is, after all, *our* saint. She knows what it is to be afraid of suffering, and she has experienced the very human desire to be rid of it.

For, the truth is, St. Colette had a constant fear of going blind. She suffered acute pain in her eyes a good deal of the time. Often her eyes burned so unbearably that she felt blindness must surely be closing down on her. She knew the measure of such a trial, too, remembering those three days in the anchorhold at Corbie when God had taken away her sight. And she who went so calmly about her daily round with constant nagging neuralgia, who walked rough roads or rode mules, heedless of her ulcerated waist and the fever racking her, prayed and pleaded that God would not take away her sight. Although she never would agree to apply any remedy to her many other ills, she was often observed putting medicine into her eyes. Perhaps God left Colette of Corbie a prey to this one physical fear for our sakes more than hers. Is she ever more ours than when she reaches for her eye drops?

Both nuns and friars felt that the abbess-general should remain longer at Auxonne before beginning the return journey to Besançon, especially with winter coming on, but Sister Colette would hear none of it. She had been away from her first daughters long enough. They tried a few more timid remonstrances, but the last of their entreaties must have died on their lips when the hour of departure arrived. For, without any previous indication of better days coming, the abbess suddenly appeared full of vitality. Her face looked young again, and the little lines were erased. Her eyes were clear and alert, with none of the false brightness of fever. "There is work to be done," was all she said to her questioning daughters.

These phenomenal temporary recoveries were to occur often, just as they did in the lifetime of St. Teresa of Avila. Serious illnesses for both saints were entirely removed by God time and time again, when some new project for His glory needed to be carried through. Afterwards, sickness would once more overpower the Poor Clare abbess, as later the Carmelite prioress.

Sometimes these instantaneous recoveries baffled Colette as well as her nuns. How could she feel so utterly wretched one minute and so well and energetic the next? "I don't know," she observed to Father Pierre de Vaux on one such occasion. "Did I have any pain and sickness, or didn't I?"

Certainly Sister Colette needed full physical vigor to face the ordeal now ahead of her. Affairs in the community at Dôle were worsening with each new day. Once he had got free of the power of the abbess' presence, Father Jean Foucault began to consider in detail what a return to the primitive Rule of St. Francis would mean in his life. No more lavish entertaining of the city's notables. The luxurious suite of rooms he occupied in a separate apartment built onto the friary would have to be replaced with a small cell. He would be obliged to appear regularly at the Office, a duty from which he was accustomed to dispense himself on very little pretext. The menu would be decidedly different from that to which he and his many visitors were accustomed.

He decided he would have none of this reform! He needed no young nun coming in to tell him, Father Jean Foucault, guardian of a community of fifty friars, how to observe the Rule. And a number of those in the community warmly agreed with him. It had been an enormous blunder to bring the abbess into their chapter room. They would see that such an infraction of the regulations did not occur again.

Many others in the community, however, had no wish to rid themselves of their new resolve. They lined themselves behind Father Pierre de Vaux and Father François Claret, and respectfully reminded their guardian that the community had formally agreed to embrace the reform at Sister Colette's departure. Father Henri de la Baume had authority from the pope to re-establish the primitive Rule in all friaries that showed willingness to embrace it. And Father Henri himself appeared on the field of domestic battle just at this turn, determined to strike for the reform while the Dôle iron was hot.

Father Jean Foucault's gift for friendship was the natural by-product of his charm, learning, and gregariousness. He was never happier than in the company of witty intellectuals, and he gloried in playing the lordly host. His private apartments attached to the friary were the scene of many gatherings of priests and laymen. And if it is true that the guardian at Dôle had strayed far indeed from the Franciscan way of life as the seraphic founder envisioned it, it is also only fair to emphasize that Father Jean was by no means an evil man.

There had been a time in the beginning of his religious life, when reading about the first years of the Order had had power to stir him deeply and move him to desire a stricter way of life than was then popular among French Franciscans. But the years had gradually stilled such responses, and he had turned his desires in the direction of a more comfortable life. He was like a re-embodiment of Francis of Assisi before the son of Bernardone had trained his sights on sanctity. Like Francis, Father Jean was a born leader, had a most generous heart, and throve on gaiety and exuberant living. Unlike

Francis, he had tried to strike a compromise between God and the world.

When Father Henri established himself in the friary at Dôle, Father Jean at first thought to make light of his coming. It was better, according to his judgment, not to make a show of indignation. That would only lend a false sense of importance to the "reformers." He preferred professing an amused aloofness. In a few weeks, the novelty would wear off these austerities and a tired community would be glad enough to flock around its charming guardian again. To show how little importance he attached to the innovators, Father Jean announced that he was going away for several weeks on business. Foucault had immense confidence in himself and his ability to rally men around him, and for the present he was glad to absent himself from the small bickerings of a community divided against itself over the matter of the reform.

When he returned some weeks later, Father Jean's amused smile must have frozen into a grimace.

Father Henri had overlooked no opportunity for redirecting the regimen at Dôle into more austere lines. Father Pierre de Vaux and Father François Claret supported him with enthusiasm, and more than half the friars were already finding the primitive Franciscan way a very rewarding one. Meals were plain now. Ornate and excess furnishings were sold and the money distributed to the poor. Hangings came down, and a new order of the day was posted up. Expensive cloth was replaced by coarse habits. Guests were politely informed that the friars would no longer be entertaining at dinner. When he entered his own suite of rooms and found them, too, considerably altered, Father Jean's normal affability deserted him entirely and he fell to belaboring Father Henri and his followers with an angry eloquence that echoed through the whole friary.

The guardian discovered more and more of what he considered the worst abuses. Among these was giving the many lavish donations the community received directly to the poor of the city. Then there was the cutting off of revenues on which he depended for all the comforts of life. Those of like mind in the community heartily encouraged their superior to resist the outrageous innovations of de la Baume and his friends. The latter, in turn, held stoutly to the authority they had been given.

Father Henri had a horror of strife and division among religious, but he knew that to yield an inch at this point was to lose all these hard-won yards for the reform. Against the promptings of his peace-loving nature, he stood his ground. Things grew increasingly tense until the climactic day when Father Jean Foucault announced that he was bringing a lawsuit against Father Henri and Sister Colette for the usurpation of his rights and the theft of his possessions. This decision and the whole sad story are chronicled by Sister Perrine and also by Father Pierre de Vaux.

Happily for the reform, this action of Foucault's served to alienate rather than confirm his followers. All but two of them were filled with horror at the notion of bringing the affair into a public court. And that Father Jean should level his accusations not only against Father Henri but also against the nun whom all of them had seen rapt into ecstasy in their own house seems to have been revolting to their sense of the fear of God as well as to their chivalry.

Father Jean Foucault, however, was not a man to lose heart easily. Let the friars desert him! He had plenty of powerful friends outside. He and his two followers engaged the ablest lawyers in Dôle to defend their claims. And Father Henri, for all his dislike of such legal involvements, was obliged to find a lawyer, Etienne de Granval, for his defense. Foucault busied himself with enlisting the full support of his wealthy secular friends, and within a few weeks he had the sympathy of the city entirely behind him. The case was called, and the Father guardian showed such adroitness in directing his lawyers and such eloquence in his own appeals that it became obvious that the judges were favoring his protests. Father Henri is described by Pierre de Vaux as unworldly; yet he was shrewd enough to see that his case was not holding up in civil court. Nor did he miss the lack of enthusiasm on the part of the lawyers he had engaged. He prepared a message to this effect for the abbess, to be delivered by the chief attorney, Etienne de Granval, who set off in a carriage for Besançon.

The fact was, de Granval himself had been losing heart for some days. The opposition was so strong. And, after all, was all this commotion justified? The community at Dôle had long been an asset to the town. Why did these rigorists have to occupy themselves with matters which were none of their concern? De Granval later described how, as such gloomy thoughts were swirling through his mind, he suddenly felt himself caught in a kind of mental vise. He felt as if his thinking processes were arrested: he seemed unable to draw any conclusions from the arguments he had been arraying in favor of abandoning the case. Worse still, he feared that he was having hallucinations. For suddenly the face of a nun seemed to be looking at him from the road, the hedges, the low-slung clouds, the bent trees, the carriage walls. He looked confusedly about him, but there was nowhere he could settle his gaze without meeting the accusation of two dark eyes.

Resolutely de Granval closed his own eyes. But behind the shutters of his eyelids, the face of Colette regarded him with sadness. He shifted uneasily in the carriage. And then, without any volition he could afterwards recall, he ordered the coachman to turn back to Dôle. Instantly he could think clearly again. And he thought primarily of how poor a case he had been putting up for the reform. Out of nowhere, arguments and persuasions aligned themselves before him.

De Granval had met Sister Colette on a number of occasions and had admitted to being impressed by her manifest sanctity and charmed with her humility and simplicity. With a profound sense of shame, he now admitted to himself how shabby he had been in his defence of her interests—no, worse, of God's interests! He leaned forward and urged the coachman to speed up the horses. And when he alighted at Dôle and was asked by a surprised Father Henri whether he had already been to Besançon and seen the abbess, the lawyer gave his enigmatic reply with vehemence. "No, I have not been to Besançon, but I have seen the abbess."

He did not linger to explain, but immediately summoned his councillors for a closed conference, proceeding to lay before them a case for the reform so convincing that they came out of the conference room full of enthusiasm. The case was re-opened the following day with a masterly address by de Granval.

Father Jean Foucault's attorneys were instantly alerted to the change. They rallied their forces to a counter-attack, but it proved no match for de Granval's new fire. The judges' sympathies began taking another road. The testimony of the witnesses for the prosecution sounded entirely different under de Granval's astute questioning. And, in the end, a decision wholly in favor of the reform was handed down. Father Henri de la Baume and Sister Colette were exonerated of all charges against them. And Father Foucault was advised either to act on the formal promises he had made the preceding year to embrace the primitive Franciscan Rule or to separate himself from the community of Dôle. In a rage, he chose the latter course.

He and his two inseparable companions took up private residence in the city, enjoying the sympathy of their affluent lay friends. It was a victory for the reform, but a triumph at the price of heartbreak. Father Henri was shaken and saddened by the defection of Father Jean and the other two friars. And when the abbess of Besançon heard of it, she was inconsolable. She had encouraged de Granval, but that such public scandal as Foucault's defection should arise from the reform was too much for her peace-loving heart to bear. She wept until she fell ill; and when the Sisters tried to comfort her, she had only one reply: "I want to die."

It seemed for a time that she was going to do just that. Without the will to live, Perrine tells us, she lay in the infirmary at Besançon where the nuns had insisted on moving her, unable to eat or sleep, her meager strength dwindling daily. People had always remarked that Sister Colette brought the peace and joy of God wherever she went. Now, she insisted, she had brought division and strife among the friars at Dôle. She had dishonored the cause of God and religion. She was worthy of damnation.

All this may seem exaggerated to us, but only if we fail to take into account the extreme gentleness and sweetness of St. Colette's character. She was always peace-loving Robert Boellet's daughter. And like St. Francis and St. Clare before her, she could not endure division. Disunity among his friars had broken the Poverello's heart and sent him off to live apart in caves and on mountains. "Let them do what they wish," was his weary reply to the nagging and bickering of his sons.

In her Rule, St. Clare had warned her daughters to "beware of all dissension and division." She begged them to be "ever solicitous to maintain among themselves that unity of mutual charity which is the bond of perfection." This horror of division within the Order permeated St. Colette as well. In a very tender manner, the seraphic foundress of Assisi showed her sympathy for her daughter, Colette.

When the abbess seemed at the very end of her physical resources, God favored her with a vision in which she saw St. Clare kneeling before the throne of God and pleading her cause. "Lord, let her die and join our company," begged the seraphic Mother.

But there was another in the vision. It was St. Francis. And, though they had never differed on earth, the saints of Assisi were differing in heaven. Far from joining in the petition of St. Clare, the little Poor Man complained to the Lord: "Alas, Sire, did You only give Sister Colette to me in order to take her away so soon?" The judges at Dôle had pronounced for the reform. The Heavenly Judge did, too. St. Francis prevailed; and immediately after this vision, the abbess of Besançon experienced unmistakable signs of returning health. Her nuns were jubilant. She was less so, but there is a rare humor in her admission to those who nursed her. "Alas! Our Father St. Francis does not wish me to die. I am not at all pleased," are her words recorded by Sister Perrine.

Pleased or not, Colette rallied her forces and took heart again. News from Dôle brought both sorrow and joy. The community there was experiencing such a spiritual renascence, and so many others of neighboring towns were showing enthusiasm for the primitive Rule, that Father Henri felt his first duty was now directly to the friars. After the long years of closest association with the abbess-general of the Poor Clares, he now had to devote most of his time to his duties and heavy responsibilities as a kind of vicar over all houses of the First Order in France where the original observance was being restored.

Wise enough to know that the future of the reform depended on the training of new recruits in the primitive way, he appointed Father François Claret master of novices at Dôle. And he sent his intimate and trusted friend, Father Pierre de Vaux, to work at the side of Sister Colette. From that day until her death, Father Pierre was confessor to the saint, her unfailing friend and adviser, and an untiring co-operator in the work of restoring the primitive observance. He also, as mentioned before, became her biographer; and his writings rank with those of Sister Perrine as the primary source of authentic information about the saint of Corbie. To the end of his days, however, Father Henri remained the abbess-general's loyalest friend. He visited her whenever possible, and together they shared the joys and vicissitudes of the reform.

If spiritual affairs were growing brighter and brighter for the community at Dôle, temporal affairs were not. Smarting under his public defeat and separation from his Order, Father Jean Foucault soothed his pride with the adulation of his secular friends. He used it as a weapon against his former community. The sympathy of the townspeople still ran strongly toward the handsome, witty friar who had made the friary of Dôle for years a favored spot for conviviality. The citizens let themselves be persuaded that they were doing a service to the cause of religion by cutting off food supplies to the friars of Dôle. If fanaticism was not nipped in the bud, Foucault argued, who could say what poisonous fruits it would not bring forth over the whole country? "They wish to fast," he reminded the people with a sardonic laugh. "Help them! Encourage them! Give them neither food nor alms." The people laughed with him and agreed.

Word of this new development reached the ears of the young abbess of Auxonne, Sister Agnes de Vaux, before it was carried to Sister Colette at Besançon, and she took prompt action. The Poor Clares at Auxonne had few enough provisions for themselves, and there were only sixty or seventy bushels of wheat in their granary at the time. But Sister Agnes at once ordered all the wheat to be used in baking bread for the hungry friars at Dôle.

Moreover, she sent word to the community of friars that she and her nuns would provide bread as long as they needed it. The offer was accepted in all Franciscan simplicity by the friars, and a lay brother was immediately despatched to Auxonne to pick up the first shipment.

He walked beside the community's donkey, a beast so diminutive of body and so droll of face that even the citizens of Dôle most indignant against the friars had to smile when they saw the odd pair. Twice a week for several months, the Franciscan brother and the donkey went to the Poor Clares at Auxonne and returned with a full supply of bread for the community of fifty men. No one was ever able to bring forward any human explanation of why the nuns' small supply of wheat never dwindled in all this time. They used it for the friars, but it was still there in the granary afterward. It is probable that both communities accepted this quite simply, as a reward for complete confidence in God.

The little donkey staggering under his burden of loaves, and the lay brother, his arms piled with loaves and more loaves strapped on his back, always singing, became a familiar sight on the country roads. There was no resisting the pair. The brother beamed on everyone he met. The donkey kept so loyally to his task. After six months, people were tired of the boycott. They lost their admiration for the embittered Father Jean Foucault and gradually transferred it to the friars whose holy living became more apparent to them each new day. At last the little donkey could be dispensed from his bi-weekly visit to Auxonne, though the lay brother occasionally returned there with little gifts which the friars were now able to provide for the nuns. Life in the friary reverted to the normal round. But the greatest good which God drew out of the evil of strife and scandal at Dôle was one Sister Colette could not yet foresee though it was to gladden her later life. That good was Father Jean Foucault. Sister Perrine, who has given us this whole detailed account of both Foucault and de Granval, leaves us the happy ending, too.

Abandoned at last by everyone, Father Jean was forced to look in upon his own soul. In the end, his pride was so lowered by God's grace that the former guardian begged to be reinstated in the Order as its least member. He was reinstated. But he became one of its greatest members, a luminary of the reform who worked until his death for the restoration of primitive Franciscan observance.

Miracles accompanied St. Colette all through her life. Father Jean Foucault, penitent, was one of them.

14   *The Monastery at Poligny*

The generous benefactions of the Duchess of Burgundy toward the spread of the Franciscan reform did not as yet seem to be yielding any tangible harvest for her husband. The affairs of John the Fearless were becoming more entangled with each new day; and in the fall of 1414, Margaret was thrown into a state of real terror when the Armagnacs (or Orleanists) suddenly sent an army against Dijon where the Burgundy palace stood, and against Rouvres, the duchess' favorite place of sojourn.

Duke John was far away at the time, laying siege to Campiègne and Soissons for the crown. Margaret feared for her life and the lives of her children, since neither Dijon nor Rouvres was well-fortified or in any way prepared to resist a strong attack. The Orleanist forces, captained by Jean de Chalon, were advancing steadily. In her panic, the duchess appealed to Sister Colette to save her.

One is reminded of the words of Christ to the centurion: "Amen, amen I say to you, I have not found such great faith in Israel." The Lord must have marvelled at Duchess Margaret's faith that a cloistered nun's intercession with God would serve to turn away the armies of de Chalon and save the house of Burgundy. "It will be all right," she told her children. And it was.

We have no record of the abbess' sending any message to the advancing forces. Perhaps she did. We know for certain that she prayed and asked her two communities to pray for the safety of their greatest benefactress and her household. And we know that the prayer was heard. It seems likely that she did intervene directly with the Armagnac armies, for the simple reason that advancing forces certain of victory do not suddenly turn tail and retreat just out of fancy. Yet, retreat is precisely what the Armagnac armies did. And it is certainly true that by this time the very name of Colette exercised prodigious power throughout all France. Women who raise the dead to life are not the common run even of celebrities. The abbess was talked of by reverent voices all over the kingdom.

Margaret of Burgundy attributed her safety entirely to the intercession, whether vocal or purely spiritual, or both, of Colette. And when her husband returned home at last in a frenzy of relief to find her and his children alive and unmolested, the duchess promptly told him what kind of action she had taken and what had come of it. John appears to have shared his wife's faith. After this, it was easy to get all necessary grants from the duke for the third Poor Clare foundation at Poligny.

In a burst of delighted enthusiasm, the duchess set about planning not only for Poligny but for three other new Franciscan houses as well. Two of these were to be for the First Order, and she sent Guillaume de Vienne to look over sites she had in mind at Sellières and Chariez. Under Father François Claret's fervent guidance, the novitiate at Dôle was flourishing both in numbers and in observance, and Father Henri was eager to start new houses of the primitive Rule for the friars so that the good influence of Dôle might begin spreading over France without delay. He had more than enough recruits, if only he had funds and houses. Margaret of Burgundy wanted to supply both, and Duke John agreed.

Father Henri had no fault to find with either Sellières or Chariez, and brought back enthusiastic reports of each to the abbess-general at Besançon. The anguish sowed at Dôle was showing God's good increase. Sellières and Chariez were to be its first fruits, and Father Henri left immediately to oversee the construction at Sellières.

Sister Colette set out for Poligny, the first of Margaret's choices for the nuns, and found that this time she had no reason to disagree with the duchess. The place won her heart at once. It kept her heart, too. Of all her foundations, Poligny was the saint's favorite. She lived there nearly seven years as abbess and returned to it frequently afterward as to a loved haven. Before her death, she promised that she herself would always keep a kind of celestial watch over Poligny, so that the observance and fervor there would never diminish. Her body remains there even now.

The site selected for the new monastery was one to rejoice the soul of anyone dedicated to an enclosed contemplative life. Poligny nestles in a mountainous recess where the Juras reach out over the rich plains close to Dôle. Surrounded by walls, as though the whole delightful town were one great cloister, Poligny was moderately wealthy and deeply religious. It had for its motto: "A Dieu playze" ("May it please God!"), and this device (which evidently appealed greatly to the abbess since she remarked on it with such satisfaction to Sister Perrine), was seen everywhere—on the city gates, on the fountains, on the numerous churches. The place had an air of quiet and serenity about it, as though it stood aside from the turmoil of France, intent on pleasing God rather than men.

The abbess was eager that work be begun at once for a monastery, but her health did not permit her to oversee the whole construction this time. Father Henri was busy with the new foundation for the friars, and Guillaume de Vienne was working with him. While she considered whom she could entrust with the building, Countess Blanche de Genève appeared on the scene. As she grew older, the countess wished more and more to be in the company of Colette, or, at least, close to her. As soon as she heard of her friend's problem, the old lady undertook to solve it. Her equerry, Jean Bon, was the man for the task.

Sister Colette talked to him and was impressed with his spirituality and good sense. She found that M. Bon was aptly named. He departed very willingly for Poligny to begin work on the third monastery of the primitive Rule, for he had the highest esteem for Colette through the reports he had heard from others. Now he was to develop a deep personal reverence for her. He later confided to the old countess that he had seen rays of light coming from the abbess as he helped her to dismount when she visited Poligny. Colette was at this time thirty-four years old. When ravaged by her infirmities, she looked much older, the early biographers lament. When temporarily relieved of them, she looked younger, they assure us.

If a reliable head for the construction crew had been found, however, the abbess soon discovered that there were to be problems of another kind at Poligny. The Duke of Burgundy had a very important arsenal there which, in his gratitude for his wife's safety, he had given over to the foundress in a document dated June, 1415. When his deputies at Poligny heard of this, they were furious. Did M. le Duc know what he was giving away? How could the arsenal be established anywhere else without great expense and strategic losses? What did praying nuns know about the exigencies of war? The indignant officials carried their complaints to the duke's chief agent, Jean de Montigny. He was in complete sympathy with the objections and refused to surrender the arsenal to the abbess, sure that John the Fearless would come to his senses and see his mistake. However, it was de Montigny who was mistaken.

Jean Bon apprised Countess Blanche of the unexpected difficulty. Blanche at once betook herself to the Duchess of Burgundy, and Margaret appealed to her husband. Duke John was not a man who enjoyed opposition at any time. When his wife's plans suffered from it, he was prepared to crush it without further consideration. Nevertheless, his letter of August 6, 1415, written at Rouvres and despatched to Poligny, is characterized more by graciousness, even sweetness, than by wrath, though de Montigny was not slow to grasp the full import of "we command and enjoin on you expressly"! He knew the Duke of Burgundy's iron hand. The letter from Rouvres was extraordinary only because John seldom wore the velvet glove. It ran like this:

As, at the request of our most cherished and beloved consort, the Duchess, and out of consideration for our cherished and beloved sister, Colette Boellet, abbess of the Franciscan nuns at Auxonne; We, having by our other letters sealed with our great seal, and for the causes and considerations which are stated in them, given free of all charges to the Church and to the said abbess our estate and house situated in the street in the upper part of our town of Poligny, there to found and build a monastery of Franciscan nuns, because from our heart we desire to spread the divine worship and to maintain our gifts and grants, and that the said monastery may be founded and built in the place of our said home and estate, and for several other reasons which have decided us, we will that the said gift and grant made by us to the said religious shall take effect, and we command and enjoin on you expressly that all the obstruction which has been caused by your orders you shall withdraw and remove, and allow the nuns to take possession.

Duchess Margaret left the abbess a free hand in planning the new monastery, only expressing the hope that the cells would be a little larger than those at Auxonne. The thought of their extreme smallness still exasperated her. Here, in a comparatively minor matter, we see the greatness of a woman who was always willing to admit her mistakes. For Colette realized she had made a mistake at Auxonne. "Assuredly, they will be larger, my lady," she said. "I did wrong at Auxonne. The cells are too small. Some time they will have to be enlarged a little." Margaret of Burgundy was accustomed to persons of repute holding it as a point of honor never to admit an error. She must have been charmed to find that the miracle-working abbess had no such fetters.

"Our Lady of Pity" was the name the saint chose for the monastery at Poligny. She always had a vast compassion for any and all kinds of suffering, and the state of France and the papacy in 1415 was enough to elicit the pity of a far less tender heart than hers. There was devastation nearly everywhere in the kingdom. The Emperor Sigismund, king of the Romans, had convoked an immense, unwieldy council at Constance, and Christendom did not know whether to hope or fear as thousands of prelates and princes continued to deliberate there.

The prestige of the Pisan "pope," John XXIII, was steadily dwindling as his thoroughgoing worldliness became apparent to everyone. Benedict XIII was fast becoming the figure of a madman, hurling daily excommunications against the former supporters who now despised him. The true pope, Gregory XII, was almost ninety, and rallying himself to rise to the really magnanimous gesture which was to elevate his mediocre life to final greatness.

England was closing fiercer tentacles around France each day. The young dauphin, son of mad King Charles VI and the adulterous Isabeau, went his giddy social round with little taste for anything higher. But in a remote village called Domremy, a little girl named Jeanne d'Arc was having her third birthday while St. Michael and St. Catherine bent over her from heaven. And in a cloister at Poligny, a thirty-four-year-old abbess was praying and doing penance with a new community of her nuns. The shadow of God's hand was moving over France and the Church.

The Poligny pioneers numbered six, including the abbess-general, but the names of only three have come down to us. There was a Sister Chevalier (not Marie Chevalier of the books and the visions) from Poligny itself, and two named Claude: Sister Claude of Arras and young Sister Claude of Courcell who became the first abbess at Our Lady of Pity after the departure of Colette in 1422. The material needs of the six nuns were few, but one constituted an urgent problem. There was no water.

Sister Colette was accustomed to miracles by this time, but she remained as practical-minded a woman as ever. She did not intend to besiege heaven for a miraculous spring if one could be discovered by any ordinary means. Experienced well-diggers were dubious about finding water on the monastery grounds, but the abbess left no possibility untried. Each day of the community's first Lent in Poligny found her out early and late, directing the well-diggers to this spot and that, encouraging their perspiring efforts, and begging them so sweetly not to get discouraged that they doggedly kept at a task they themselves felt was hopeless. However, by the fourth week in Lent, even the smiling encouragement of the abbess was not sufficient to put their shovels into action again.

They had sounded every foot of ground on the place, they insisted. They were sorry, very sorry; but the monastery of Our Lady of Pity had no water. "All right," the abbess said, "but please come back tomorrow." The foreman started to protest, but something in her face must have stopped him. "Oh—all right," he replied.

Ever since their arrival at Poligny, two out-door Sisters had been walking daily to the well in the town to draw the community's supply of water. It was hard work; worse, it involved much loss of valuable time. Everyone in friendly Poligny had to stop the Sisters and chat a bit. The affair was getting to be more than an ordinary nuisance, as both Father Pierre de Vaux and Sister Perrine are at pains to mention.

Sister Colette, they tell us, went to the choir and laid the case before our Lord. And Sister Perrine adds that she did so "piteously." She told Him she had done everything possible to supply her community's needs. It wasn't enough. He would have to take over. She urged the other nuns to pray with her. It was Friday of the fourth week in Lent, and the gospel of the Mass was St. John's account of Christ's meeting with the Samaritan woman at Jacob's well. (According to our present arrangement, this gospel narrative is read on the third Friday in Lent.) When Colette read the woman's words: "Lord, give me this water," she had a powerful inspiration.

When she went into the garden afterward, she found a crew of disgruntled well-diggers. They knew their business. There was *no water here*. The abbess did not argue, but simply bent down and began to "knock at the ground and hollow out some earth," as Perrine describes it. Then she said: "Dig here." They dug. And they shortly uncovered three separate springs which they directed into one well.

Even in seasons of drouth through the years, this well at Our Lady of Pity in Poligny never went dry, and it is significant that Father Pierre and Sister Perrine describe its water in exactly the same words: This "beautiful water," they say, was "so good that there was none better in the city or the whole country." The "beautiful water" has remained a testimonial to the faith of six nuns.

If Sister Colette had so solicitous a heart for the physical needs of her community, her care for their spiritual welfare was even more tender. Death came to visit Poligny only a short time after the foundation was made. One of the young novices she had brought from Auxonne fell very ill and grew worse so quickly that her death seemed imminent. Everything possible was done for her, but neither medicines nor prayers availed. The child seemed to have no fear of death, asking only that her abbess should be with her at the final hour.

Sister Colette nursed the novice herself a great deal of the time, refusing to leave her unless she was obliged by some great necessity. When it happened one day that she did have to leave the infirmary, she stationed another of the nuns at the bedside, strictly charging her to come at once and call her if the novice seemed in immediate danger. The nun took up her post, but shortly fell into a sound sleep. While she slept, the poor little novice entered into her agony and died alone.

This incident is given in Father Pierre's biography and also in Perrine's chronicle, and both describe the abbess as sick at heart when she learned of the novice's lonely death. Negligence must have been involved, and not merely overpowering fatigue on the part of the watcher, for Colette reprimanded her with a severity she seldom showed, and she added to her reproof a dreadful prophecy: "Because you did not carry out the directions I gave you, I tell you now that you will die alone; no one shall be present at your death." The stern words are given in both chronicles, and it appears that Colette did not temper them with any consoling additions.

We grieve for the young novice unassisted in her last agony, but it is hard not to feel pity for the miserable watcher, too. When this Sister was in her last illness "a short time after this," as the early biographers place it, she lost her power of speech for six hours. She was sure death was imminent, and she had not received the last Sacraments. Yet she lay there, powerless to call anyone, miserable in the recollection of her abbess' dreadful prophecy, and aware that the others knew nothing of her being *in extremis.* One did know, though—the abbess.

The sick nun was weeping as Colette entered her cell and walked quickly to the bedside. She took the nun's hands in her own and began to pray. Suddenly the sufferer's power of speech returned to her. The abbess went at once to summon the confessor, probably Father Pierre himself.

The priest came and heard the Sister's confession, administered the last Sacraments, and left a peaceful patient quietly and resignedly awaiting the moment of death. The Sisters who had been summoned then left her, feeling there was no immediate danger. Their abbess knew better. She kissed her dying daughter on the forehead, traced the little sign of the cross she had drawn there so often during the nun's life, and left her. The nun died alone.

It was to the monastery of Poligny that the chronicler of this incident and so many others, Sister Perrine, presented herself as an aspirant in 1417. The entrance day of Father Henri's niece must surely have been one of extraordinary joy for Sister Colette, whose recollections of the circumstances of Perrine's birth must have been vivid.

It was a common thing in the fifteenth century for very young girls to enter monasteries where they lived a semi-religious life, taking part in many of the community exercises and completing their education under the tutelage of the abbess or some other nun. Thus the primitive Rule of St. Clare makes provision for "the young ladies who are received into the monastery before they have reached the proper age," decreeing that they "shall be clothed in religious garb of such sort as may seem befitting to the abbess" and that "when they have reached the proper age they shall make their profession, clothed after the manner of the others."

St. Clare's own youngest sister, Beatrice, entered the monastery when she was twelve or thirteen. Perrine de la Baume came when she was ten, but officially entered the Order only several years later, making profession of vows when she was about eighteen. She remained by the side of the abbess-general more or less continually for thirty years; and, as she grew in years and maturity, became Colette's closest confidante. Perrine had been the child of her prayers. Sister Perrine became the daughter of her soul.

Before Colette left Poligny, death came to the monastery again, but from a different direction. Countess Blanche had aged noticeably in the years since the Poor Clares had left Auxonne to establish the house at Poligny. She talked more and more of her approaching death, and the abbess did not contradict her friend's predictions. "There is only one thing now," Blanche would repeat over and over to Sister Colette: "I want to be buried wherever you are at the time." "Maude," she would insist to her niece, "you must bring my body to Colette."

Sister Perrine tells us that the two gave their word to the old countess. Blanche died, happy in their promise, in 1421, while Colette was still acting as abbess at Poligny. Countess Maude had the body brought in state not to the burial vault of the counts of Geneva where the remains of the old countess' brother Clement VII lay, but to the little Poor Clare monastery at Poligny. Maude built a new and impressive chapel onto the monastery in memory of her aunt. The chapel has since been destroyed, but the body of Countess Blanche de Genève, who had been the first to hear from Father Henri in 1406 the strange tale of a young anchoress in Corbie destined by God to restore primitive Franciscanism in France, remains at Poligny even to the present day.

The old countess sleeps near the saint of Corbie, waiting for the great day when she will rise in company with her illustrious protégée for the general judgment. Things should go well for Blanche de Genève on that day, with St. Colette beside her. One likes to hope that, on Blanche's account, they may also go well for her misguided brother Clement VII, first of the anti-popes in the Great Western Schism.

This has been a look into the future. It was now only 1416, and a peaceful year and more had passed for the nuns at Poligny. Things were not so peaceful, though, for the councillors at Constance, now in session for nearly three years. Emperor Sigismund had had a very personal interest in convoking the Council of Constance, though it is only fair to credit him with the higher motive of working for the end of the papal schism also. Sigismund could not be crowned as emperor in Rome until Western Christendom again gathered around one spiritual leader. This powerful prince had determined that Christendom *was* going to be reunited—and soon.

Claiming the right by his imperial authority, he had convoked the sixteenth Ecumenical Council at Constance. Practically everyone of note in Church or state had moved to answer the convocation. Cardinals and bishops of all three obediences had come pouring into Constance. The greatest secular princes in Europe had also come either personally or by proxy. The immense heterogeneous assemblage was saved from being merely another schismatical council like that of Pisa by the action of the true pope, Gregory XII. The aged pontiff had sanctioned the convocation of the Council of Constance and endowed its proceedings with his authority. One can thank God for this inspired action of Gregory's which saved the Church from the very possible curse of a fourth "pope."

Meanwhile, the Pisan pope, John XXIII, seemed oblivious of his waning popularity and contemptuous of Gregory's show of authority. He arrived at Constance with a huge retinue, expecting to hear enthusiastic cries of "Viva il papa!" He found instead a hostile throng, and what he heard was the long document drawn up by the canonists at Constance and read aloud for his benefit. It amounted to a listing of all his crimes. And its length was considerable. John XXIII knew himself defeated. After another look at the threatening crowd, he knew more than that. He fled.

It was only when Emperor Sigismund's deputies pursued him and gave him the emperor's personal guarantee of safe conduct that the frightened "pope" could be induced to return to the council. Thoroughly intimidated, and aware that all was lost as far as his claims to the papacy were concerned, John accepted the council's sentence of deposition. After a period of imprisonment, he was reinstated in the Church as Cardinal-bishop of Frascati, in which high post he seems to have behaved himself admirably, considering his past record.

The council then turned its considerations on the other two papal claimants, but this was the hour of Gregory XII's immortal achievement. The old man humbly handed in to the council his formal resignation of the papacy. It was a superbly magnanimous gesture, and he was loved and respected for it as he had been neither loved nor respected during the long years of stubbornness and travail. He was asked to accept the appointment as Cardinal-bishop of Porto, and he did. He remained at that post until his death two years later in the autumn of 1417.

If the council expected the third claimant, Pedro de Luna, known as Benedict XIII, to follow Gregory's example and resign, it was disillusioned in short order. The Spaniard would have testified to the sincerity and integrity his admirers had always claimed for him had he resigned with dignity at this point. Instead, he manifested only an insane jealousy for his "rights," rewarding the advice of those who really loved him with fresh excommunications. Thus, instead of a resignation, it was a deposition which ended Benedict's reign.

Even when this terrible sentence was delivered against him, Pedro de Luna remained unmoved. To the end of his tragic life, he continued to hurl his "papal" thunderbolts against all and sundry. He was forced to leave Avignon and went to end his days at Perriscola in Spain, a pope without a Church. Two cardinals remained loyal to him to the last; and when the pathetic old Spanish friar was dying, he charged this "college of cardinals" to see that he was buried in the full insignia of a supreme pontiff.

Perhaps the two cardinals still believed in Pedro de Luna's claims to the highest authority in the Church. Perhaps they remained with him only out of affection and pity. Without any such conjectures, we know there was an abbess in the cloister of Poligny who realized now that his claims were false and her own former belief in him unjustified, but who remained loyal in prayer to her benefactor. Often, in those days, her nuns found Sister Colette weeping. After awhile, they no longer asked anxious questions, for her answer was always the same: "I weep for Pedro de Luna. May God have mercy on him."

The papal throne was at last vacant, and a valid election could be held. It took two years of deliberation after the deposition and resignation of 1415, however, for the cardinals to agree on a successor to the former Gregory XII. Finally, on November 11, 1417, the electors settled on Cardinal Odo Colonna, who became Pope Martin V. That a member of the powerful and hated Colonna clan should wear the papal tiara could scarcely have delighted most of Christendom. Still, the new pontiff's personal life was blameless; and after he had courageously refused the overtures of the French for establishing the papal see at Avignon and those of the emperor for moving it to Germany, his fierce and numerous family cleared his way to Rome and made order of Roman chaos with a sweep and despatch possible at that time only to the Colonnas.

Martin V ascended the papal throne almost immediately after the death of the erstwhile Gregory XII, then Cardinal of Porto. It seemed a divine chronicling of events, so that Martin's election followed Gregory's death as naturally as a succession in normal times. Christendom—whatever the dislike of most of its members for the Colonnas—took courage again. So did the abbess at Poligny. Very soon after Martin V's accession, the new pope issued bulls confirming all the privileges and authority granted Colette by the antipopes. She set herself with even greater zeal than before to train her nuns in the way of Franciscan perfection.

"I, little Brother Francis, promise reverence," St. Francis had vowed in a century when men's reverence, whether toward the clergy or directly toward God in divine worship, left much to be desired. In the midst of a society which openly sneered at its covetous and sensual priests, Francis moved with the awe of a small and humble man for his betters. There is the famous incident of his visiting a town where the parish priest was a public sinner. The people thought they had cornered Francis, with all his talk of reverence for priests, this time. "Shall we respect this fellow with his feasting and his concubines?" they asked. But the saint of Assisi was not worsted this time or ever. He loved the Christ who saved the adulterous woman and invited a man with no sin of his own to cast the first stone at her. Francis knelt down before the sacrilegious priest and kissed his hands. "Whether he is a sinner, I know not," the saint declared, "but these hands alone give me the Lord of heaven and earth."

It was the same with reverence for the house of God and His

worship. The careless who remained apathetic to exhortations were strangely moved by the sight of St. Francis and his friars prostrating themselves on the ground each time they entered or even passed a church. They were fascinated to see the father of hundreds of religious himself busy with a broom in dirty, neglected little wayside shrines. The soul of St. Clare was imbued with this same simple reverence. So was the soul of St. Colette. She insisted especially that the Divine Office be discharged with all possible reverence, dignity, and devotion. "If earthly kings and worldly lords," she said, "are served with such great care and reverence, with how much greater care and reverence ought we not to serve the King of kings and Lord of lords?" An especially telling comment on the importance the saint attached to the Divine Office is made by Father Pierre de Vaux when he tells us that Colette, despite her zeal for poverty, had breviaries imported from Germany for the use of her nuns. They were more beautifully and accurately executed than those she could obtain in France, and Father Pierre writes that she "would not have it that there should be any fault in the divine service because of faults in the books."

The abbess used her gift for reading hearts to great practical advantage in this matter of the Divine Office. A nun who stood in the choir, Office book in hand, but with thoughts flying in four directions, might have Sister Colette walk over to her and calmly take the breviary out of her hands. The blushing nun would know why. And when the culprit had humbled herself before God and recollected herself, she would be rewarded with the return of her breviary by a smiling abbess. Sister Perrine makes the demure comment that "The knowledge that their holy Mother read their hearts was a great check on the Sisters' idle and useless thoughts, and a spur to keep themselves recollected." No doubt.

She loved silence, too, and knew it for the guardian of reverence. "Where there is no talking," she remarked, "there is little need for rules." To preserve a greater spirit of recollection, she devised many little signs which the nuns were to use during the day to curtail speech even about necessary matters. These are still in use today. When all were gathered together at some common work, the abbess wanted all unnecessary talk strictly avoided. Yet, she was anything but a mere externalist. It was silence of soul that she wished above all to be observed, and she would caution her nuns that "exterior silence is of little account if the passions and affections make a tumult in the heart."

So humble herself, she was merciful toward her young daughters, who often entered the cloister with an interior luggage of pride they themselves did not suspect was there. In general, she was patient in helping them unpack and dispose of it; but when there was a question of pride in worldly rank, she lost her smile.

Young Sister Agnes Wissmelle was still a novice when she learned the abbess' views on family pride. During dinner one day, Sister Colette gave the lector a copy of a certain legal act which she wanted read aloud to the community. In it there was mention of Isabeau of Bavaria, Queen of France. Novice Agnes wriggled importantly on her bench and cleared her throat. "That's my aunt," she whispered to the novice sitting next to her. Doubtless her fellow-novice was impressed. So was the abbess, who had caught the stage whisper, but for a somewhat different reason. She called the whisperer to her and rebuked her severely. "You are never to speak of your relatives again," she commanded. Sister Agnes never did, except to tell this story to Sister Perrine years later.

By 1417, with the papal schism ended, the abbess-general knew she must begin planning a fourth foundation. She still had Margaret of Burgundy's offer of Seurre, and there would soon be well-trained subjects enough to fill a new monastery. Before establishing it, however, she realized she must set about putting in writing the regulations which were still being handed from monastery to monastery only by oral teaching and example. Consequently she undertook the all-important work of writing her Constitutions, which would show her future daughters St. Clare's Rule in action. The Franciscan saint was just beginning this task in earnest when a Dominican saint came to call on her.

15 *The Cross of Vincent Ferrer*

During the ten years since the establishment of the first community
of the reform at Besançon, St. Vincent Ferrer had been laying the
firebrand of his eloquence and zeal on religious apathy in Spain and
France. Like Colette, the Dominican friar had been a staunch ad-
herent of Benedict XIII and had even acted as the anti-pope's confessor for some time. Pedro de Luna, in his turn, reverenced Father
Vincent. And when the fiery Spanish preacher got himself embroiled
with the Court of the Inquisition through the native impulsiveness
which sometimes left certain of his statements open to theological
question, the Spanish pope rescued him and cleared his name.

Vincent Ferrer left the papal court at Avignon out of a conviction
that God wished him to devote his energies exclusively to preaching,
but he remained in close communication with Benedict for many
years. It was only when that pontiff began to show a fierce attachment
to his claims, refusing any talk of conciliation with the pope in Rome,
that the Dominican friar was enlightened to see his error in supporting
Benedict XIII.

He prayed earnestly as he restudied the old quarrels and the beginnings of the great schism more than a quarter of a century before.
As a result, he ascended the pulpit in the cathedral of Perpignan on
January 6, 1416, and solemnly delivered a public retraction of his
allegiance to Benedict XIII. He had already counselled the kings of
Aragon, Castille, and Navarre to withdraw their support from one
who he now saw clearly had never been anything but an anti-pope.
And so great was the influence of Vincent Ferrer that after this public renouncement of his, all Spain followed his lead and separated
itself from Pedro de Luna.

This solemn act and its consequences must certainly have cost
the Spanish preacher real anguish of heart. He was a man fashioned
for undying loyalty, and he knew how much he owed to Benedict

XIII. Like Colette, he suffered to the end of his life on account of the tragic Spanish pope.

If Father Vincent Ferrer had been mistaken in his first convictions about the validity of Benedict's papal claims, he was certainly not mistaken in his convictions about his own ministry. With his gift for reaching the most hardened hearts, he became the outstanding preacher of the century. He could conquer seemingly invincible sinners and persuade the most lethargic souls to embrace a militant Christianity.

He was at the peak of his popularity in 1417 when the people of Poligny received the great good news that he was coming to preach in their city. They decorated the streets as though for a visiting prince and went to meet the preacher at the city gates. Vincent was a colorful figure, and the people could recognize him when he was still far in the distance. They raised a great shout of welcome. The Dominican always carried a large wooden cross which he used as a staff on his long journeys on foot over Europe (he despised more comfortable means of travel), and which he planted in the ground or stood in the pulpit beside him whenever he spoke to the people. He remained several days in Poligny, preaching to the townspeople during the day and addressing the Poor Clares in the evening at their grate. He had been eager for a long time to meet the abbess, whom people were already calling a saint. He had also, as he later revealed, been granted a vision of her conversing with our Lord, in which God had told him to go and confer with Colette.

Father Pierre de Vaux has left us the account of this vision, recording words which Vincent Ferrer, during its course, "overheard" spoken by our Lord to Sister Colette. They were in answer to the young abbess' pleas on behalf of sinners. "My daughter, what do you wish Me to do? Each day they attack Me with new injuries! They wound Me by their blasphemies. I am cut into pieces and mangled by the multitude and diversity of their crimes."

This vision of Vincent Ferrer's has a curious parallel in a vision of Colette's some time earlier, in which the Mother of God showed her a kind of platter on which the flesh of an infant cut into bits was spread and told her this was what sin had done to her Divine Son.

Colette was thirty-six and Vincent Ferrer sixty-seven when the two saints met. They talked first of the great schism and of the

Council of Constance. Together, they composed a letter which they despatched to the councillors, urging them to make no compromise which would further injure the principle of the papacy, and encouraging them to act boldly for God's sake. We have no way of knowing what precise effect a joint letter from the cloistered Franciscan nun, known all over Europe now for her miracles, and the Dominican preacher, renowned for his preaching and his holiness, had on the council; but it must have been considerable. The fact that it came from two erstwhile supporters of the anti-pope could not have failed to give it added human impact. At any rate, after the long impasse which had left the papal throne vacant for nearly two years, the cardinals of the council did unite shortly after this in their choice of a new pope, Martin V.

Schisms and councils apart, however, the Dominican had a very personal curiosity he wished to satisfy without further delay. He had been told by his good friend, Father Henri de la Baume, that the Poor Clare abbess had in her possession an exquisite gold and pearl reliquary containing a splinter of the true Cross. Father Vincent had venerated relics of the true Cross before, and he does not appear to have been a collector of precious reliquaries. But Father Henri had confided that this reliquary had come directly from heaven.

It had happened one day during the first years at Besançon when the abbess was meditating on the Passion of our Lord. Since her childhood, when she had first heard from her mother the story of Gethsemane and Calvary, Colette tells us she had the tenderest devotion to the suffering Redeemer. Her visions in the anchorhold at Corbie of the thorn-crowned, bleeding Savior had inflamed her compassion to such an extent that she frequently fell into an ecstasy when meditating on Christ's Passion and death. Her ardent devotedness to the crucified Lord also aroused in her an intense desire to visit the Holy Land and see for herself the scenes of the sacred Passion. It was a longing she knew a cloistered nun could never hope to satisfy on earth, and she could only ask God to accept desire for deed.

What she could not surrender, however, was her longing for a relic of the true Cross. She had several times tried to secure one, but her efforts had been unsuccessful until the hour when God Himself delivered the prize into her hands. She had been praying in the choir this particular day, when the remembrance of Christ's sufferings again lifted her out of herself into a spiritual realm where her nuns could not follow her. When she returned to herself and once more became aware of earthly realities, she discovered one reality she could not explain. She held in her hands a small golden cross bearing an image of Jesus crucified.

On the back, where the arms of the cross joined, Sister Colette saw a sparkling red stone set into the gold. There were four pearls around it, and four small blue stones flanked each pearl on its outer side. At the foot of the cross was a fifth pearl. The head on the figure of the dying Christ was very slightly inclined. The arms were stretched wide in agony, and the hands held in place by nails. The sacred feet were fastened next to each other with two more nails. Pilate's superscription was marked just above the joining of the cross.

When the face of the cross where the image of Christ hung was turned back, the miraculous gift was discovered to be a reliquary. A large splinter of the true Cross was fixed inside, clearly identified with an inscription.

(This cross was kept at Besançon until the monastery was suppressed during the French Revolution. Afterward, having been kept secretly during the days of chaos, it was enshrined at the restored monastery of Poligny and then returned to Besançon in 1879 where it remains to this day. A picture of it appears in *Les Annales Franciscaines* published by the Capuchin Franciscan Friars.)

At this time Sister Colette still tried desperately to keep from the public anything extraordinary in her own life. She continued to hide in her cell when people acclaimed her. But with her daughters, she sometimes showed a charming simplicity about her wonder-working powers. Once, caught "red-handed" in a miracle, Sister Perrine writes that Colette told her nuns: "You could do much more than I if you would spare nothing to gain the heart of our Divine Redeemer." She had just restored a dead child to life. It is interesting to speculate on just what greater things the nuns were encouraged to do! Perhaps their abbess meant that they might accomplish the greatest miracle: the total surrender of themselves to God. With similar candor, the abbess showed the little cross to her nuns and to Father Henri. They were convinced that it came from heaven.

Of course, no one is obliged to accept the gift of the small reliquary as miraculous. It is neither an article of faith nor an indispensable element in the life of the Corbian saint. However, to dispose of the sudden, strange appearance of the precious cross on natural grounds, it is necessary to evoke a series of conventual near-impossibilities: first, that a nun had kept a gold and jewelled reliquary in her own possession without the knowledge or permission of her abbess, although this abbess had the gift of reading hearts; second, that this deceitful religious all of a sudden decided to place the treasure in the hands of her abbess while the latter was rapt in ecstasy, held back by no awe of such a state; and third, that no other nun in an enclosed community knew anything of either the first or the second circumstance. Always ready to subscribe a purely natural explanation to the strange events in her life, Colette could find none for this one. Perhaps others can.

She told all this to Father Vincent Ferrer, and she had a rapt audience. Without a word, the old Dominican merely held out his hand. When Sister Colette showed him the miraculous prize, Father Vincent fell on his knees. The abbess looked at the great preacher, known all over Europe as "the trumpet of the last judgment," now quite oblivious of her, engrossed with his Lord and his love. She herself was carried away into an ecstasy at the sight.

When Father Vincent finally turned back to Colette, he saw her face streaming with light, as the peasants outside Besançon had seen it, as the friars at Dôle had seen it, and marvelled. Typically, Father Vincent Ferrer settled down to enjoy the sight.

We are told that the two saints remained like that for more than an hour; and when Colette at last opened her eyes on earthly things again, it could have been with no feeling of embarrassment. There was no need for social conventions with Vincent Ferrer. After all, such things as these were nothing extraordinary. She told him quite candidly that she had learned something of his future while she was—"away." Pressed for the information by the Dominican, Sister Colette declared that he was to die in less than two years.

The great old man appears to have accepted this without comment, for Sellier and Douillet report that he merely announced his intention of returning to his native Spain. Surely this made it more painful for Sister Colette to deliver the rest of her prophecy. She told him that he would never return to Spain. He was to die in France.

With this burden of knowledge upon him, and perhaps in exchange for it as well as in token of his having little further need of his mission cross, Father Vincent Ferrer gave Colette the famous staff which many a prince in Europe would have given a fortune to possess. The old preacher blessed her and turned away, suddenly a strange figure without his familiar cross.

St. Vincent Ferrer died at Vannes in Brittany on April 5, 1419. When he got his first look at earth from heaven's perspective, he must have seen his mission cross propped up just outside Sister Colette's monastic cell where we are told she customarily kept it. The famous cross, "le baton de Maître Vincent" as people used to call it, is preserved even today in the Poor Clare monastery at Besançon. The black wood is greenish now, but the suffering Figure fastened there has not changed. The corpus is carved in the Spanish style, expressive of real agony. It was this great crucifix which St. Vincent touched to the dead whom he commanded to rise in the name of Christ crucified. It was this cross which the saint held high before the thousands of eyes riveted on him when he preached in the great cathedrals of Europe or on the open plains. It is one of the greatest treasures of the Poor Clares.

Sister Perrine and Father Pierre de Vaux do not mention the joint letter of Sister Colette and Father Vincent Ferrer to the Council of Constance. However, Father Ubald Alençon, editor of the original manuscripts of their biographies, inclines to the opinion that such a letter was written although it has not been preserved. It has the force of very strong tradition in its favor, and its omission in the two early biographies carries no definitive judgment against it. Both writers are often inclined to pass over important historical events in favor of some homely detail about their saint. Thus Father Pierre describes with care the appearance from nowhere of a little chicken one Easter morning, how it obligingly laid an egg beside Sister Colette, and how the saint ate this Easter feast with joy, having no need of further food for three days afterward, while he makes no mention whatever of her interviews with St. John Capistran, meetings which nearly ended her whole work of restoration. This choice of subject matter accounts at once for the charm and the exasperating qualities of Pierre de Vaux's biography.

The departure of the renowned Dominican left all the nuns at Our Lady of Pity spiritually reinvigorated. One admonition which Colette gave her nuns after the visit of St. Vincent was repeated again and again in her later life, so much importance did she attach to it: "As long as charity and peace shall reign among you, our Lord will not forsake you, and our houses shall endure and prosper. But as for those who will trouble our monasteries by breaking the bonds of charity, our Lord will permit that they have continual suffering. Purgatory will begin for them here on earth; and if they do not amend, they will surely perish."

The abbess' own greatest satisfaction was to see joy reigning in her communities. Like St. Francis and St. Clare, she knew that joy is the fruit of charity. She would not tolerate any least show of antipathy; and, above all things, she execrated petty jealousies, the scourge of community life. She suffered to see even a shadow of disagreement between two Sisters; and it was her practice, Sister Perrine writes, to call such pairs to her at once and reconcile them. Kneeling before their mother, the faultfinders forgot their findings; the complainers had no complaints. (However, as good a psychologist as Colette was, she would certainly know that such contrived reconciliations can be effected only in given circumstances and with certain types of characters. With those of difficult temperaments, more harm than good can result from joint interviews with the superior.)

Just as when she had acted as novice mistress in the early years at Besançon, the abbess of Poligny kept a continual watchfulness for signs of despondency in her nuns. If she knew when one of them was wilfully distracted during the Divine Office, she also knew when any of them was beaten down by depression and interior trails. Once a nun at Our Lady of Pity was enduring very acute interior sufferings. Tempted to despair, she believed herself cast off by God. It required an immense effort of will to disclose her sorrow to the abbess, but she determined to make the effort. She could not go on in this state any longer.

Wondering how to begin the account of her trials, and afraid her very real anguish would sound negligible—perhaps even unintelligible—when put into words, the fearful nun was inspired to make a little pact with God. "If our Mother receives me with more kindness than usual, if she gives me some small, special proof of affection, I shall not lose my hope of being saved." God heard this pathetic prayer and evidently entered the pact. Before the nun could approach her abbess, Sister Colette sent for her.

When she stood before her superior, expecting to be given some chore to do or perhaps to be corrected for some fault, the Sister saw her abbess sitting very quietly, looking at her. It was no task she had to impose, no correction to make. Nor did she offer any preamble to the words which dispelled the little nun's suffering and must have bloomed in her heart until she died. "My dear daughter, I love you so much—as much as I can love any Sister in our entire Order."

"Some small, special proof of affection," the nun had whispered to the Lord. She was told there was none in the whole Order to surpass her in the abbess' affections!

Sister Perrine tells us there were many instances where Colette "knew the secret desolations of her daughters" and how she "would secretly and sweetly call them to her, consoling them in their trial." Perrine offers one example "out of many." The one just given, reported by later biographers, is undoubtedly another out of the many.

This tenderness for those suffering genuine trials sent by God did not at all, however, carry over to those ostentatiously "enduring" self-imposed penances. The abbess-general had a real horror of nuns who panted after theatrical austerities, "great vigils, and a multiplicity of prayers," as she specified. She knew that the penances of the common life were quite sufficient for her nuns; and when she founded a monastery, she never failed to caution the new abbess against receiving postulants "not willing to be like the others in all the observances of our holy state."

"Professional vain devotees" was her disgusted appraisal of those loving singularity and never satisfied with the common practices. "They are full of secret vanity and self-love which accompany them during their whole lifetime. They have little docility and submission, and too great attachment to their practices of piety, preferring their own unseasonable devotions to their duties in the community and to the orders of obedience." She added wryly: "The confessor of the community is never to their liking, and they must have several; for in the world they tried every confessor that came along, without remaining with any." The abbess at Poligny, for all her ecstasies, always had the pulse of her communities. If no one equalled her in sanctity, it is very probable that no one equalled her in shrewdness, either.

By 1419, the year of St. Vincent Ferrer's death, Sister Colette was beginning to select the Sisters who were to form the nucleus of her next community at Seurre. She was called from the happy seclusion of Poligny, however, not to look over properties at Suerre, but to support the Duchess of Burgundy in her bereavement. The abbess had been planning to discuss with the duchess her plans for the new foundation. Instead, she talked for hours of God's mercy and unfathomable love to a new widow. The Duke of Burgundy had been assassinated at the bridge of Montereau on September 10.

16 *The Monasteries at Seurre, Moulins and Décize*

The Duchess of Burgundy seems to have been won at first sight to the cause of Colette and the reform. Her husband, however, was not much given to immediate capitulation to friendship, any more than to the surrender of lands. In the beginning, John the Fearless had spilled out grants and privileges to the Poor Clares with a free hand solely because of his love for his wife. But as the years passed, the formidable genius of Burgundy began to make observations of his own. By 1415, when she founded the monastery at Poligny, things had got to the place where Sister Colette could freely give spiritual and even military advice to the man before whom many a prince and captain trembled. Her letters include several to John the Fearless; and, at least on one occasion, she managed to keep him out of a battle she knew would be disastrous.

John was preparing for a huge combat with the Armagnacs, and full of the jubilation his war-loving heart always experienced at such times. Colette sent him no less than three separate messages, begging him to withdraw from the field. "M. le Duc will be defeated," she insisted. It is a pity we do not know for certain the names of all the three friars brave enough to confront the bellicose duke with exhortations to retreat written by a cloistered nun! Very likely one of them was Father Henri de la Baume, and some of the later biographers maintain that Father Pierre de Vaux was certainly another.

Both de Vaux and Sister Perrine write of a miraculous ring placed on Sister Colette's finger early in her work of restoration by St. John the Evangelist, "by his own right and on behalf of the sovereign King and Prince of virginity and chastity." Father Pierre describes the ring as "of gold, very precious and beautiful," and tells that, although Colette customarily kept her treasure in a gold or silver case (did she have two?), she sometimes showed it to "her friars, confessors, and other persons who were much gladdened and consoled by the sight of it." He adds that she frequently gave the ring to friars she sent on some difficult mission so that "sufferings and dangers might be averted." In another place he tells us how the abbess-general fortified her friar-messengers with a good glass of wine before despatching them on a journey for her. She poured a generous portion, Father Pierre recalls, "so full that not another drop would go in the glass." Surely an expedition into the battle-tents of John the Fearless was an occasion calling for both ring and wine.

This miraculous ring, says the Benedictine Dom M. Notel in his *Vie de Sainte Colette* (1594), was given to the Benedictines of Saint-Pierre in Ghent after the saint's death in 1447. It disappeared in the sixteenth century.

In the third of her messages to the Duke of Burgundy, the abbess told him plainly that she had had a vision from God in which she saw the two armies at battle "with great slaughter and spilling of blood." Perhaps this did not much affect the militaristic John, but the rest of the revelation did. He was informed he would lose the battle!

We never see the conflict in the nature of the enigmatic duke highlighted more than here. Eager to get at ripping the Armagnac forces apart, assured as always of his superior prowess, urged on by his men to strike out into battle, John of Burgundy wavered because a nun told him she had had a vision. He read the messages over and over again, pacing up and down. And, in the end, to the rage of his captains and the amazement of the Armagnacs, he changed his mind. There was no battle.

If the duke had similarly heeded Colette's advice in 1419, he would not have felt a knife blade between his shoulders on the bridge at Montereau. But he is always the same contradictory John. Instead of listening to the nun who warned him that the proposed meeting with the young dauphin, Charles, was a trap, the Duke of Burgundy listened this time to the silken encouragement of his mistress, Dame de Giac.

Some time earlier, there had been a formal reconciliation between the dauphin and John the Fearless. Young Charles had pardoned his redoubtable cousin for his part in the murder of Louis of Orleans. To what purpose, then, this second meeting, also supposedly for purposes of reconciliation? Colette thought she knew. Treacherous Dame de Giac and the Armagnacs most certainly did. But the duke agreed to it, showing himself at least this one time John the Fool. He and his retinue arrived at the bridge of Montereau as the dauphin and his entourage approached from the opposite side. When the cousins met, the duke pulled off his velvet cap and bent his knee before the future king of France. At that moment, he was stabbed in the back.

John's followers raised a cry to rend the heavens and fell upon the dauphin's party with a bloodthirstiness that promised to wipe them out in seconds. They might not have spared even the dauphin, but Tanneguy de Chatel swept the royal heir up into his own strong arms and ran with him to safety. When the dreadful slaughter was over, the few survivors slunk away, leaving the dead bodies where they had fallen. Robbers came to finish the day's work, stripping the murdered nobles of all their rich trappings. When the body of the Duke of Burgundy was reclaimed for decent burial, there was only one article of his effects to carry home to the duchess. No one had dared to touch his breviary, which is preserved in Paris to the present day.

In this mysterious circumstance (for it was a very handsome breviary and would have brought any robber a comfortable sum), Sister Colette found a spark of consolation for the anguished widow. With untiring tenderness, the abbess rehearsed for Margaret again and again the accounts of her dead husband's charities, his goodness to the downtrodden, his attachment to Holy Church. And it is true that Europe, and especially France, mourned the dead duke as a fallen idol. There must certainly have been depths of genuine goodness in this strange man for whom thousands shed sincere tears. They could hope and pray he was not eternally lost.

The duchess snatched at the words of comfort, and gradually some of her native energy and resolve returned. They must do more than hope and pray! They must raise up more and more houses of prayer and penance! They must outnumber John's crimes with monasteries. In an agony of desire, Margaret of Burgundy begged Sister Colette to begin at once the building of a new house of the reform at Seurre. The abbess agreed, and entered, in 1420, on the greatest period of activity in her life. There had been three monasteries founded in the past ten years. In the next decade, there would be three times that number.

The new friary at Sellières, completed in 1415, was now flourishing; and work on the next house for the First Order at Chariez was not yet begun. Father Henri de la Baume could afford to assist the abbess personally for a time. They went together to Seurre to inspect the place. Both were charmed with the little town which lies in a fertile valley of the Saône, and they made two important friends there at this first visit.

Jacques Charton and his wife had never been blessed with a family. Far from settling down into a selfish embitterment, however, the wealthy couple spent their money and their energies on works of charity. Charton had been planning to build a church in honor of the Blessed Virgin Mary at Seurre just at this time; but when he talked to Sister Colette and Father Henri, he decided to make his prospective church the chapel of the new Poor Clare monastery—that is, if they wanted it. They did indeed!

Mme. Charton, equally won by the two Franciscans and their

glorious enterprise, urged her husband to give them a house he owned in Seurre to serve as a monastery; the chapel could be joined to it. The well-intentioned couple had little notion of a monastic building, for even poverty-loving Colette could see that the house they proposed to give was hopelessly small. However, she accepted the generous offer with thankfulness, deciding to leave the rest to God. The Lord took over at once, inspiring another wealthy townsman to donate a house of his which adjoined that of the Chartons. Guillaume de Vienne, by now resigned to aiding the spread of the reform in secondary positions, obtained the important remission of taxes for the new foundation. The Duchess of Burgundy took care of everything else.

Margaret herself laid the cornerstone of the monastery at Seurre which Sister Colette named the Poor Clare Monastery of the Nativity. She had been inspired to give it this title by the fact that the site of the chapel was that of the former Charton stables.

When the building and reconstruction were finished, the duchess wished to be present again at the dedication of this first Poor Clare foundation made since the death of her husband. She was staying at Rouvres in October of 1421 when the monastery was ready for occupation; and her faithful chamberlain, Guillaume de Vienne, came to escort her from there to Seurre. Margaret would have liked her son, Philip the Good, to take her personally; but the young duke was absent at the wars. The murder of his father resulted in twenty-two years of warfare during which more than a million men were to be slain, and Duke Philip was already busy avenging the death of his famous father with a military drive worthy of John the Fearless himself.

Another old friend, Archbishop Thibault de Rougemont, who had welcomed the first community of Colette's nuns into his archdiocese of Besançon in 1410, came to Seurre to bless the new monastery. He journeyed by way of Rouvres to join the Duchess of Burgundy and her party. The procession to Seurre was a mournful one, however, without any ceremony. The duke's funeral was still too recent an event for any Burgundian pomp to be allowed.

The abbess-general had selected seven nuns for the Seurre foundation, among them Sister Marie Sénéchal from the Besançon monastery, her childhood friend and one of her first two followers.

Young Perrine de la Baume from the house in Poligny came along, too. Accompanied by Father Henri de la Baume and another friar, the Poor Clares set out from Besançon, intending to transact a few pieces of business en route to Seurre. One of these concerned a certain M. Rollins who lived in Neublans and owned a fine forest of oak trees. Sister Colette had her eye on some of these oaks for the furnishings of her new monastery; and when she learned on her arrival that M. Rollins was away from Neublans just then, she decided to wait for his return. Oaks were oaks, and who could say when another such excellent begging-opportunity would present itself! Father Henri arranged for the eight nuns and Perrine to stay in an old castle near the church until Rollins' return.

Meanwhile, the Duchess of Burgundy and her party had arrived at Seurre. Margaret was still in a state of extreme nervous tension, and she became greatly agitated to find only an empty monastery awaiting her. She despatched an excited message to the abbess. The note must have been almost frenzied in tone; for when the perspiring runner delivered it to Sister Colette, she determined to leave Neublans at once and take the shortest route to Seurre, doubtless with a sigh for the oaks.

Now, taking the shortest route to Seurre meant crossing over the river Doubs which had just flooded its banks. The eleven religious went down the hill on which the old castle stood and walked to the river's edge. Colette and the friars saw and heard the angry, rushing waters of the swollen Doubs; and Father Henri may have been preparing to deliver an ultimatum against anything so foolhardy as attempting to cross the torrent when a voice forestalled him. "Where is the flood we have heard so much about?" inquired Sister Marie Sénéchal.

Colette evidently took the startling question as a sign from God. Perhaps Father Henri was still hesitant, for there is a gentle reproof in the abbess' words: "What of Divine Providence which has guided you and me for so many years?" She made the sign of the cross over the waters that remained invisible to the other nuns; and then Father Henri did likewise, stepping out after Sister Colette and Perrine. The other nuns and friar followed them, and all arrived quickly and safely at the other side, quite dry. As soon as they did, the rushing waters of the overflowing Doubs became very visible to them all, and audible, too. Perrine could have been no ordinary teen-ager if she did not deliver herself of a few good screams at that point.

Father Pierre de Vaux and Sister Perrine describe the miraculous crossing of the swollen Doubs tersely and without any reference to date or exact company. They add that some ill-intentioned persons who tried to follow the saint and her party in the crossing were instantly sucked into the swirling waters and drowned. Later biographers place the miracle as given here, and it is one of those most frequently the subject of paintings of St. Colette.

Margaret of Burgundy welcomed the abbess and her party with obvious relief. She had come to depend on Sister Colette for spiritual support more even than she realized, and the thought that some accident had befallen the nun who was now both her protégée and her mentor had tormented her. The day of the dedication of the Monastery of the Nativity at Seurre was the first really bright one in her life since her husband's tragic death, and she returned to Rouvres full of hope for John's salvation and already busy with plans for more monasteries when Colette should have nuns to staff them.

Actually, Seurre was to be the last of the Burgundian foundations. The duke's assassination had pulled at the very roots of his devoted wife's own life, and it would not bloom much longer. Sister Colette and Father Henri may have suspected this when they said goodbye to Margaret at Seurre.

The abbess herself remained at the new monastery only for a space of a few months, for she was now involved in an extremely delicate situation. As early as 1415, after the massacre of the French nobility at Agincourt, the Duchess of Bourbon, Marie de Berry, had expressed the desire to have a Poor Clare monastery of the reform in her own dominions. Sister Colette would have been willing enough to establish a house at Moulins as the duchess wished, and she certainly rejoiced that the royal house of Bourbon was looking with favor on her work; but the affairs of the Bourbons and the Burgundians were hopelessly entangled in enmities. Colette had feared to alienate the Duke and Duchess of Burgundy, who had already done so much for her, by venturing into Bourbon

domains in 1415, though she assured Marie de Berry of her desire
to fall in with the plans for a monastery at Moulins.

Marie de Berry's husband, John I, Duke of Bourbon, was a man
of high principle, utterly loyal to the king of France. After the battle
at Agincourt, he had been carried off to London by the English
and imprisoned there. He remained a captive of the English
for twenty-nine years, released only by death. From his prison, he
had appointed his duchess as regent; but the elder of his two sons,
Charles I, Count of Clermont, became the acting head of state. Not
for long, however. In 1418 John the Fearless captured Charles of
Clermont and his young brother and imprisoned them both in the
Tour du Louvre.

The Duchess of Bourbon, in anguish, threw herself on God's pity,
promising to build two monasteries for the Poor Clares of Sister
Colette's reform as a royal alms to accompany her prayers for the
release of her husband. In fact, Duchess Marie was so driven by
multiplying trials that she had undertaken to seek the pope's
authorization even before settling the matter with Colette.

Martin V, the Colonna pope whose election in 1417 by the
cardinals at Constance had ended the great schism, had already
given his full approval to Sister Colette's work of restoring the
primitive Rule among the Poor Clares. He had issued new bulls to
ratify all the authorizations given her by the anti-popes. Benedict
XIII, Alexander V, and John XXIII; and he had greatly encouraged
the abbess-general in her difficult mission. When he received the
Duchess of Bourbon's petition, he had been delighted to grant it
at once. In a bull dated September 12, 1420, he authorized the
erection of a Poor Clare monastery of the primitive Rule at Moulins
and another at Aigueperse.

Bonne d'Artois, Countess of Nevers, was another of the Bourbons
who had suffered cruelly from the massacre at Agincourt. Whereas
John of Bourbon had been carried off to England as a prisoner, the
Count of Nevers had been carried off to eternity. The young
countess was inconsolable in her loss for some years after the
tragedy of 1415. The more she learned of Colette and her monasteries throughout the domains of Burgundy, the more she longed
to have the abbess establish a foundation in Bourbon dominions
in memory of her beloved husband.

Bonne d'Artois was the sister-in-law of the Duke and Duchess of Burgundy, her husband having been the brother of John the Fearless; but, whereas Bonne's husband had given his life for the cause of the French king at the tragic battle of Agincourt, John the Fearless had not even appeared on the scene. Very likely, the Countess of Nevers, daughter of the Duchess of Bourbon by a former marriage, was instrumental in bringing her mother and the Duchess of Burgundy to an agreement in the matter of the Poor Clare monasteries extending through the territories of both, since her marriage to the brother of John the Fearless made her, in a sense, a woman of double perspectives on the political intricacies of France. It was Sister Colette's own persuasions, however, which finally sealed the pious bargain between two of the greatest ladies in Europe.

Even before Duchess Marie de Bourbon had appealed to Pope Martin V for the bull authorizing the foundations at Moulins and Aigueperse, the vigorous young Bonne d'Artois was in possession of a bull for her own projected foundation at Décize. It was dated 1419. Thus in chronological order of authorizations, the monastery at Décize precedes the two established by the Duchess of Bourbon; and all three Bourbon foundations are earlier than the foundation of Seurre, the last of the Burgundian houses. However, in point of actual establishment, Seurre ranks first. The community, headed by Sister Marie Sénéchal, began monastic life there in 1422. Moulins was begun in 1423, Décize sometime after that (the exact date is unknown), and Aigueperse, which was to cause the saint so much sorrow, in 1424.

Happy at the generous grants but alarmed over the state of affairs between the houses of Burgundy and Bourbon, Colette and a companion went to the Bourbon court at Moulins for the first time early in 1421. It is almost certain that Father Henri de la Baume accompanied her on this all-important visit. The last thing the loyal friar wanted was a painful involvement for Colette with the two great houses, much less an alienation from the Duchess of Burgundy. The cornerstone for the monastery of Moulins was apparently laid during this visit. Work at Moulins proceeded very slowly, however, and without publicity. With the Duke of Burgundy dead little more than a year, and Margaret still in the first anguish of her grief, Colette could not consider approaching her old friend on this delicate new venture.

To complicate matters further, Margaret's youngest daughter, Agnes, was affianced to Charles of Clermont, son of the Duchess of Bourbon. During his last year, John the Fearless had released the Count of Clermont from prison on condition that he would support the Burgundians and repudiate his fiancée, Catherine, daughter of the king of France, in favor of John's own daughter, Agnes. Charles of Clermont must certainly have been at the last outpost of desperation to agree to such terms, but he did. He was released from the Tour du Louvre; and Agnes, a mere child, was sent off to the court of the Bourbons. However, John the Fearless was no sooner removed from the scene by assassination than Charles sent his child-fiancée home to her mother. It was too late to retrieve his Catherine, though; for the royal princess' treacherous mother, Queen Isabeau, had by then shaken the whole realm by espousing the girl to Henry V, king of England. Later, in 1425, Charles of Clermont and Agnes of Burgundy were actually united in marriage; but by that time Margaret of Burgundy had gone to God, leaving a France that seemed hopelessly riddled with intrigue.

Colette's powers of persuasion were never more evident than in her almost incredible achievement of reconciling Burgundy and Bourbon to a common purpose. Barefoot and meanly garbed, the Poor Clare abbess passed from one warring domain into another, respected and loved by those held by no common bond on earth save their reverence for her. She slipped in and out of Burgundian and Bourbon castles with the assurance of a queen and the humility of a peasant. The same winning blend of deep respect and artless simplicity she had shown when she was a small girl in Corbie kneeling to kiss Dom Raoul de Raye's abbatial ring still characterized her in her dealings with the greatest princes in Europe.

Sister Colette never acted as abbess at Seurre. As soon as the new monastery was dedicated, she gave its authority into the hands of her beloved Sister Marie Sénéchal. What a moment this must have been for the two nuns, with their shared memories of childhood games in Corbie, girlhood confidences, and that unforgettable day when Colette Boellet had told Marie she was going to spend the rest of her life as a recluse! Forty-one years had passed since Mme. Sénéchal had rejoiced that her neighbors, the Boellets, had a little girl of their own.

Neither Father Pierre nor Sister Perrine, however, has left us any details of Sister Marie's appointment, content merely to chronicle the event. Perhaps Sister Colette kept memories of this kind to herself. And, typically, Pierre de Vaux hurries on to tell us of more miracles, recording, with the same juridical detachment, how a little ass ate Colette's palm leaves, and how the saint healed a number of sick persons by the sign of the cross.

It happened on Palm Sunday, writes Father Pierre, that the glorious Mother, Sister Colette, was walking in procession in the monastery with her nuns. Like the others, she carried a branch of palm, newly-blessed by the priest. As the procession moved along, Colette became more and more profoundly engrossed in thoughts of our Lord's sufferings and death. Then, suddenly, she told the friar afterward, she beheld the Savior "humbly mounted on a little ass," and so close that she "could have touched both Lord and beast." If Sister Colette did not avail herself of this opportunity, out of reverence and awe, the small ass was deterred by no such corresponding timidity. "When," says Father Pierre, "the little ass perceived that green palm, she took it in her mouth from out of the [saint's] two hands, and the said palm vanished from sight as the ass ate it, every last bit of it." He does not explain how Sister Colette felt about the matter, walking along empty-handed, or whether the nuns' chants of "cum ramis palmarum" bore the cadence of a saint's laughter. As always, de Vaux tells the thing in his spirit of "take it or leave it, but it's true."

Twelve postulants entered the new monastery at Seurre within a few months, and Colette felt that her presence in the fast-growing community was not demanded any longer. Sister Marie Sénéchal could be depended on to train these numerous young recruits in the best traditions of the primitive Rule. So the abbess-general left the last "Burgundian foundation" with a thankful heart and set out to establish the first "Bourbon foundation" at Moulins.

On the way, she stopped at Rouvres to see the Duchess of Burgundy. It proved to be their last meeting, for Margaret of Burgundy died at Dijon in 1423. Her death marked the end of what might be called the Burgundian epoch in the Poor Clare reform and inaugurated the Bourbon epoch. For, in that same year, Duchess Marie de Berry's first monastery of Moulins was completed; and the very next year, 1424, was to see Colette setting up monastic living for still another group of her nuns at Décize on the Loire, the house so long desired by the Countess of Nevers, Bonne d'Artois.

Both the Moulins and Décize monasteries thrived as far as subjects were concerned, but the prodigious amount of work involved in establishing two houses in such quick succession took great toll of Colette's strength. Besides the physical strain, she had to deal at both places with resident priests who made it plain they wanted no primitive Franciscan nuns for close neighbors. This was the kind of trial that always caused the abbess the acutest pain. But her sufferings in this sphere at Moulins and Décize were to prove as nothing to what lay ahead at the third Bourbon foundation at Aigueperse.

17 *The Monastery at Aigueperse*

Weary, and weighed down with her increasing responsibilities, the abbess-general selected seven of her nuns from Poligny and Besançon for the monastery of Moulins and gave its governance into the capable hands of Sister Marie de Corbie, formerly a nun in the Seurre community, appointed another group of nuns for Décize, and set out for Aigueperse in low Auvergne. The Duchess of Bourbon had a castle close by at Montpensier, where Colette frequently stayed while the new monastery was under construction. No matter how exhausted she might be, and although she often could not oversee all the work of building as she had done at Auxonne, the foundress always managed to direct the beginning of the construction and make certain that all would be in line with her ideals of poverty and simplicity.

Duchess Marie's older son, Charles de Clermont, had laid the cornerstone for his mother's second Poor Clare foundation on November 4, 1423; and all promised to go smoothly. It had been a happy day for the Bourbons, although the duchess fell to weeping at the sight of her son performing the offices that really belonged to his captive father. Marie had quickly regained her composure, though, reminding herself that great spiritual gains for the house of Bourbon would undoubtedly follow on this foundation. Perhaps her John would be released by the English when the new monastery was completed! Her young son, Louis de Montpensier, had been present at the laying of the cornerstone, too. He was a most engaging child and won Colette's heart at once. This was the boy who was to fight so valiantly for the French king by the side of St. Jeanne d'Arc six years later.

The abbess-general left Aigueperse for some weeks to visit her other monasteries, for she kept a close maternal watch on her multiplying communities and especially on the two at Moulins and Décize still so very new and inexperienced. When she returned to the castle at Montpensier, she found the duchess in a state of great agitation. While her strong-willed son, Charles, had been on hand to supervise the building at nearby Aigueperse, all had gone well enough, despite the murmuring of the canons of the collegiate church against Colette and her reform. However, when Charles was recalled to the royal court to act on behalf of his imprisoned father, the disgruntled canons were quick to take advantage of his absence.

Accustomed to a very comfortable kind of life, these well-contented gentlemen of the Church had no intention of letting their lives be silhouetted for the people of Aigueperse against the bright light of the Franciscan reform. The citizens might begin making comparisons and drawing conclusions embarrassing to the canons. They determined at all costs to prevent the Poor Clares' occupying the new monastery. With this resolve the parish priest of Aigueperse and his assistants hurriedly allied themselves.

When continuous petty persecution availed them nothing, the canons and the parish clergy turned to violent measures. Their arguments that the proximity of the new Poor Clare monastery would interfere with the divine services in the collegiate and parish churches must have sounded very odd even to the credulous towns-folk. And since the priests dared not voice their true reasons for rejecting the nuns, they grew desperate. One night they so far forgot justice and common decency as to tear down the half-built walls of the monastery. Colette came to Aigueperse to inspect her new building. She found ruins.

However, if the canons and parish priests had forgotten chivalry, they had also abandoned caution. The townspeople were scandalized at the sabotage. And if the Duchess of Burgundy was agitated, her son was roused to action. A message was despatched to Charles de Clermont, and he came hurrying back to Aigueperse in full fury. He brought the case to court, where the canons were heavily fined, and he himself returned to attend to the completion of the building.

It is perhaps out of delicacy that Father Pierre de Vaux and Sister Perrine pass over in silence this scandalous demolition and the legal action taken by the Bourbons. The story is easily verifiable in the archives of Aigueperse, and Father Douillet and other reliable biographers give it in detail. "The canons," writes Douillet, "destroyed by night what was built by day." He adds with a certain satisfaction that when they were condemned by law, they "had to pay a good sum which just about sufficed to finish the convent."

The marauding canons suffered a fatal loss of face with the people of Aigueperse, whose sympathies naturally swung now to the cause of the nuns. The duchess was relieved. Count Charles was jubilant. Colette was neither. Her reverence for priests was as boundless as her love of peace, and she bitterly accused herself: "I have brought strife to Aigueperse."

As she grew older, Sister Colette's judgments against herself were increasingly stern. She blamed herself mercilessly where she was obviously blameless, yet her sincerity is evident in her pathetic pleas that her nuns make reparation for their mother's crimes. Thus, in a letter to Agnes de Vaux, abbess at Auxonne (whom, incidentally, she gives the title "Mother" which she would never tolerate for herself) she plunges without preamble into a description of her misery:

Alas! my Mother . . . when I see all the time how stupid I am and consider my misery, which you know well enough, I fall into anguish, into a great sadness which God knows is perilous indeed. But it is my opinion that I damn myself in religion and that hell is not sufficient to punish me. When I think about my sins and my abysmal ignorance, I am like a desperate person. . . . Oh, my Mother, my Sister, my friend, have pity on me before our Savior Jesus Christ . . . and please ask Sister [Jeanne] Roberdelle, Jeanne de Digeon, Beatrice, and my other Sisters, to pray the *Miserere mei* seven days, one whole week, for my faults. . . . I do not know what to do. . . . May God take care of you all, as I desire.

Sister Colette

It is typical of the saint that she pauses in the midst of this agonized outpouring with a thought for a certain "Brother Gerard and his mother."

It was not only strife, though, that Colette brought to Aigueperse or any other place, despite her fears, but new spiritual vitality and unnumbered blessings. The canons and parish priests had tried to defame her. God was swift to defend her, and with miracles. Just at the time of the building scandal, Father Pierre de Vaux tells us, the town bailiff was suffering from a violent attack of what was then called quatern aigue. (It was, perhaps, a variant of malaria.) Colette saw him pale and shivering, and as always, the sight of another's suffering was sufficient to make her forget her own. She intended to assure the sick man of her prayers for his recovery. Instead, on sudden inspiration, she heard herself say: "Have courage, monsieur! You must get well without delay, for you have to help us finish the monastery." She made the sign of the cross over him, and he was instantly cured.

It is safe to say that no building superintendent ever worked harder than the town bailiff of Aigueperse on the Poor Clare monastery! It was finished in record time, and dedicated on June 26, 1425. The abbess-general at once installed a small colony of her nuns chosen

ing life as King of Naples. He did not know that he had secured as a wife one of the foremost shrews of the century. He discovered it soon enough. Once she had the debonair Jacques under her royal thumb, Queen Joanna proceeded to make his life as miserable as possible. She strove to withhold from him all the prerogatives which rightfully belonged to him, even to the title of King of Naples which he had especially coveted. And when he became too obstreperous, she simply locked him up in prison in her so-called "Egg Castle" on the Neapolitan coast.

The Court of Naples was a miniature of the French court so far as intrigue and ambition were concerned. Thus the same courtiers who flattered Queen Joanna and laughed at her new husband were quite capable of becoming loudly loyal supporters of Jacques de Bourbon when it seemed to their interests. When the tide of enthusiasm ran toward him, King Jacques would find himself released from his prison by nobles suddenly moved to deplore the unqueenly behavior of Joanna. And Jacques' first act upon being freed was invariably to throw his queen into prison in her turn. It was, all in all, something less than a model Christian marriage.

The last of King Jacques' marital imprisonments lasted nearly four years, and this time he was released only through the intervention of powerful French nobles and Pope Martin V himself. By then, 1421, the disillusioned Bourbon had had enough of kingship, even though the nobles of the court of Naples so feared his fierce reprisals that they now fell upon him with every show of deference and hailed him as their true and well-loved king. He retired to Venice and remained there for the next four years, keeping a close surveillance over his daughters through the guardians he had appointed for them, but rarely seeing them.

Still known and hailed as the King of Naples, the embittered Jacques was leading a life almost monastic in its simplicity and seclusion when his eldest daughter, Bonne, asked his permission to enter the Order of Poor Clares. He went to Castres to talk with Bonne and also to arrange for the marriage of his second daughter, Eleanor, to young Bernard d'Armagnac, captain of the Bourbon forces since the death of the older Armagnac in the Paris massacre of 1418. While he was occupied with these negotiations, his youngest girl's petition to enter the monastery at Aigueperse reached him.

Retired or not, Jacques kept himself well-apprised of national affairs. And by 1425 the life and doings of Colette Boellet were considered national affairs. Wonder-worker! Saint! Seer! Her titles multiplied. The whole of France and half of Europe followed her every move with keenest interest. If Jacques de Bourbon had been curious to meet this extraordinary woman for a long time, his interest was certainly whetted when two-thirds of his family announced that it wanted to join her reform.

King Jacques gave both girls permission to enter and resolved to go himself to interview the Poor Clare foundress at the earliest opportunity. With the entrance of his daughters into the cloister, their ageing father, then fifty-five, seems to have experienced the beginnings of a desire for a more spiritual life. In token of his new resolve, he built a chapel near the famous monastery of St. Antoine in Dauphine. The chapel was no sooner standing than Jacques decided he, too, would be a monk! Doubtless the powerful drive of his impulsive nature would have forced the door of the nearest monastery save for the fact that Queen Joanna, his termagant wife, was still alive and vocal. Desertion by her handsome consort had touched the quick of her vanity, but Jacques was lost to her beyond retrieving.

It will be necessary to go in advance of our story here to follow the events of Jacques de Bourbon's life to its close. He set out in late 1427 or early 1428 to visit his daughters, who had informed him that they were both going to Savoy with the abbess-general as members of the community chosen for the new monastery in Vevey. His middle daughter, Eleanor, and her husband, Bernard d'Armagnac, went along. Young Claude d'Aix, Jacques' natural son, made an embarrassing addition to the party; but Claude's meeting with the abbess-general, and probably with several of the friars, too, evidently had a profound effect on the boy. We are told that he later entered the Franciscan Order and lived as an exemplary friar until his early death.

The erstwhile King of Naples was the very soul of impetuosity. His reunion with his oldest daughter, now Sister Marie de Bourbon, and his vivacious youngest child, the novice Isabeau, rocked him with emotion. These two loving yet remote creatures with their bare feet and poor habits touched him profoundly; and, once he had talked with their abbess, his mind was made up. He, too, would be a Franciscan. He, too, would place himself under the direction of Sister Colette. Typically, he advised the foundress of these "irrevocable decisions" in a letter as colorful as his speech and signed with a flourish by "le sérénissime roi, Jacques, votre fils."

One is tempted to an unholy envy of the nuns who saw Sister Colette's face as she read this remarkable message! If there was anything in Vevey she cared less to annex than a penitent king of Naples, Colette would certainly have been hard-pressed to name it. But when Jacques dubbed himself "votre fils," the thing was done. Sister Colette had to reply to "mon fils."

The abbess, who was always possessed of that most desirable trait in a superior, the ability to appraise character and capability accurately, knew, however, that beneath the theatrical surface of Jacques de Bourbon's personality there was real spiritual nobility. Father Henri de la Baume, who was in Vevey at the time, had the same conviction. Even if she sighed as she did it, Colette undertook the spiritual direction of the King of Naples. It is surely a safe wager that no Poor Clare abbess ever had a more singular disciple.

After she had established her monastery at Vevey and was obliged to push on to Orbe, she was kept advised on her royal protégé's progress; and she wrote him many letters in return. He became a Franciscan tertiary and settled himself in a small house near the Franciscan Friary at Besançon. His life there was exemplary in every detail. He devoted his time to prayer and works of charity, and gradually the townspeople stopped gaping at the sight of the still-handsome king of Naples doing the lowliest service for the poor and the sick and keeping entirely aloof from even minor social diversions. He still longed to enter the First Order, but for once in his tempestuous life Jacques was forced to be patient. Queen Joanna seemed to have no notion of dying, and it was not until 1435 that she finally obliged him. The potential friar minor was then sixty-five, though contemporaries insist he could have passed for a man of forty-five. His aristocratic face was still unlined, and his powerful physique showed no signs of sagging.

Shortly before Joanna's death, King Jacques had drawn up his will, perhaps the simplest document he had ever drafted. With two of his daughters in religion, and one the wealthy wife of Count d'Armagnac, he had no dependents. Consequently, he left all his possessions to the poor, only reserving for his soul stipends for a rather striking number of Masses—ten thousand! Jacques evidently harbored no illusions about the possibility of his passing directly from earth to heaven. That was the whole of the will, save for the one poignant provision that he should be buried near Sister Colette "in whatever place her body shall repose." It was an echo of the last desire of Countess Blanche de Genève expressed to her niece, Countess Maude: "You must bring my body to Colette." There is something uncommonly touching in the childlike simplicity of these earthly great who wanted only a cloistered nun for companion in death. Records show that Father Pierre de Vaux and Father Henri de la Baume were named "solicitors" (executors?) for this will.

The news of Queen Joanna's death reached her husband at Vevey, where he had gone to visit his Poor Clare daughters. With a wild jubilation happily rare among new widowers, he sent Colette the good word that he was free at last to enter the First Order. She, in her turn, lost no time in making arrangements for his entrance at the friary in Besançon. She must have felt a great happiness in her own soul that her colorful disciple was finally to realize the hope of many lonely years. If she did, the mood of quiet thankfulness was shattered by the news the horrified friars brought her a few days later. Their postulant was en route to Besançon—reclining in a scavenger's cart and with a whole royal train of attendants on foot behind him!

Jacques de Bourbon was often exasperating, but surely this was the triumph of the old swashbuckler's deplorable taste for the sensational and theatrical. It would not have been the King of Naples to enter religion simply as a king or simply as a penitent. He must show he was both. And no one but himself could have cast and directed the fantastic pageantry of the Besançon processional march.

As he travelled from Vevey to Besançon, the whole populations of towns turned out to stare at him. Jacques wore a coarse grey robe and the white Franciscan cord, and added a white hood which he tied under his chin. He reposed in the scavenger's cart on some straw and dung. Had the wretched cart been divorced from its following, it would still have proved enough of a spectacle to most persons. The fact that immediately behind the cart walked scores of monks and clerics beholden to the Bourbons, Jacques' entire former household staff, two hundred of his horses fully caparisoned and led by their jewelled bridles, and finally carriage after carriage filled with his arms, his equerries, and numerous retainers all magnificently attired, rounded off a panorama sufficient to make Cecil B. de Mille quiver with appreciation.

One can imagine what effect this ridiculous display had on an abbess-general so averse to ostentation of any kind. She did not hesitate to rebuke "mon fils," but the damage was already done. A century later, the entry of Jacques de Bourbon into Portalier and the other towns on the way to Besançon was still a subject for mockery. The old king himself saw nothing deserving of reproach in his behavior, and he was amazed at Colette's reactions. It is true that no one could remain irritated at Jacques for long. There was something so utterly disarming about his perennial youthfulness and his curious blend of urbanity and naïveté.

He made his novitiate in the friary of Dôle; but there is no record of his ever having made profession in the First Order, whether because the friars thought it unwise or whether because in the end the old man humbly preferred to remain a tertiary. He certainly gave his fellow-Franciscans nothing but edification, however, happy in the humblest menial work at the little Franciscan hospice on the Rue St. Vincent in Dôle where he later lived with four of the friars. Whenever possible, he visited Colette when she was stopping at her monastery in nearby Besançon; and he himself died in that city.

That Colette had a deep affection for her royal disciple is testified by the fact that she had him brought into the chapel of the Poor Clare monastery at Besançon in his dying hour. Jacques de Bourbon, King of Naples, died there at the grate in the presence of the saint after making the humble assertion that he "depended entirely on the Lady Colette to get him into heaven." He was buried according to his wish without coffin or bier of any kind, simply lowered into the "mother earth of all human beings," as he had expressed it in his will. They still preserve at Besançon Jacques' spoon of mother-of-pearl and his cup of olive wood, the two pathetic reminders he kept of his past earthly grandeur.

All this has been a reach into the future. Sister Colette seems to have suspected nothing of the part she was to play in the life and conversion of Jacques de Bourbon when she asked Father Henri de la Baume in 1426 to solicit the great man's permission to receive his daughters, Bonne and Isabeau, into the Order. She was mainly occupied at that moment with a proposal from the Viscountess Claudine de Roussillon that she make a foundation in Polignac, and with the pressing demands of the Duke of Savoy for a monastery at his own Chambéry. She had also just recalled Sister Marie Sénéchal from Seurre to take over the office of superior at Aigueperse, and had to find the best replacement for capable Sister Marie at Seurre. She probably gave no particular thought to Jacques de Bourbon except to pray that he would give the permission his charming daughters so much desired.

The Viscountess Claudine was evidently a large-hearted woman, for she offered to hand over to Colette her own imposing castle at Polignac for a monastery. The great mansion, however, was everything that the abbess did not want for her nuns, with ineffaceable luxuriousness at every turn. The same tact that had won many another noble to her way of thinking, persuaded Claudine de Roussillon to Sister Colette's views in this instance, too; and the viscountess agreed to finance a monastery in the neighboring town of Le Puy instead. She and Colette went there with Father Henri de la Baume to select a site which the viscountess purchased at once. Almost as promptly, a lawsuit was brought against her for rights attached to the property.

The abbess-general had had quite enough of lawsuits, and she would have withdrawn at once save that the viscountess insisted on contesting the suit in her own name and with no involvements for the Franciscans. Wearily, Colette agreed to it, so long as she would have no part in the affair. Lawyers were engaged to defend the viscountess, and Sister Colette was glad enough to leave the place until matters should be settled. It is as well that she did, for the lawsuit dragged itself out over a period of several years; and the new monastery was completed only in 1432.

It was an exhausted abbess that turned to Savoy, expecting smoother paths to open before her. She especially rejoiced at the prospect of a foundation at Chambéry for Father Henri's sake. Her first and most faithful friend in the reform was now past sixty. She herself was forty-six, and her youthful vitality had deserted her. It would certainly work both of them immense good to go to Chambéry, where Father Henri's own friary stood; it had long been his dream to have a monastery of the reform there.

It may be that the little lamb described by Father Pierre de Vaux, which Colette received as a gift, trotted along the road with the group bound for Chambéry. We are told that it followed Colette everywhere, even into the oratory to assist at Mass! Father Pierre is solicitous to tell of the lamb's piety, writing how, "at the elevation of the Precious Body of our Savior, it would go down on its front legs as though to kneel." He tells us the lamb was given to Sister Colette by a certain person who realized its significance as a pet for one who so loved even the symbols for purity, and that "many times her spirit was comforted at sight of this little lamb."

She was to need comforting at Chambéry of Savoy. It was now twenty-one years since Father Henri had left there to make his pilgrimage to the Holy Land, only to be deflected to an anchorhold in Corbie.

18 *Further Foundations*

When Father Henri had solicited permission to visit the Holy Land in 1406, his hope had been to receive graces and enlightenment there about the state of the papacy and about the conditions in the Franciscan Order. He had trusted that when he returned to France and his own Chambéry, perhaps in 1409, issues would be clearer in his own mind, and affairs of Church, state and religion in better order. In 1427, he walked through a France which, although now acknowledging the one true pope, Martin V, was already laying the foundations for a new papal schism in 1437. He went toward the house of his Order to find that affairs were incomparably worse than he had left them.

The old friar who had been guardian of Chambéry when Father Henri departed was long since dead. The new guardian showed nothing of his predecessor's enthusiasm for Franciscans of Father Henri de la Baume's ilk. "Trouble-makers and fanatics" was his disposal of them. He looked with great disfavor on the re-establishment of primitive Franciscan observance at the friary in Dôle and regretted that that house should already have begotten two more of its kind at Sellières and Chariez. He especially disliked the idea of a friar spending a good part of his life tramping about France with this nun, Colette Boellet. He was aware of her reputation, and he did not intend to have her intrude on his own way of life. Had not the Urbanist Poor Clares in the town been appealing to him for weeks to keep Colette out of Chambéry? They wanted no part of her, any more than he did. And most of his community felt the same.

Amadeus, Duke of Savoy, had not seen the abbess-general for a number of years, but he had his memories of his first meeting with her in 1406 when she was returning to Corbie with Father Henri and Baroness Isabeau de Brissay after their interview with the ill-fated Benedict XIII. Duke Amadeus had been young and impressionable then, but he told how he had kept all these years a deep reverence for the tall nun with the beautiful face, so poorly clad and so humble in manner. He had followed her activities with the keenest interest, and for a long time he had envied the Burgundians and Bourbons their patronage over her. It was time the house of Savoy had a monastery of primitive Poor Clares to its own credit. He had offered her his castle in 1406. Now he would offer her any site she wished in Chambéry.

When he won Colette's acquiescence early in 1427, and shortly afterward received from Pope Martin V the papal authorization he had sought for a monastery of the Second Franciscan Order in Chambéry, Amadeus supposed the affair was settled save for the actual building of the house. He would attend to that. Money was the least consideration. Only let the abbess come and select a site for the new foundation.

The totally unexpected opposition from the Urbanist Poor Clares and the Franciscan friars in Chambéry was a stunning blow. The duke was almost fifty now, and since the death of his wife had been living a retired life in company with three or four other noblemen of genuine spirituality who shared his love of solitude. Indeed, they lived almost like monks. Such men would find it difficult to comprehend the feeling against the saintly abbess in their own Chambéry. Apparently Amadeus decided not to inflame public feeling further by a spirited defense of her. How, though, was he to explain to her this wholly unlooked-for turn of events? And she was even then en route to Chambéry!

The Duke went outside the city to meet the little party of five nuns and two friars, and he must have had another shock when he saw Sister Colette and Father Henri. We are told that the friar looked ill and weary. The abbess seemed older than her forty-six years. Father Pierre de Vaux has written of the many attacks the devil levelled against Colette around this time, which certainly did nothing to counterbalance the effects of natural exhaustion from her works and journeys. We read of Satan's striking the saint, tormenting her during the few hours she allowed herself for sleep, and in general, harassing her with ingenuity and perseverance. Father Pierre quotes her as "saying familiarly" to some of the friars who knew of the torments she suffered: "To the glorious martyrs in paradise, God gave a great grace and a good bargain; they just ran the gauntlet or were roasted or had their heads cut off in a hurry."

Sister Perrine tells us of Satan's once taking Colette bodily and doubling her up into the little window of her oratory which looked into the church. The nuns found her there in the morning, wedged so tightly into the small frame that their concerted pullings could not dislodge her. These nuns were obviously products of their practical abbess' training. They turned to the friars for help; but Perrine notes that it was especially Brother Pierre Renault they begged to come, because "he had been a carpenter in the world."

When the chivalrous Amadeus of Savoy went on one knee in the road to salute the saint, however, he must surely have won the smile with which she customarily dismissed any trouble of her own. And Colette's smile could throw a transforming radiance over the marks of her suffering. Despite Colette's protests, Amadeus assisted the nuns into his carriage; the friars insisted on walking the rest of the way. As the carriage swayed along into Chambéry, the duke delivered his unhappy news. Chambéry did not want her.

The early biographers have not described the effect of this news on the nuns in Sister Colette's party, but it is interesting to speculate as to their reactions. If young Isabeau de Bourbon was true to her ordinary impulsiveness, she must have rallied from disbelief into protests. Her abbess! The saint! The nun whose wishes were accepted as heaven-sent commands by the Burgundians and the royal house of Bourbon! They did not want Sister Colette in little Chambéry! But we may suppose that novice Isabeau felt her abbess' hand on her elbow at that point, and closed her mouth again. Sister Marie de Bourbon would certainly have shared the duke's embarrassment and misery, and Sister Perrine, too; but the other nun in the party was a mysteriously serene person. Amadeus learned later that her name was Sister Marie Chevalier, that she was reputed to be a saint, and that she had written two very remarkable books, it being whispered that our Blessed Lady and the Holy Child had appeared to her on the completion of the second book, which was a life of our Lord, in token of their approval.

The duke need not have feared that his report would shock the abbess-general. Colette knew only too well the hostility of those who could not be content to go their own way and let her go hers, but felt they must defame her to defend themselves. Misunderstanding of her aims, sophisticated scorn for her ideals, small cruelties and great scandals—she was familiar with all that dreary company. In 1427, the abbess-reformer had run the gamut of men's malice from parlor gossip to public lawsuits. She was no longer surprised. "We shall have to go somewhere else, then," was her calm acceptance of the situation.

But what of Father Henri? It appears that his tired heart broke entirely over the affair. He went into his old friary and saw inimical faces. The few who sympathized with him dared not express any friendliness. He was told that affairs in the Chambéry friary were going along very well. The community needed no nun's assistance to keep the Rule. As for the Poor Clares, there was already a monastery of the Second Order in Chambéry. A second one was not needed. Father Henri de la Baume had stood loyally by Sister Colette's side in every crisis and sorrow of her life since 1406. Now, in this hour which was bitterer for him than for her, she stood by him.

Once the painful state of affairs was clear, Duke Amadeus hurried to outline an alternate plan. Could Colette not establish a house at nearby Vevey on the shore of Lake Lemon? It was a very charming, secluded place. He would pay for everything. He would get the best constructors. He would oversee the work personally. After Sister Colette and Father Henri had visited the place, she readily agreed to accept the offer.

As to the reception Chambéry had given to her and to its own son, Father Henri, the only recorded comment of Colette's is contained in a prophecy she made before the party left it for Vevey. Duke Amadeus would not hear of her walking further, and partly, no doubt, to relieve his embarrassment over the whole distressing affair, she acquiesced in his wishes. As she stepped into the ducal carriage, she looked back over Chambéry. "It will not always be like this," she said. She pointed down to Sister Marie Chevalier, standing just below her. "There stands the first abbess of my reform at Chambéry." Sister Marie Chevalier accepted the appointment without any recorded comment.

The prophecy was fulfilled in 1454, but neither Sister Colette nor Father Henri lived to see Sister Marie Chevalier restore the primitive Rule of St. Clare in the city that had treated them so unkindly.

As the party travelled toward Vevey, Sister Perrine tells us that young Isabeau pulled at her abbess' arm and invited her to admire the beauties of Geneva as they passed through it. It was lovely, Sister Colette agreed. Novice Isabeau wanted to know more, though; and Colette must have smiled at the eager young girl. "Yes, one day we shall have a house in Geneva." Then, Perrine says, the saint's face saddened, and she added: "But it will not exist for long." Actually a monastery of the primitive Rule was later established in Geneva. Unlike the one at Vevey, which suffered much in the Protestant Reformation but did survive, the house at Geneva was totally destroyed. The razing of the Geneva monastery points up the distinction between the two concepts of "reform." Colette's reform was a matter of restoration. The Protestant Reform was an affair of mutilation and destruction.

The reception given the little party at Vevey was far different from that at Chambéry. There was a very large monastery of Dominican nuns there; and while the Franciscans at Chambéry had closed their hearts against the abbess, the Dominicans at Vevey literally ran out to meet her with open arms. She could scarcely have failed to be reminded of the day when St. Francis and St. Dominic had first met in the streets of Rome. Saint had recognized saint, and the two founders had simply embraced each other without an introductory word. It was the beginning of the traditional close friendship of the two great Orders which endures to our own times.

In 1959, Franciscan friars and Poor Clare nuns still preface their thanksgiving prayers after dinner on the feast of St. Dominic (August 4) with the singing of an antiphon which is an affirmation of the Franciscan-Dominican friendship: "Apostolicus Dominicus et Seraphicus Franciscus ipsi nos docuerunt legem tuam, Domine." ("The apostolic Dominic and the seraphic Francis, they have taught us Thy law, O Lord!") Because the two saints have done just that, their children add the stirring psalm: "Laudate Dominum, omnes gentes!" ("O praise the Lord, all ye nations!") On October 4, the feast of St. Francis, they repeat this little ceremony. In Dominican houses, the same song on both feasts testifies to the same friendship. But this is looking forward five hundred years. Vevey looked back two hundred years, on that day in 1427, to St. Francis and St. Dominic as the Dominican nuns came out to welcome the Franciscans.

Colette opened her arms wide in turn. Sister Perrine tells us that the abbess kissed each nun lightly and smiled into the friendly eyes, doubtless pretending not to notice the frank reverence they showed for herself. But one nun held back. The white-robed Dominican stood apart from her Sisters and made no slightest move toward Sister Colette. In all simplicity, she turned to the Dominican chaplain and pointed at the nun standing alone. "Shall I not kiss her also?" she asked. The chaplain was embarrassed. "She is a leper, Reverend Mother. She cannot live with the community. Over there is her house." He indicated a tiny building some thirty yards away. "We are sorry to distress you," he continued. "It would have been better for her to stay away, but she wanted so much to come."

Without another word, Colette walked directly to the leprous nun, put both arms around her and kissed her "even more warmly," says Perrine, than she had kissed the others. While the nuns fell back in alarm and the Dominican chaplain stepped forward to pull the Poor Clare abbess away, Colette merely assured them that everything was all right. Everything was indeed all right for the leprous nun. She had not felt a human embrace for many years, and she drew back from Colette in horror that she had contaminated the body of a saint. But she had not. The Dominican convent of Vevey no longer had a leper.

Vevey was Colette's eighth monastery, and one of the happiest of all her communities. Perhaps because it was founded on the cross of Chambéry, it flourished betimes. Duke Amadeus' own daughter, Blanche de Savoy, was one of the seven postulants who entered at Vevey almost as soon as the monastery was standing. Among the first colony of professed nuns was Sister Agnes Wissmelle, niece of the Queen of France, whose pride in her family had been so sternly mortified by Sister Colette years ago at Poligny.

Sister Clair Labeur was summoned from the Ave Maria Monastery in Auxonne to be the first abbess of Vevey, thus helping fill up the measure of a prophecy Colette had laughingly made some time before this, and which both Father Pierre de Vaux and Sister Perrine have recorded. Rising from table one day, in the monastery at Poligny, Colette had looked around thoughtfully and then turned to Sister Clair Labeur. "What would you say if you had seen nine abbesses at our table today?" she said. Sister Clair's rapid blinking indicated that she did not know what she would say. "Well," continued Sister Colette, "that is what I see: nine abbesses!" The nuns at table must have looked at one another speculatively. The community was still young. Half those present were only novices. But the abbess had known whereof she spoke. Sister Clair Labeur herself was to be abbess of Vevey. Vivacious young Agnes Wissmelle would govern the monastery at Seurre. And seven others were to become abbesses of the reform.

The Duke of Savoy had no objection to his daughter's becoming a Poor Clare. In fact, he so associated himself with the new monastery that he changed his favorite residence from Chambéry to Vevey, continuing his life of seclusion and prayer in the shadow of the Poor Clare foundation. Amadeus was more than a model nobleman of France. He seemed very close to heroic sanctity. One wonders whether the abbess to whom so many future events and secrets of hearts were revealed by God knew what an infamous title the Duke of Savoy would annex before another ten years had passed. Did she guess there would be yet another papal schism, and that her friend, Duke Amadeus, would accept a false papal tiara and call himself Felix V? If she did, she confided the terrible secret to no one. Instead, she only publicly thanked God for the marvel of sisterly love which was her young community at Vevey and, after her famous first meeting with Jacques de Bourbon, King of Naples, whose tempestuous career we have already followed to its peaceful close, moved on to Orbe.

Father Henri would have much preferred that Colette remain at Vevey for a year at least and try to regain the strength poured out on six foundations in as many years. But again, it was a great noblewoman who summoned her, and the abbess felt she could not refuse Jeanne de Montfaucon-Montbéliard's offer. Jeanne was the wife of the Prince of Orange, Louis de Chalon; and she was impatiently awaiting Colette at her castle of Nozeroy. As was the practice of the Burgundians and the Bourbons, Princess Jeanne had armed herself with a papal bull of authorization for the foundation she wished to finance at Orbe. It was dated November 17, 1426. Father Henri and the abbess-general agreed that the princess had chosen a most suitable site; and, as Jeanne was a woman of action, work was begun on the new monastery without delay. After giving detailed instructions to the workmen and overseeing the first stages of building, Colette left Orbe early in 1427.

The monastery built by the Prince of Orange and his wife was not to be completed until 1428, but Jacques de Bourbon was already urging the abbess to come to Languedoc. He was ablaze with plans for no less than three Poor Clare monasteries of the reform there, and he was not a man famous for his patience. Sister Perrine tells how, with her physical forces thoroughly depleted, and with Father Henri grumbling at her side about the importunate demands of the French nobility, Colette began yet another journey. She took Sister Mathilde de la Baume with her this time, in addition to young Sister Perrine de la Baume, who had become her nearly inseparable companion. So it was quite a family group that took the road to Languedoc.

Sister Colette laid the foundations for two new monasteries, at Castres where King Jacques' own ancestral castle stood, and at

Lezignan. The Bishop of Castres, Raymon d'Avilhun, had the greatest esteem for the renowned Poor Clare abbess. He greeted her with every deference, and she was at first edified by his piety. But as the saint came to know the bishop better, she discovered in him a strain of ambition which saddened and alarmed her.

Father Pierre de Vaux writes of this prelate's coming one day to the new monastery where Colette, despite her fatigue, was directing the workmen as usual. Bishop d'Avilhun was in the greatest good humor. He was about to leave for Rome, he told her, and he wanted her to pray especially for the successful outcome of some business he had there. Sister Colette made no reply, and the prelate appeared uneasy under her level gaze. Perhaps he remembered things he had heard about her gift for discerning hearts. Maybe he feared she had already read his own and knew that the business he had in Rome concerned the obtaining of a cardinal's hat for himself. Father Pierre describes him as "laboring, in secret, to be a cardinal." Raymon d'Avilhun had powerful friends in Rome who were working with him in this dubious cause, bringing their pressure to bear on Pope Martin V. They had advised their candidate in Castres that the time was now ripe. He should hurry to Rome.

When the bishop finished describing the route he would take, he looked at the abbess again, this time probably a little nervously. "So, you will pray for me?" he asked again. "Yes," answered Colette slowly. "I will pray for your lordship." After a long moment she added: "It would be better for you to be thinking of the journey to eternity, which will not be long delayed." If Bishop Raymon d'Avilhun was shaken by this information, he made no serious comment on it. "Eternity?—oh, that is far away, my dear Mother." He blessed her, and departed for Rome. When he arrived there, however, it was no cardinal's hat he received, but a most unwelcome visitor, death. The nuns at Castres prayed for the soul of their bishop, who might have stood less in need of suffrages had he heeded the warning of their abbess.

As soon as the community life was established at Castres, Sister Colette moved on to Lezignan and set herself to supervise construction there. With King Jacques pressing the workers on and pouring Bourbon funds into the new monastery, the building rose with a speed that amazed even the abbess-general. Early in 1429 it was finished, and a small community of nuns chosen from the older houses was installed. Without allowing herself any respite from this intense activity, Colette returned at once to Orbe, where Princess Jeanne de Montfaucon-Montbéliard's monastery was now completed. Evidently efficient Jeanne was still no match for Jacques de Bourbon in getting things done with despatch, but Sister Colette was much pleased with the results of the princess' efforts. The house at Orbe was entirely in keeping with the abbess' ideals, and she appointed one of her dearest daughters as the first abbess there. This was Father Henri's niece and Perrine's sister, Mathilde de la Baume.

Sister Mathilde was nearly forty now, but her memories of the day in 1406 when her father had led a travel-rumpled nun to her mother's deathbed could scarcely have dimmed. The little sister Mathilde had held in her arms on that momentous day in Alard de la Baume's castle at Frontenay stood beside her now as twenty-two-year-old Sister Perrine. Perhaps Father Henri de la Baume set down some details of this dramatic moment of Mathilde's installation as abbess at Orbe in that manuscript which Sister Colette, unhappily for us, consigned to the flames.

The abbess-general left an enthusiastic young community at Orbe and returned with Father Henri and Sister Perrine to Lezignan to rest a little before attempting the third of King Jacques' proposed foundations in Languedoc, that of Beziers. The friar heartily approved. Colette should remain at Lezignan at least six months, living quietly and peacefully in the enclosure again, with no trials of journeying and building and warring nobles to trouble her during the respite. She could finish the minor revisions she wished to make on her now completed Constitutions without constant interruptions. It was an excellent plan. And Father Henri had taken everything into account—except his own state of extreme exhaustion.

The little group had no sooner returned to Lezignan than the friar fell so ill that the nuns despaired of his recovery. That is, all but Colette did. In something akin to frenzy of soul, she pulled at heaven to spare her friend. Here we see her again so much a partner to our own fears and our wavering detachment. Yes, she would give God anything! She was prepared to suffer any trial, any separation. But God must not ask Father Henri of her! The trial of losing the holy friar's wise counsel and perfect understanding was outside the sphere of the conceivable. Colette knew all too poignantly how much she depended on Henri de la Baume.

She alarmed her nuns by keeping so constant a watch at the sick friar's side that collapse seemed imminent for her, too; but she would not hear of leaving him. She prayed unceasingly for an extension of Father Henri's life. When she won it, and the sick priest began to rally noticeably, Colette, far from collapsing, showed a renewal of energy. Leaving the convalescent friar in capable hands, she and Sister Perrine set out with Father Pierre de Vaux and his companion and a few other nuns for Beziers. After so many anxieties and so much hostility and opposition, the abbess-general found one of the happiest surprises of her life awaiting her there.

There was in that town a community of Urbanist Poor Clares. After her recent experience in Chambéry, she must have approached Beziers with dread. Useless to explain that she respected and loved the Urbanist Poor Clares. Unavailing to insist that a monastery of the primitive observance would in no way reflect ill on theirs or interfere with their quite separate Rule. In Chambéry, they had simply refused to believe her.

What must she have felt, then, to find that the Urbanists at Beziers not only believed her, but that before her arrival they had agreed among themselves to embrace the primitive Rule of St. Clare —if Sister Colette would accept them. Did she remember, at this moment of such unexpected joy, Sister Simonette in the Besançon monastery in 1410, and the day when the old nun had timidly asked to be allowed to attempt keeping the primitive Rule? Surely there were few days in the life of St. Colette to equal in gladness the day when she received a whole community at Beziers into the arms of the first Franciscan observance.

Given so much good will, she found little difficulty in establishing the ancient observance in the monastery of Beziers. She remained to govern it for some time; and when she felt she could leave the community in other hands, she returned to Moulins, appearing younger and more rested than Sister Perrine had seen her look for a long time. Her happiness at Father Henri's recovery, along with her delight at the attitude of the nuns at Beziers, seemed to have transformed her. Because all the monasteries of Languedoc were destroyed in the sixteenth century by the Huguenots, archives along with buildings, we know little of the three Bourbon foundations there except what has just been set down. But it is enough. They made an island of joy in the bitter waters she so often breasted.

It was autumn of 1429 when Sister Colette returned to Moulins. Her nuns welcomed her back with boundless joy; and the people of Moulins were most enthusiastic over her return, too. "The saint" was their ordinary tag for her now. But there was another saint in France, though not all knew it as well. And she, too, came to Moulins late in 1429. She was not a nun, but a soldier. Her name was Jeanne d'Arc.

19 *Colette and Jeanne d'Arc*

In 1429, the famous Maid of Orleans was at the height of her brief career. Everyone in the kingdom talked of her; and if all were not convinced that she was a saint, all were agreed that she had some kind of superhuman power. The seventeen-year-old girl had rallied the noblest French hearts around her in a campaign to restore the wretched dauphin, son of mad Charles VI and adulterous Isabeau of Bavaria, to his royal rights and crown him King of France. In one of the greatest sieges in history, Jeanne d'Arc had succeeded in taking Orleans for the crown, and the flower of the French nobility as well as the common people hailed her as the heaven-sent rescuer of the nation.

When she rode into Moulins in the winter of 1429, the familiar red cape billowing out over her bright armor, she had, in a sense, already fulfilled her mission. The dauphin had been crowned King of France as Charles VII. The house of Bourbon and half of France were wild with joy. The other half was desperate with hatred of this girl with her flashing sword and her beseeching eyes that could summon lethargic noblemen to peaks of heroism.

The Duchess of Bourbon, Colette's old friend, loved Jeanne d'Arc as a mother loves a favorite daughter. And the duchess' young son, Louis Montpensier, was the warrior saint's loyalest lieutenant. They were a picturesque pair: the tall peasant girl in doublet, breeches, and high boots, her young face shining with dedication under the cropped hair and soldier's cap; and the handsome young nobleman who reverenced his girl-captain as a saint.

Charles de Clermont, Duchess Marie's older son who had come hurrying to Sister Colette's assistance during the unhappy days in Aigueperse when the canons of the collegiate church had destroyed her half-built monastery, had a much more equivocal attitude toward Jeanne d'Arc than his mother and young brother. There were times when he fought gallantly with Louis at her side. There were other times when he listened to the court slanders against her and coldly withdrew his support. However, during the recent coronation of Charles VII at Rheims, Charles de Clermont had stood before the throne next to Jeanne, and perhaps the supreme satisfaction of that hour had thrust temporarily into the background the Duchess of Bourbon's anguish over her husband's continued imprisonment in England.

The Bourbon palace at Moulins occupied a whole shoulder of the town. Sister Colette was a frequent and honored visitor there on her journeys from one monastery to another. Jeanne d'Arc was considered a daughter of the house. Now, reason balks at supposing the Duchess of Bourbon never brought her two saintly protégées together. Then, there is the undebatable fact of Colette's being everywhere hailed as France's wonder-working saint, and Jeanne being acclaimed as France's savior. How could it be possible that the two never met? If the sinful and the saintly alike flocked to the Poor Clare abbess to beg her prayers for the ending of family quarrels, for a happy marriage, or a successful negotiation of business, would only Jeanne d'Arc make no move to solicit the contemplative nun's prayers for the ending of the quarrels that divided France, and for the torn country's wedding with peace at last?

On the other hand, when Colette's heart so agonized for the state of her country, would she have held aloof from the valiant girl who alone had been able to rally France to its king? The abbess thought nothing of remaining whole nights on her knees in prayer for one condemned criminal. What must she have done to win from God new strength and blessings for the young leader of France's armed forces?

It is strange that we have no written record of their ever meeting; but the suppositions which have been offered to explain such a mystery are reasonable enough. Jeanne d'Arc was on fire with a holy impatience to free her country. If the former dauphin was content to sit on his throne as Charles VII and enjoy his royal prerogatives, the Maid of Orleans could not rest until her loved country was entirely free of the English toils. She was heartily hated by every unworthy prelate and scheming noble in France. And she was thwarted by the Truce of Burgundy which, in 1429, protected a part of enemy country.

Colette was as patriotic a Frenchwoman as the girl-soldier. She would never hear of establishing one of her monasteries in a part of France occupied by the English, though she would have been welcomed by English and French alike. However, her mission was not Jeanne d'Arc's mission. The Poor Clare abbess was as much beloved by Burgundians as by Bourbons, and to the house of Burgundy she owed the construction and protection of her first monasteries. Jeanne laid siege on Burgundian territories, and her life was constantly in danger. Colette walked out of Bourbon dominions into Burgundian domains as spiritual queen of both. It is surely easy enough to deduce, from this state of affairs, reasons that the meeting or meetings of Jeanne d'Arc and Colette Boellet should be kept secret.

Too, if there is no written testimony to the two saints' meeting, tradition is entirely and vehemently in favor of it. The best writers of France, from Gabriel Hanotaux down to Charles Péguy, take for granted the friendship between the young warrior and the middle-aged nun. In his *Mystère de la Charité,* Péguy has Jeanne d'Arc cry out: "To have given up!—that is worst of all! Madame Colette would never have given up!" And besides the strong tide of tradition in favor of the saints' friendship, there is the telling fact that the archives of the town of Moulins, where the most reliable traditions place their meeting, were badly burned and half-destroyed during the French Revolution. There is also the troublesome reality that this very period of Jeanne's life is the one concerning which documentary evidence is the most meager, and in which her own "Itinéraires" are most often inaccurate in matters of detail.

It is left to each one's decision, then, whether Jeanne d'Arc and Colette of Corbie met at Moulins in 1429. The Maid of Orleans arrived in the autumn and remained for several weeks, awaiting the supplies and ammunition she needed so desperately for her assault on La Charité. During this time, she is known to have spent three full days in the chapel of the Poor Clares, making a kind of private retreat. During those same days, Sister Colette was just on the other side of the altar grille, chanting the Divine Office with her nuns. Whether she saw the abbess or not, St. Jeanne d'Arc certainly heard St. Colette's voice chanting the psalms. It is not at all difficult to imagine the excitement of the Poor Clare Sisters in Moulins over the presence of the armored girl in their chapel! And the most reasonable conclusion in the light of all we know of both saints seems to be that Sister Colette not only saw the young saint of the battlefield at the parlor grille, but that she brought all her nuns to the parlor to see her, too.

Soon after Jeanne d'Arc left Moulins for the historic siege of La Charité, Sister Colette went to Décize to visit her community there. Now, Décize was a Burgundian town, while Moulins was one of the greatest Bourbon strongholds. Accustomed to acting freely as a neutral party, the abbess calmly despatched a messenger from Décize on November 1 to find out how things were going with Jeanne d'Arc at La Charité. And for the first and apparently the only time in her life, Colette fell under political suspicion.

Décize was swarming with Burgundian men-at-arms, and the whole town was stretched taut with fear and apprehension. The soldiers turned distrustful eyes on the nun who had just come from Moulins and was sending letters to the seventeen-year-old warrior of the king. In such a state of tension and alarm, the soldiers were ready to seize on the most innocent circumstance as being part of a plot. It was certainly unfortunate that at such a time, the sacristan at the Poor Clare monastery in Décize should make a very wide-margined error in ringing the church bell for the nuns' night Office almost three hours in advance of schedule. Sister Perrine describes the sleepy sacristan as awaking (more or less!) between nine and ten o'clock and, taking it for granted it was time for the midnight Office, going at once to peal the great bell. Perrine obviously feels that it was an understandable mistake, and any Poor Clare would agree. Insomnia has never been the occupational hazard in their vocation. If a nun in good health wakes up in the middle of the night, it is obviously because it is time for Matins. She has been aroused by the bell or by force of habit, maybe both. It is merely typical that the sacristan at Décize believed herself awakened by her sense of duty and nothing else.

The men-at-arms were accustomed to the midnight peals of the tower bell which roused the Poor Clares for the night Office. When they heard the great bell ring before 10:00 P.M., they sprang up in full battle-cry! Everyone knows that church bells have often been used as signals in war time. The Poor Clares were sending a warning to the enemy! "We are betrayed!" captain shouted to captain. And with a common impulse of fierce reprisal, the soldiers rushed toward the monastery. Almost at its gates, they froze where they were. Sister Perrine records that the great clock in the town belfry struck one.

When the Burgundian soldiery gathered its collective wits again, the leaders decided on a magnanimous gesture. They would go on to the monastery as they had planned, but to apologize, not to threaten or imprison. It is a rare tribute to Colette of Corbie that these fighting men who had actually done no least harm to her or her nuns except by half-formed intentions, felt compelled to humble themselves before her. Everyone knew the abbess read hearts. Evidently these rough men took it for granted she could discern theirs, and that they owed her an apology for even a thought against her political integrity.

We can picture Sister Colette, as a terrified little sacristan ran to her cell with the news that she had rung the Matins bell almost three hours early. In any Poor Clare monastery, getting the tired nuns off their straw mattresses so previously would be considered a tragedy of no small proportions. With suspicious soldiers thronging the city in wartime, it was a public calamity. Probably the unfortunate bell-ringer cried loud and long, with practical-minded Colette urging her daughter to sob on more of a decrescendo while she herself figured a way out of this impasse.

One can also see the heavy-eyed nuns beginning to gather around their abbess. Barring an accident such as had happened to the unfortunate sacristan, anyone who has slept every night for years in two sessions, so to speak, knows exactly what hour of the night it is when she is aroused. Brother Ass is in such-and-such a mood at midnight. If he gets up feeling that life is very worthwhile, he knows he has overslept the bell for the midnight Office and got in several illegal hours on the straw. Or, if he is awakened considerably before the hour for the night Office, he refuses to subscribe to any reality at all. The nuns at Décize in 1430 were one of the rare exceptions to this; for, though it was more than two hours earlier than they were accustomed to rise, the suggestion that Burgundian soldiers would probably be pounding on the enclosure doors in a matter of minutes shook them immediately and irrevocably awake.

Evidently one or more of the Burgundian captains made public confession of what he felt was a sinful judgment against Sister Colette and her nuns, for Sister Perrine gives their "gracious reprimand of themselves" in direct quotation: "We are wicked men to think evil of these good and devout religious who serve God so faithfully and guard us by their holy prayers better than we could protect ourselves."

What followed had not only the soldiers but all the citizens of Décize blessing themselves and looking at the heavens. This was that dawn broke that morning in accordance with the mistakenly-rung Matins bell, and not in accordance with nature. The sky turned pink and pearl three hours earlier than usual. "Dawn appeared as if it had really been after midnight when she rang the bell," is the way Sister Perrine expresses it, adding that "the Sisters were full of a great wonder when they perceived this." Doubtless one sleepy citizen after another shook his timepiece and scolded at its running three hours slow. But when the delicate dawn remained suspended until the normal time for it to ripen into full day, the people stopped muttering about timepieces and feeling tired. They feared God and blessed His name.

Sister Colette graciously pardoned the soldiers and sent them away, chastened and confirmed in their reverence for her. And certainly the whole community never recited with greater fervor than they did that night the prayer their abbess had taught all her nuns.

Familiarly titled "Blessed be the Hour," the prayer had been revealed to Colette in the first years of her foundations. The original
copy, in the saint's own hand, was kept at the monastery in
Besançon. To this day, the prayer is recited in every house of the
Order sprung from St. Colette's restoration and is held in greatest
veneration by all her daughters. Here is a faithful English translation:

Blessed be the hour in which our Lord Jesus Christ, God and Man,
was born. Blessed be the Holy Ghost by whom He was conceived.
Blessed be the glorious Virgin Mary of whom the God-Man was
born.
May the Lord hear our prayers by the intercession of the glorious
Virgin Mary and by the remembrance of the most sacred hour in
which the God-Man was born, that all our desires may be accomplished for Thy glory and our salvation.
O good Jesus! O Jesus our Redeemer, do not abandon us nor
punish us as our sins deserve, but hear our humble prayer and grant
what we ask, by the intercession of the Blessed Virgin Mary and for
the glory of Thy holy Name. Amen.

The Poor Clares love to say this treasured prayer after their midnight Office. How the nuns in Décize must have savored the words
that historic night of alarm and rescue. Blessed . . . be . . . the
. . . hour!

In 1432, the Viscountess of Polignac, Claudine de Roussillon,
sent the abbess word that the new monastery at Le Puy was at last
completed. The troublesome lawsuit brought against the viscountess
for property rights on the site she and Colette had agreed would be
ideal for a monastery had dragged out for nearly seven years; but
at last everything had been settled amicably and the building was
finished.
The abbess left immediately for Le Puy with Father Pierre de
Vaux and a companion and a few nuns from Décize. The viscountess
was right in thinking that Colette would be pleased with the neat
and humble dwelling she found at Le Puy. She at once established
a small community of nuns there. Another oblique proof of the
friendship of St. Jeanne d'Arc and St. Colette is that in 1431, the year
of St. Jeanne's cruel martyrdom, the King of France had made his

first personal gift to the abbess-general of the Poor Clares. Charles VII had sent one hundred and twenty gold ducats to the unfinished monastery of Le Puy to be used as Colette thought best. Was it a pathetic attempt on the part of the pusillanimous king to quiet his agony of conscience by sending a royal alms to the friend of Jeanne d'Arc?—he who sat on his throne only because of the labor and loyalty of the girl from Domremy, and who had sat there without lifting a finger to save her from months of imprisonment and death in the flames?

Sister Colette had her Constitutions in final order now, but she wisely preferred to give them an even longer test of time and usage before submitting them to the Minister General of the Franciscan Order and to Pope Martin V. Those who have lived by these Constitutions during five centuries and those who find them as practicable in 1959 as they were in 1439 can thank the prudence of a woman in whom God's grace built on mental acumen and profound insight. When her Constitutions were submitted to Rome in 1933 for revisions according to the new code of Canon Law, the five-centuries-old Statutes needed only the most negligible of adjustments. Cardinal Cerretti, into whose charge the Constitutions had been given for possible revision, remarked on the singular marvel by which St. Colette's legislation has remained so eminently practicable, so even "modern."

The years after the foundation at Le Puy were relatively peaceful years for Sister Colette. Although, like St. Paul, she was "in journeyings often" from one of her thirteen monasteries to another, she did not establish any more new ones for several years. She busied herself with the spiritual guidance of her daughters, whose number now reached into hundreds, never so occupied with major issues as to overlook an individual nun's needs, and ever showing herself the soul of simplicity as concerned the extraordinary events of her own life but the very heart of compassion as regarded the small trials of her children. Her maternal tenderness endeared her more each day to her nuns, but sometimes her casual simplicity about the phenomenal disconcerted them.

There was the unforgettable day described by Sister Perrine on the testimony of Sister Colette Prucet who was present at the time, when several Sisters were gathered together in the choir, praying silently before the tabernacle. All of a sudden, a white phantom appeared at the grille, visible to them all. The nuns stood up in terror, and some were already making long strides toward the exit when the abbess softly clapped her hands in pleasure. The fleeing nuns, as well as the few stalwart ones who had remained in their places, turned and looked at Colette. Her eyes were fixed on the grille, and her face was alight with joy. The nuns looked back at the grille and saw that the ghostly figure was still there. Nothing to beam about, surely! But then their abbess spoke aloud in her delight at seeing an old friend again and so unexpectedly. "Here is Father William," she announced enthusiastically. Now Father William Turéal was a Franciscan friar. And he had died a year previously!

Not all visits from the dead were causes for rejoicing, however. Dom Raoul de Raye had been dead for several years before Sister Colette confided to Sister Perrine that the Benedictine abbot appeared to her each year on the anniversary of his death. The visits were prefaced, Perrine writes, by a terrifying "clanking of chains and very great noise." The man who during his lifetime had not defended Colette in the hour of her great trial in Corbie now came to her in death, and seven separate times.

It seems that the abbess never supplied any details about these awful anniversary visits from her old guardian, though as years passed, she grew less secretive about the fact of the apparitions. Once she was conversing with a group of her nuns at recreation when she heard the familiar clanking and shouting. She pushed the nuns away; and Sister Perrine adds: "She said to us: 'Go away! It is the enemy. It is that abbot.'" We can only guess at the suffering these visitations caused her, that she so feared her daughters might see what she saw. The saint's words to her daughters and the noise of chains seem to suggest that the soul of the abbot was eternally lost. On the other hand, his appearances on the anniversary of his death for seven successive years point more to solicitations for prayers. Colette draws no conclusions for us. We can only hope that the man who had genuinely loved the carpenter's daughter was saved.

To counteract the anguish Colette endured because of Dom Raoul came another of the friends of her youth in Corbie. It was Father Jéhan Pinet, the friar who had first received her into the Franciscan family as a tertiary and then advised her to become a recluse. No dragging chains or cries accompanied his visits. Father Jéhan appeared to her in glory. Sister Perrine informs us that the friar "appeared to our glorious Mother once a year" and also furnishes the charming detail that Father Jéhan was solicitous, even in heaven, for Colette's continuing in humility. "He would sometimes demand," Perrine writes, " 'Colette! Colette! Where is the fervor of your anchorhold days now!' I myself have heard our glorious Mother tell this."

Father Jean Bassan, the saintly Celestine who had encouraged her to vow her virginity perpetually to God when she was a girl of eighteen, was still living. Now the general of his Order, he wrote each year to his former disciple whom all France now acclaimed as a saint. And the saint was showing more and more of St. Francis' own traits and powers these days. Like him, she had a tender affection for all small creatures, especially birds. They responded to her, as to him, with trust and affection. Father Pierre de Vaux tells us of a beautiful lark which flew about with her and settled itself familiarly beside her, quite without fear, to "sing God's praises." He writes of "many other little birds" who flew into her oratory and sang their accompaniment to her prayer, of how they ate and drank along with her, receiving "their little refection from her as payment for their praises of the Creator."

De Vaux also describes a "little animal all white and beautiful," which came into the enclosure and which no one could identify. Evidently the small strange creature did not want to be catalogued, for Father Pierre says that one day when "the little handmaid of our Savior ran after the said beast, along with the other nuns, both she and the little beast vanished, and the said religious did not know which way to turn because the two of them were quite lost to view." This picture of Colette hot in pursuit of her strange pet, her nuns fast after her, would appear to be one of the rarer ones we have of her.

Father Pierre is also at pains to inform us that if the glorious Mother had a great fondness for birds and animals, she had as great a horror of "bugs and evil odors." He explains that she was able to bear these two trials "sweetly" only because of her love "for Him who bore the stench and vermin of our sins."

As she entered into her late fifties, the delicacy of Sister Colette's love for her daughters became more and more evident. Each was an individual child, not to be judged quite as any other. There was, at this time, one young nun in particular who caused the abbess distress. Against the advice of the older nuns in the community (and it is a telling comment on the saint that her nuns did not hesitate to advise her!) Sister Colette had received this girl, who seemed unstable from the first. Nearly everyone in the community doubted her vocation; but the abbess was so sure of her that, in the end, the others put aside their own views and voted in the novice's favor. She made her vows, but continued wavering and uncertain. Young Sister Marie's perseverance seemed dubious to all but her abbess, who had so strong a conviction of her being truly called by God that she refused to lose faith in her.

Not long after her profession, Sister Perrine records, the young Sister became very ill and lost the power of speech. After some days, the doctors declared that the sickness was beyond their power to help and that death was imminent. She lay in the infirmary in a deep coma. But Sister Colette had no intention of letting her daughter die without the last Sacraments. She tried to rouse her, but could not. She knelt at the Sister's bedside for hours on end and would let no one persuade her to rest. Like many a natural mother, Colette had a particular affection for the daughter who caused her most anxiety.

One day, quite exhausted from her long vigils, the abbess buried her tired head in the invalid's coverlet and cried. The other nuns stood by helplessly, but then Colette raised her head and looked once more at the dying nun's face. "Oh, Marie, speak to me!" she begged. Sister Perrine says that she repeated this command two or three times and that "the invalid then turned to her and spoke to her clearly."

The abbess helped her prepare for death, and the daughter whose vocation all but Colette had doubted died like a saint, smiling and radiant. "She is saved from great pain," announced Sister Colette; "she is on the road of salvation." Perhaps no one but Sister Marie's abbess had guessed what heroic struggles against temptation had kept her faithful to her vocation, or what reward God has laid up for the weak whose trials the strong cannot comprehend.

On the other hand, writes Sister Perrine, what appeared to the other nuns to be the most promising vocations sometimes left the abbess quite unimpressed. Once, against her firm judgment, Colette yielded to the importunities of the community that she receive a handsome and highly talented girl into the cloister. "She has no vocation," Sister Colette said flatly; but the nuns were so much in favor of the gifted young lady that the abbess finally accepted her. After only a few weeks, the new postulant lost all her enthusiasm for a life of prayer and penance, which had lost its glamor at such close range. She packed her numerous valises with alacrity and returned to her home, leaving a community of nuns looking sheepishly at an abbess who assuredly did not say, "I told you so." The incident shows more than Colette's shrewd discernment of souls. It demonstrates her humble willingness to yield to her own subjects even when she knew they were mistaken.

If these years were untroubled ones so far as making new foundations was concerned, they were quite the opposite in regard to the activity of Satan. He tormented the saint, sometimes with violence, sometimes with petty persecutions, such as repeatedly putting out her lamp when she was trying to recite the Office she had missed in choir. Once he overturned the lamp on her breviary, and the oil had soaked through page after page of the book before she could rescue it.

Sister Colette never showed herself a truer "ordinary nun" than in her reaction to this catastrophe. Poor Clares are trained from their postulant days to turn the pages of their breviaries with the utmost care. To plant one's thumb in the book is considered a most heinous nun's crime. The idea seems to be that, after a nun has used her breviary for fifty years or so, it should be in perfect condition to pass down to some new novice. Colette always handled her own breviary with scrupulous care. When she saw her precious book hopelessly greasy with lamp oil, she was stung in what is every nun's Achilles' heel. After all, a breviary is the only expensive appurtenance allowed by St. Francis and St. Clare to their children, and Father Pierre de Vaux says that Colette "greatly cherished" hers.

The next morning, she called Father Pierre to the parlor grille and told him what had happened. "The devil has ruined our breviary," she complained, doubtless in accents of tragedy. And she gave out the oil-soaked book through the turn. Father Pierre was perhaps less stricken by this occurrence than a nun would be. After all, the devil had done no physical harm to the abbess herself, and he was sufficiently grateful for that. A breviary was, relatively, a small thing. However, he was prepared to be properly sympathetic over the greasy mess.

Father Pierre reached for the book; but as he turned page after page, he found no oil. The book looked quite new. Was it a joke? He handed the breviary back to Sister Colette, asking for an explanation. Seeing her oil-soaked breviary clean again was real cause for jubilation, but it is Father Pierre's comment which puts the last delightful touch on this vignette. "I don't even see those thumb-prints of yours that used to be in the book," he observed. If Sister Colette asked him just what he meant by that remark, Father Pierre de Vaux did not note it in the account he wrote of the affair, which has also been recorded by Sister Perrine.

The affection she showed for her daughters was returned to the abbess in hundredfold measure. One of them, recalls Father Pierre, was so ingenuous in her devotion to her ageing superior that she set herself to protect Colette from the attacks of the devil. One day, when she saw her abbess grow suddenly pale and shrink back, the brave nun, teeth chattering withal, stepped in front of Colette and spread her arms protectingly wide before her. "Come, attack *me!*" she invited the demons she could not see, but that she knew were present. "Attack *me*," she repeated, "but leave my Mother alone!" Surely the abbess must have caught her trembling little defender to her heart.

Her interest in the friars was as solicitous as that for her own daughters. When she heard that Father François Claret, one of her and Father Henri's oldest friends and for all these years the novice master at the model Franciscan community in Dôle, was dying, she begged God to spare him. Both Father Pierre de Vaux and Sister Perrine write that the sick friar then made so unexpected a recovery that all in his community marvelled. Father François himself stoutly declared that he had been already dead and Sister Colette had pulled him back to earth. The friars believed him. However that may be, it certainly testifies to the kind of opinion the friars in Dôle had of the nun whom the ancients among them had seen in ecstasy in their own chapter room in 1412. They had no difficulty in believing that she could bring a dead Father François to life.

But early in 1439, just after the abbess arrived at her monastery

in Besançon, death came to another friar, the dearest of them all
to Sister Colette. It was Father Henri de la Baume. And this time
the abbess did not ask God to spare him. At seventy-three, the
saintly old man was weary of earth and eager for heaven. For thirty-
three years he had trudged the roads of France at Colette's side.
He had advised her and consoled her. When she had been slandered,
he had defended her name. He had warded off from her as far as
lay in his power every attack of the evil and malicious, and protected
her with the gallantry of a knight errant for his lady. No one had
ever understood Sister Colette as Father Henri had. It was a heart-
rending parting, but when Colette looked into the faded eyes of her
best friend on earth and read in them such longing for the vision of
God, she could not find it in her own heart to beg to keep him
longer.

Instead, she had him carried to the grille of the monastery choir,
and there she prayed with him, her nuns weeping around her. She
would not let Father Henri out of her sight during these last hours
they had together on earth. When he was to be anointed, she begged
the friars to do it in the monastery chapel. They agreed, and simply
laid him down at the foot of the altar where he had so often offered
Mass for the Poor Clares. Afterward, they carried him back to the
grille, and while Father Henri looked up at Sister Colette from the
chapel side, she knelt on the enclosure side, whispering words of
consolation to him. Thus he died, without agony or outcry, only
closing his eyes like a tired man settling down to sleep.

It was at this same grille and under the same loving eyes of Colette
that the King of Naples, Jacques de Bourbon, whose life we have
already followed to its close, was to die some years later.

Even in death, the abbess would not agree to separation from the
partner God had given her in the work of restoring primitive Franciscanism. She begged Pope Eugene IV, who had succeeded Martin V
in 1431, to grant her permission to bring Father Henri's body into
the cloister. The pope agreed, and Sister Colette placed her loved
friend in the nuns' chapter room. He was given temporary burial in
the cloister until the tomb she ordered built for him was completed.
Her grief at his going was undoubtedly sweetened by her conviction
that he was already in heaven. But, though she was to live eight more
years, something of death entered into Colette's own heart with

the death of Father Henri de la Baume. This is evident in her letter to her various monasteries, announcing the death of her friend and father:

February 26, 1439

Very dear and much-loved Sisters in God, I wish to tell you that recently deep sorrow has come upon me, with anguish and bitterness both of soul and body, and not without good cause; for on Ash Wednesday last, after Matins, our Reverend Father, Frère Henri, became much more grievously ill, so that on the following Thursday, shortly before midnight, he was brought to our chapel, and there . . . he received very devoutly the precious Body of our Lord Jesus Christ . . . after this, he said farewell to all the Sisters. . . . At six and a half hours after midday, while saying his prayers and speaking to our Lord, he gave up his beautiful and glorious soul tranquilly and piously to God our holy Creator. Which soul, with all possible love and affection, I recommend to you, begging of you with my whole heart, that if you loved him loyally in life, your love may not be lessened after his death but rather increased; that you should do your duty as well as you possibly can by praying to God for him, knowing as you do how much he deserved this. And although I believe there is greater need that he should pray for us than we for him, I recommend his beautiful soul to you all . . . He was ever to us a true father. . . . And I recommend my own poor soul to your good prayers and devotions.

Your unworthy servant,

Sister Colette of Jesus

20   *John Capistran and the Reform*

Once when one of her nuns had asked Sister Colette what she considered the most painful thing that could happen to her, the saint had replied without hesitation: "To pass a day without suffering anything for God." Apparently she never experienced this "most painful thing." The wrench of parting from Father Henri was barely past when another friar just as saintly as de la Baume—one who, indeed, was to be raised to the honors of the altar—came to bring her a measure of anguish she had never anticipated. This was Father John Capistran, co-worker with Father Bernardine of Siena who was laboring so indefatigably for the restoration of primitive Franciscan observance in Italy.

Born in the same year as Colette of Corbie, Bernardine of Siena never met the nun who was laboring in France for the same end he hoped to attain in Italy; but he followed her progress with the liveliest interest. More than that, the famed Italian friar had unbounded admiration for the abbess-general and publicly declared that he wished to be known as "the disciple of Sister Colette." Father John was as Father Bernardine's other self. We would expect that his coming to Besançon to visit Colette would constitute one of the happiest periods of her spiritual life. Instead, it meant her time of climactic trial. Perhaps it was during John Capistran's sojourn in Besançon that Colette gave a few of her nuns the confidence which Sister Perrine has recorded for us: "I feel as if someone had split my heart across the middle, filled it with burning salt, and sewed it up again."

It is the familiar tale of saint polishing saint. Teresa of Avila admitted that no suffering was so bitter to her as misunderstanding and persecution by good and pious people. We have seen how a great doctor of the Church and a son of St. Francis, Bonaventure, had tried only a few short years after the death of St. Clare to impose a new and mitigated Rule on all her daughters. Certainly St. Bonaventure acted from the highest motives, however obscure they may appear to us. Just as surely, the friar who was to be honored on the Church's altars as St. John Capistran was actuated only by selfless zeal for the good of the Franciscan Order when he came to the Poor Clare monastery at Besançon to propose that the abbess merge her life's work in compromise with the mitigants.

If Bernardine of Siena and John of Capistrano had been following Colette of Corbie's restoration with joy and thanksgiving, the abbess was just as aware of the friars' work in Italy. She knew their ideals were one with her own. But she also saw the focal point of their difference. Because the minister-general of the Franciscan Order belonged to the "Conventual" Franciscans, distinguished by this title from the "Observant" Franciscans who wished to follow the primitive Rule of St. Francis without change or mitigation, the Observants had appealed to the pope for a vicar-general in the Order to whom they could turn in their needs and who would be prepared to understand their particular difficulties because he shared their ideals.

This privilege had been granted to the friars, but Colette wanted none of it for her nuns. Although she clung to the primitive Rule, she had managed to keep the good-will and even the affection of the Conventual minister-general. Father William of Casal wrote to her frequently, and the letters still preserved in the monastery of Besançon reflect an admiration for the saint of Corbie which reached to paternal fondness. Sister Colette had no intention of letting her work of restoration be cut off from the official head of the Franciscan Order. It was the triumph of her tact and humility that she did accomplish the feat of remaining subject to a minister-general who personally thought her way of life too idealistic for the entire Order, yet respected her with real devotedness.

William of Casal had approved her strict Constitutions in 1434 with words whose authority is rendered strangely poignant by their tenderness. He was undoubtedly a great man, for only greatness of soul could give approbation such as this to Statutes for women far eclipsing what he felt could be imposed on men:

Father William of Casal, Minister-General of the Order of Friars Minor, and Servant and Master in Sacred Theology, to his Religious Sister in Christ, Colette, foundress of many monasteries of the Poor Ladies of the Order of St. Clare that have been at the present time established in France and are to be established . . . health in the Spouse of Virgins, Jesus Christ!

How the most renowned merits of the admirable Virgin Clare have been multiplied under the guidance of Francis, her leader in poverty and sanctity, and how they shine forth in the Holy Church of God . . . is most joyfully proclaimed . . . by the unceasing devotion of the faithful and by the great multitude of virgins who, drawn by the odor of her sanctity, even in these times flee from the perils of the world to the safe harbor of her Order.

For this should we render all the greater thanks to the Most High, in that nature being more prone to relaxation, little plants, nevertheless, are seen to spring up within this Order, who do not deviate from the ordinances of Father Francis and the footsteps of Clare, but desire with great fervor to have the Rule and the Form of life, given them by the most holy virgin, Mother Clare, fortified by the aid of suitable Constitutions, to the end that they may be accounted true followers of so great a Mother. . . .

Again he wrote to her, and in his own hand:

My very dear daughter in Jesus Christ, I have heard out your confessor, Father Pierre, on the subject of approving and confirming [your] Constitutions which appear, at first consideration, to be very severe on certain points. . . . It seems to be blameworthy, on the one hand, not to yield to your devotion, so glowing with zeal for God and the salvation of souls; but, on the other hand, I feared to lay too heavy a burden on our Sisters and daughters. I have been given my decision by our Lord Jesus Christ and through the merits of St. Anthony of Padua . . . God has made me understand, by the merits of my patron saint I do believe, that yours is a special work of God. That is why I am resolved not only to confirm it, but still more to approve it, to promulgate it, to give it the force of law, and to sign it with the seal of the Order.

I desire very much that the family of St. Francis of Assisi should be reformed by your holy means for the glory and honor of God and the salvation of souls.

Brother William of Casal,
most unworthy Minister-General of the Order of Minors

Father John Capistran knew all about the minister-general's reverence for his Poor Clare daughter. Why could it not be appealed to for effecting a complete transformation of the whole Order? Could not the abbess suggest to Father William that the Observants and the Conventuals might strike a final and happy compromise so that all sons and daughters of the seraphic founder would be united under one discipline?

It was a glorious canvas which Father John painted: a vast and bright-hued Franciscan chorus following a way of life from which all abuses and relaxation had been pruned but which was adapted to the strength of the generality rather than the chosen few. If Colette would not fall in with this plan, she had, of course, no other alternative than to place her reform under a vicar-general of the Order. It was preposterous to think she could go on acknowledging the supreme authority of a minister-general who neither himself lived by the primitive Rule nor generally encouraged its restoration. As he brushed in these last details, Colette knew him for a man possessed by his idea. Douillet describes him as "dominated by one great idea: that of re-establishing perfect unity in the Franciscan Order, wishing, having uprooted all abuses, to mitigate the Rule and render it accessible to all." What did these two saints, equally zealous, equally sincere, discover when their eyes met?

Aeneas Sylvius, who had seen John Capistran at Constance, described him as "a small man, toil-worn and wizened, he looked all nerve and bone; yet he seemed happy and full of energy in his labors." He was fifty-four when he came to the monastery in Besançon, clad in a ragged habit and walking barefoot. His face, almost emaciated from his austerities, and tanned and seamed by sun and wind, was dominated by the great brilliant eyes. They gave one an overwhelming impression of a spirit consuming the body.

Colette was fifty-eight at this time; her face, lined beyond her years, was still arresting. The swelling in her legs which troubled her so often now had slowed her brisk gait, and her tall frame was slightly bent. Yet, probably to John Capistran's surprise, she did not appear emaciated. And we are told her dark eyes looked out over the world with ever-increasing compassion as she grew older. Compassion, though, must certainly have given place to alarm as the friar sketched his plan.

"Well?" Father John asked at last. And without heat of argument, Colette explained to the friar why his plan did not seem feasible to her. That she should divorce her communities from the direct authority of the minister-general was unthinkable. And as for this proposed compromise, surely Father John, so much wiser and more experienced than a simple cloistered nun like herself, realized the inevitable outcome of such attempts. The Observants would be unhappy in their surrenders, and the Mitigants would chafe under austerities they had never bargained for. Was it not still true that the "Spirit breatheth where it will"? Certainly the Conventuals, with full approbation from the Holy Father on the mitigations they desired, were pleasing to God and to St. Francis in their sincere piety, just as the Urbanist Poor Clares were. Did it lie in John Capistran's or Colette Boellet's province to force on these worthy religious an observance they declared to be beyond their strength, and to which they were not drawn?

On the other hand, why should either her nuns or the Observant Franciscan friars abandon the vocation to which they were called, surrender their privilege of poverty, and give up their strict adherence to the primitive Rule? She spoke very humbly of the mission God had entrusted to her, that she was to restore the primitive Franciscan Rule, neither forcing it on anyone nor compromising it for anyone.

Then Colette reminded Father John that the matter had already gone beyond her jurisdiction. The minister-general and the Holy Father had approved her Constitutions in 1434. For the past five years, strict enclosure, absolute poverty, recitation of the Divine Office by day and night, intellectual and manual work, silence, and perpetual fast and abstinence had been matters of law for her nuns. It was too late for any reconsiderations or compromises, even if she wished them.

Perhaps the abbess felt her first alarm at Father John's proposal diminishing as she explained all this to him. After all, no one could any longer threaten her work when she had it sealed by both the minister-general and the pope. But John Capistran drew out of the large pilgrim's wallet he carried a sheaf of documents and tapped it with the back of his bony fingers. "Pope Eugene has been good enough to draw up new Constitutions for your nuns. I have worked with him. And I believe God has inspired us with a plan that will unite the whole Franciscan Order at last."

The friar insisted that there was nothing to be upset about, but Abbé Douillet describes the abbess-general as "saddened profoundly." He tells us flatly that Sister Colette "would not consent to the destruction of the reform," and also that Father John Capistran "continued insistent." "It is in your hands, Madame Colette—the unity of the Franciscan family!" he said (it was the eloquent voice that thousands in Italy knew so well); "What do you say, Madame? What do you say!" The low reply from the other side of the grille was certainly not the one he had hoped to hear: "I ask you to give me three days to consider."

John Capistran agreed, however. He strode out of the parlor and returned to the friars. And Sister Colette went to tell her nuns that the restoration of primitive Franciscanism was hanging in the balance.

The year when the friar arrived with his armful of documents fresh from Pope Eugene's pen was the second last of the pope's nine years of exile from Rome. Eugene IV had been living in semi-retirement at Florence, slowly regaining his lost prestige. Memories of the past eight years' catastrophies for the pope must have mingled with Sister Colette's new and personal grief as she left the monastery parlor. Just when she had rejoiced that her life's work was nearly accomplished, her Constitutions approved, and monasteries of the primitive Rule multiplying, John Capistran had come to topple the whole structure, and even to threaten its papal foundations with new briefs from Pope Eugene IV. And this was the pope for whom she and her nuns had so prayed and suffered since his ignominious flight from Rome in 1432!

Eugene had literally run, and in very terror of his life, from the swords of the Colonna; and it was only the pity of a Tiber boatman, moved to give the frightened pontiff shelter and passage to Florence in his flimsy skiff, that saved his life. When Colette had ordered the *Te Deum* sung in all her monasteries for the pope's safety, she could scarcely have dreamed he would live to attempt—with however good intentions—the redirection of all her endeavors.

Pope Eugene's predecessor, the Colonna pope, Martin V, had repaid his relatives well for their services to him following his election in 1417 at the Council of Constance. This was the council which had deposed John XXIII and Benedict XIII and accepted the resignation of the true pope, Gregory XII. It had ended the Great Western Schism. But Martin V had endeared himself to few outside the Colonna clan. He knew the power of his family; and with the Colonna troops always at his service, he apparently felt that a tactful consideration for the views of his cardinals was beneath his notice. He became a real tyrant, and a contemporary historian described him as crushing all his cardinals to the extent that "they go red and pale by turns when they speak in his presence." We have been born and reared in a tradition of paternal popes, and it strains our imagination to picture a despot like Martin V. Yet the species was plentiful enough in the fifteenth century.

Pope Martin owed his election to an ecumenical council, but he had no affection for such gatherings. Although, in the first flush of his elevation to the papacy, he had enthusiastically agreed to summon general councils of the Church at regular intervals, he regretted this commitment soon enough. Martin V meant to rule alone, and he did. It was only when the unrest and dissension which his tyrannical policy begot in the Church had intruded themselves on even his detached notice that he was forced to advert to his promise, summoning in 1423 a council which he presently dissolved on the grounds of poor attendance (there was an outbreak of the plague at that time), and in 1431 another at Basle. Evidently he expected trouble at this convocation, for he had armed his legate with papal authority to conclude any meeting and even to disband the whole council whenever he thought it prudent. Such a provision was bound to infuriate the cardinals, but scandal at Basle had been temporarily averted by death. Martin V died in 1431, just before the prelates were to have convened.

Sister Colette's powerful friends among the nobility had kept her painfully well-informed of the new disastrous turns in papal affairs. She must have experienced a vast sense of relief that the Council of Basle had not convened in Pope Martin's lifetime, for she had realized that neither he nor the impassioned conciliar fathers had been in a mood for compromise or even for calm discussion of differences.

When the cardinal electors had come together in a Roman convent to elect a successor to Pope Martin V, they had been of one mind on the point that the next pope should not be allowed any leeway for such dictatorial powers as the Colonna pope had exercised. And it was only when the Venetian Cardinal, Eugene Gabriel Condolmieri, solemnly promised to delegate a large part of the governmental authority over both papal states and the Church at large, that they had elected and crowned him as Pope Eugene IV.

The papal crown, however, had sat uneasily on Eugene's head from the first. Like many a ruler before him, he had found that concession demands concession, and that certain subalterns are swift to seize on the fatal weakness of parcelled and promised power. With the new pope's worried consent, the proposed Council of Basle had assembled only five months after his coronation. And before another five months had elapsed, Pope Eugene had realized the tragedy of his initial mistake.

Most of the fathers of the council had been heady with assurance of their superior power, as a body, over the pope. As soon as Eugene had recognized the council's insubordination, he had declared it disbanded; but the council members had replied, with cool defiance, that they had no intention of obeying a command which they considered the pope had no power to issue.

To add to the pontiff's anguish over a now schismatic council, the gathering fury of the Colonnas, ousted on the accession of Eugene IV from the high positions they had been given by Martin V, had broken in a revengeful storm such as even Rome seldom witnessed. It had been in the midst of this cyclonic Colonna rage that the pope had escaped to sympathetic Florence. When Father John Capistran visited Sister Colette, Eugene was at the high tide of his popularity with the Florentines and, with the help of the ruler of Florence, Cosimo di Medici, was preparing to return to Rome and take up the reins of government again. Unfortunately, at this same time, the Council of Basle, sputtering its last after the long years of schismatical harangue, was planning a final and what was to prove a fatal coup: the election of a new pope on its own tenuous authority.

After thirty-four years of journeying and laboring and suffering, Sister Colette could have considered that she had made no advance at all since 1406. Affairs of the papacy, though not so complex as during the great schism, were anything but well-ordered. Rome had not seen its bishop for eight years. And her reform? A friar she felt sure was a saint of God had just told her she must sacrifice it on the pyre of compromise. Father Henri de la Baume, the friar who had always comforted and advised her in crises, was dead. But Colette would not submit to defeat. This was a question of God's interests. Douillet writes that "she did not carry the case to the tribunal of men" (apparently he thought that she well might have) but "she prayed and set others praying."

As we have observed before, there was a good deal of the general in Sister Colette. Abbé Douillet describes the despatch with which she divided her community at Besançon into prayer squadrons so that one group was always before the Blessed Sacrament with "insistent supplications." If John Capistran, God's familiar, had known the substance of Colette's own prayer, he could have run up the white flag then and there. For the abbess "humbled herself and demanded of her soul whether it was not her own faults which were exposing to ruin the work God had entrusted to her," pleading that He should not let His plan be thwarted by her sins. There has been and will be no record of the Almighty resisting such a prayer.

Still, Colette had to admit that she had had no definite answer from God when the end of the three-day reprieve came. She asked for and received (whether grudgingly or magnanimously we do not know) another.

This time, one of the nuns suggested that maybe they could have some processions to pray that Father John Capistran would take a different view of things. It was a typical nun's way of facing up to crisis or disaster. A procession around the monastery was obviously all that was needed to make the whole thing come out right. The abbess agreed. And when someone else asked whether the procession might not go on its collective knees instead of on foot, the others enthusiastically seconded the idea. So did Colette.

For three days, every nun in the community went around the choir and through the cloisters on her knees, praying the ancient litanies and battering at the mercy of God for—they knew not what. It did not matter. *He* knew. Abbé Douillet writes that the route of the procession was marked by the blood from the torn knees of the nuns. "It was," says Douillet, "enough. The Lord ended the ordeal."

Father John, meanwhile, was growing increasingly anxious to get away from Besançon. He was staying at the friary, and he feared that the incessant praises of Colette which his confrères sang into his ears were having a harmful effect on him. Why, there had even been a few bad moments in which he, unshakable John Capistran armed with documents from the pope, had doubted the rightness of what he was demanding of Sister Colette. This would not do at all. But when the nuns' painful processions were ended, the great Italian preacher heard more praises of Colette. This time they came directly from Christ, Who appeared to Father John in a vision, and showed him that His will lay in the direction of the abbess' views and not of John's.

The affair was settled, and John Capistran returned to the Poor Clare monastery. When Sister Colette came to the grille, he asked for the return of his documents from the pope. He wasted no words, says Douillet, in his explanation: "I have been seriously in error, and I ask your pardon. I was wrong to interfere with you; but I shall never again molest you in this way, for I believe that your reform is according to God and St. Francis. Persevere as you have begun, because God is with you."

It is John Capistran at his greatest, beyond what rapt congregations in crowded Italian churches had ever heard or would have been able to appreciate. And from that day forward, Father John was one of the abbess' staunchest friends. "These two great souls," writes Abbé Douillet, "entered then into a most perfect union. Peace and calm returned to the monastery." In that peace, the abbess-general began making plans for a trip to Germany.

A foundation in Heidelberg had been the desire of the saint for some years past. Now she had both subjects and the promise of funds for it. Preparations for the journey were halted abruptly in early summer, however, when Father Pierre de Vaux brought news of the Council of Basle. It had elected a "pope" on June 25 and, with incredible insolence, declared Eugene IV deposed. There was again a papal schism. And the anti-pope, unbelievable as it seemed, was the abbess' faithful and devout friend, Duke Amadeus of Savoy.

Father Pierre, as well as Sister Perrine, declares that Sister Colette had "known and predicted three years before this" that the Council of Basle would cause new division in the Church and elect an anti-pope to be known as Felix. It does not appear, however, that she had foreknowledge of Felix' identity. If she had, would she not have tried to forestall her friend's tragic action? We are not told of her sending Duke Amadeus any message until after his assuming the "papal" dignity. Then her pen flew over page after page in a tender and anguished appeal to her old friend, "my lord Amadeus," not to wear the false tiara. But as soon as she finished the letter, she tore it into bits. "It is my business to pray and to suffer, and not to interfere," she told the nuns.

The mere existence of this kind of uncertainty lets us gauge the depth of Colette's pain. She had never before hesitated to advise her friends among the nobility when she thought it necessary; one recalls her messages reaching the battle-tents of John of Burgundy. But that the Duke of Savoy, whom she so respected and loved, should be a party to a fresh schism in the Church seemed too much for her. Perhaps she feared that if so deeply religious a man as Amadeus was deaf to conscience, he could scarcely be expected to hear any words of hers. Blustering, brutal John the Fearless and prayerful, penitential Amadeus of Savoy presented wholly dissimilar cases. But having destroyed her letter, she was so overwhelmed the next morning by the fear that she was neglecting her plain duty by remaining silent, that she feared to receive Holy Communion.

She confided her problem and confessed her possible guilt to Father Pierre de Vaux. He insisted that she must at least make an attempt to save the Duke of Savoy from his delusions. Father Pierre was of the opinion that it was not so much a case of the duke's ignoring the warnings of his conscience as of muddled thinking and having too willing an ear for the specious arguments of certain Fathers of the Council. Had not the great Cardinal Julian of San Sabina written to Sister Colette of his own anxiety over the confused reasoning which had taken hold of the Council?

Obediently, Colette wrote another long letter to my lord Amadeus; and this one was delivered. Those who were present when the duke read it informed her later that Amadeus had fallen sad and silent. In the end, however, he was not proof against the persuasions of the prelates of Basle; and on December 23, 1439, the Duke of Savoy was crowned "pope," having first been hastily ordained priest and consecrated bishop. He called himself Felix V, an ironic title for one who bade farewell to felicity that day.

There could have been no sadder Christmas in Sister Colette's life. Yet she refused to let either her personal grief or her lively sense of gratitude to the man who had been ready to give her his whole ancestral castle, whose daughter was one of her nuns, and who had built her monastery at Vevey, blind her to her duty. She drew up a circular letter to the nuns in all her monasteries, warning them against giving obedience to Felix V. "Beware of him," she wrote, "for he is an anti-pope."

Felix V never commanded a great following outside his own territory of Savoy, though for a while he had the loyalty of Switzerland and the support of certain European universities. His uncertain authority steadily diminished through the years, but surely the incessant prayers of Sister Colette and her nuns had a part in the duke's finally recognizing and admitting his colossal mistake. The aged Amadeus was so sincere in his repentance at having allowed himself to be styled Pope Felix, so almost pathetically eager to undergo public humiliation to ease the burden of his shame, that Pope Eugene's successor pardoned him magnanimously and gave him an honored place in the college of cardinals. The abbess who had suffered so much on his account did not live to see this happy ending to the duke's "papal" career. It came to pass in 1449, two years after her death.

"Carrying a great grief in her heart" over Duke Amadeus' coronation, as Sister Perrine describes it, Colette set out for Germany early in 1440. She may have realized she had not many years left to work at restoring the primitive Rule, for there is an air of urgency about her going. Father Pierre de Vaux and Sister Perrine went with her on this historic journey which marked the initiation of her mission outside France.

For the past eleven years, Louis of Bavaria and his wife had been urging Colette to establish a monastery in Heidelberg at their expense. Duke Louis was the nephew of old Duchess Margaret of Burgundy, wife of John the Fearless. It was this young relative whom the Duchess of Burgundy had been so eager to see married to Countess Maude, niece of Sister Colette's first aristocratic benefactress, Countess Blanche de Genève. Both Margaret and Blanche had been dead several years when the desired marriage was finally arranged; but the two old friends must have busied themselves in heaven praying for the happiness of the young couple, for the match proved a singularly happy one.

There were several children, the first of whom was named for Louis' sister, Duchess Elizabeth, who had entered the Poor Clare monastery in Besançon. Little Elizabeth followed her aunt into the cloister when she was not yet twelve years old, just as Perrine de la Baume had done years before; and the precocious child was very dear to the abbess-general.

Louis of Bavaria had heard the praises of Colette Boellet chanted since his childhood. His wife, Maude de Genève, knew the abbess personally, and her admiration for the nun had gone on increasing since the day in 1410 when she had sat opposite her in Archbishop Thibault de Rougemont's carriage as Colette entered Besançon to take over the old Urbanist monastery there. If the saint felt beholden to both Louis and Maude because of the tremendous help given her work by their families, she was also as eager as they to extend the work of the restoration beyond the borders of France.

We have few details of this foundation in Heidelberg; but we know that the elder Elizabeth of Bavaria was among the nuns the abbess selected for the new community, and that Colette also brought little Elizabeth, then about fifteen, on the strenuous journey so that she might have the pleasure of seeing her parents again. Sister Colette evidently did not belong to that school of spirituality which considers it a duty to close off every natural avenue of joy.

The territory around the French-German border was infested with bandits in 1440. One group of these outlaws decided that the strange-looking travellers might be worth stopping. Their clothes were poor, but still, each one carried a bag. There was no harm in trying! So the rough men accosted them and demanded that they hand over their belongings.

Quite unafraid, the abbess stepped forward and interrupted Father Pierre's excited French appeals to the robbers' chivalry. Pierre de Vaux was probably just as glad to stop. He did not seem to be fetching up any signs of gallantry. His French eloquence was quite wasted on the German bandits, in any case. If the outlaws wondered at the bravery of the nun who dared to confront them, they certainly marvelled much more when she spoke to them. For she was obviously a Frenchwoman. Yet she was speaking German, perfect German. And in their own German she reproached them, but, writes Father Pierre, "sweetly and kindly." He goes on to marvel how "at the sound of her sweet voice, their cruel violence was changed into charity."

When the leader took off his cap, the other bandits did not laugh. They took off theirs, too. And then they held a short conference. At its conclusion, their chief stepped forward to beg pardon of Colette and her companions, and also to warn them. There were lots of other bandits in this country. The religious ought to have some protection. Would madame accept his humble offer? Would madame let him and his "men" escort her party wherever she was going?

Sister Colette did not need to consider. Had St. Francis stopped at merely converting robbers? Certainly not. He had received some of them into his Order! Similarly, writes Father Pierre de Vaux, Colette accepted the chivalry of the bandits, "thanking them very charitably and humbly for their offer." Maybe they bowed from the waist. Most certainly, they knew they were knights now.

Under the safe escort of these outlaws, Sister Colette carried the ideals of St. Francis' primitive Rule into Germany.

21 *Prophecies*

It was summer when Sister Colette left Heidelberg, accompanied by Sister Perrine and Father Pierre de Vaux. She must have longed for the familiar seclusion of her cloister in Besançon, but there was still another foundation hanging fire in 1440. In fact, the wish of the Duke and Duchess of Lorraine to have a Poor Clare monastery at Nancy dated back to 1425 when Charles II of Lorraine had drawn up his will and bequeathed "one hundred florins of gold to the very devout nun, Colette, of the Order of St. Clare, to be given to whichever of her convents she wishes."

After Charles' death, the dowager-duchess, Margaret, made it plain which convent *she* wished. It was to be built at Nancy. However, for the same reason the abbess had years ago resisted the Duchess of Burgundy's plan for a cloister at Dijon, she refused the Duchess of Lorraine's offer to build a monastery at Nancy. In 1440, that city was far too much a center of court life and splendor for Colette's taste. Her preference was for nearby Pont-à-Mousson. And just as she had persuaded Margaret of Burgundy to build in little Auxonne instead of gorgeous Dijon, she persuaded Margaret of Lorraine to put aside Nancy for Pont-à-Mousson.

By the summer of 1440, when the fifty-nine-year-old abbess-general could finally give her attention to this foundation, the duchess was already dead. King Réné of Anjou had acquired the Duchy of Lorraine by his marriage, and was now its ruling duke. He and his Isabel were as desirous to have one of Sister Colette's monasteries in Lorraine as old Margaret and Charles had been, and they agreed to Pont-à-Mousson. All details regarding it were completed in short order, and Colette remained there only long enough to see the building commenced and to select the nuns who were to make up the first community. One of these, Sister Perrine tells us, was Sister Colette Prucet of Besançon whom the abbess had miraculously restored to life thirty years earlier. If the young nun still preserved the abbess' veil which her father had wrapped around her at Sister Colette's direction, Colette Prucet must surely have worn it—and with what reflections!—when the saint selected her as the first abbess of Pont-à-Mousson.

Too weary to make any more plans for the future when she left Pont-à-Mousson, Colette, writes Abbé Douillet, now "returned happily to Besançon." She seems always to have returned there as a homing-bird to its nest. The years left to her now were few, and she said that she knew it. What she apparently did not know, when she left Lorraine, was that the monastery would run into so many minor difficulties during its building that it would not be completed for seven full years. She was to assist at the dedication of Pont-à-Mousson in 1447, but from heaven.

It was late autumn of 1440 when the abbess-general arrived at Besançon. When the excitement of her homecoming had abated a little, the nuns could not have failed to notice how worn she appeared. The pain of relentless neuralgia had bent her head slightly to one side, giving her the endearing air of an inquiring mother-bird. She walked much more slowly now. And she was more than ever concerned about her failing vision. Yet, any admission the nuns might wrest from her about the extent of the swelling in her legs or the searing pain in her eyes or the heart attacks she was beginning to suffer, would be almost immediately followed by an expression of self-contempt. "How I grumble about every little thing!" Father Pierre remembers the saint remarking with distaste. Nuns who sometimes did grumble and about really little things may have felt an accusing warmth on their cheeks and made some resolutions for the future.

If illness plagued this sojourn of the saint at the first house of her restoration, the devil did his hateful best to mar it, too. She had seen him and his infernal company when she was a young girl in the anchorhold of Corbie. He came again at Besançon, sometimes as a roaring black lion, sometimes in loathsome human guise. And he tormented her most particularly at the time of her confessions. Certainly she had no bundle of crimes to be unloosed, but she appears to have suffered from scrupulosity, since she once wrote to the abbess of Auxonne, Agnes de Vaux: "I do not know if I ever make a confession pleasing to God." With the devil beside her, it is easy to understand that she would wonder.

One day she was telling Father Pierre de Vaux of Satan's latest attacks on her when she suddenly conceived the inspiration that the devoted friar might understand her situation better if he, too, could once behold the father of lies in visible form. She prayed that the snarling black lion which she could see and hear so clearly might be made manifest for a moment to Father Pierre. Her prayer was promptly answered. Just as promptly, the confessor fainted. Probably the embarrassed abbess had to speed to the parlor and have another friar summoned to revive Father Pierre. We like to hope that she gave the resuscitated priest permission to tell his confrères what had transpired in the box, so that nobody hazarded any guesses about which nun's confession had caused the Father confessor to faint dead away.

Poor Father Pierre had his own trials. On a certain other occasion, his saintly penitent fell into an ecstasy while making her confession. Her voice trailed off, and he could elicit no least further response from her. No doubt he had been worried for some time past about her failing health; and this anxiety, along with the frequent confidences of the other nuns, who feared their Mother might not be spared to them much longer, led him to think that Colette had died in the confessional.

He was so sure of it that he went at once and tolled the monastery bell the prescribed number of strokes for announcing the death of a member of the community. The silent cloister came alive, with twenty-five nuns pouring out of cells and workrooms and laundry. Word ran like flame on dry tinder: "Our Mother is dead!" But just as the chorus swelled to a wail, "our Mother" emerged from the confessional, radiant as she always was when returning from her ecstasies. The nuns fell silent in a moment, and knelt down where they were. The shock of sudden grief, followed by the shock of seeing the shining face of the supposed corpse, left them unsure for a time whether they were looking on their living abbess or a vision of her in glory.

Yet, for all their conviction that she was a saint, Sister Colette's daughters were completely familiar in their relations with her. Like simple children they pelted her with questions about her ecstasies, and she did not rebuke them. She, too, had grown more and more simple with the passing years, and Sister Perrine has written of many instances which demonstrate Colette's increasing candor with her daughters about her visions and spiritual gifts. For example: "Sister Dominique at Auxonne just died," she announced one day at Poligny as she came to recreation. "I saw her." According to the Rule of St. Clare, when any nun dies, the other members of the community are to assemble at once in the choir and recite fifty Paternosters for her. As regards the nuns of other monasteries, one must, of course, wait for the obituary notice to arrive. Things were different during the lifetime of Sister Colette, when a dying nun in any of the communities could depend on getting her fifty Paternosters the moment she exhaled her final breath!

Sister Perrine has also told us how she often heard the saint repeat through an entire night the simple query which was the prayer of St. Francis before her: "Lord, who art Thou, and who am I?" Perrine remarks that when they were staying for a time at a monastery where the abbess-general's personal regimen was not generally known, Colette "would act as though she were settling down to sleep"; then, the faithful scribe adds, "she would not sleep at all." Perhaps Sister Colette supposed her ruses succeeded with her secretary, too; but Sister Perrine points out in her dry way: "I slept in a little cubicle near her. I could hear her praying and weeping for sinners all night long."

After these few precious months in the Besançon cloister, the abbess put on her mantle again. She was going to Hesdin, where there must by now be a completed monastery awaiting her. Philip of Burgundy, son of Colette's old patrons, Margaret of Burgundy and John the Fearless, following what had become the accustomed procedure for French nobles desiring a Poor Clare monastery in their dominions, had applied to Pope Eugene IV in 1437 for a papal bull of authorization for a foundation at Hesdin. The Holy Father had obliged him in a bull dated that same year, but, although Sister Colette had accepted Duke Philip's offer, she had been unable to go to Hesdin that year. Acting contrary for once to her principle of overseeing at least the beginning construction of all her monasteries, Colette had this time left matters in the hands of Philip and his wife, Bonne. Perhaps she comforted herself that Duchess Bonne of Burgundy knew what kind of building the abbess desired, since she was no other than the daughter of the old Duchess of Bourbon, and had built the Poor Clare monastery at Décize in memory of her first husband killed at the battle of Agincourt in 1415.

Bonne had been a very young widow when the Décize foundation was made, and handsome Philip of Burgundy had dried her tears in 1424 when he married her. The match was one of the real masterpieces of Burgundian-Bourbon marital entanglements; for the young widow's first husband, it will be remembered, was the brother of John the Fearless, Philip of Burgundy's father. Philip, therefore, married his aunt.

Sister Colette got one of her rudest disillusionments about trusting duchesses to be good construction bosses when she arrived at Hesdin. Instead of a completed monastery, she found a mere shell of a building. And everything, absolutely everything about it, was wrong. The chapel, relates Abbé Douillet, was not yet built at all. The whole place was very small, even too small for Sister Colette's modest desires. Yet she had to convert the largest of the rooms into a temporary chapel and thus leave the nuns' living-quarters smaller still.

Illness and exhaustion notwithstanding, the abbess who had confounded the workmen at Auxonne nearly thirty years previously with her enterprise and drive rallied her forces again and set about repairing Duchess Bonne's blunders. After all, Hesdin was the death place of her beloved Father Jéhan Pinet. Even on his account alone, she said, she would not abandon it as the site for one of her monasteries. Then, just to complete the cycle of disasters for the Hesdin foundation, Colette fell one morning when alighting from the borrowed carriage which her infirmities had forced her to use. She broke her arm.

It must have been a severe fracture, for Sister Perrine writes that "it caused the glorious virgin great pain and anguish." Whether there was no doctor available to set the arm, or whether the ministrations of a local quack only aggravated Colette's suffering, Perrine declares that "nothing could be done to help her." Then she hurries on to the happy circumstance of Father Jéhan Pinet's appearing to the abbess-general whom he had invested with the Franciscan habit nearly forty years earlier, and himself healing her arm. Sister Colette told her secretary that Father Jéhan had scolded her for not enlisting his services at once: "Colette, why did you not turn to me before? I would have made you well." Sister Colette declared that her broken arm was then immediately mended.

Perrine gives us further proof of the familiarity of the nuns with the abbess when she adds how the saint's astonished companions at Hesdin, "the good Mother Agnes de Vaux, Sister Marie d'Ormon, and myself," saw the arm healed and "demanded" to know the details of the miracle. With satisfaction, Sister Perrine reports that "she answered us: 'My good father, Frère Jéhan Pinet, came to see me and made me well. He scolded me because I had not turned to him before.' "

It took nearly a year to rectify all the mistakes that had been made and get the Hesdin building to a stage where it was no longer possible to deviate from her plans. And all this time, she was receiving impatient messages almost monthly from Ghent. Did Sister Colette not remember she had promised to establish a house in Ghent as early as 1427? Did she not know that the people of Ghent loved and revered her and had seen that her plans for a monastery were followed to the least detail? Had not Father Pierre de Vaux told her that the monastery completed in 1440 was everything she could ask? The abbess sent one loving letter after another to the excited townspeople, saying that she was coming with all possible speed. It was no lack of love for Ghent, nor apathy about seeing the new building, that kept her in Hesdin. When she did arrive in Ghent, on August 3, 1442, she was given a welcome to equal any she had ever received. "The saint is coming!" the ecstatic people shouted to one another. The town emptied its houses into a great procession to meet her. Colette's tired and burning eyes must surely have been washed with tears when she saw them.

Thirty years before, she had chafed under the praises of the citizens of Besançon when she entered their city. When anyone whispered "saint!" she had scolded and threatened. It was so different now. Like St. Francis in his last years, Colette had become quite indifferent to what people said of her. If it pleased their good hearts to suppose she was a saint, then God be praised for the pleasure they found in their gross error. When her enemies slanted all manner of malicious calumnies against her (for, even in 1442, Father Pierre tells us that she was still called "ambitious, covetous, vainglorious"), she was just as unconcerned. She had slipped beyond the praise or blame of men to breathe the rarefied air of her Father St. Francis' finished spirituality, the condition in which he had repeatedly said: "A man is just what he is in the sight of God, and no more." In the sight of God, Colette was sure she was the greatest of sinners. And when she said as much to Father Pierre de Vaux, she meant it. No one is really qualified to speak of sin except the saint.

Sister Colette remained at Ghent less than two months, but she conceived a particular affection for the town and for the monastery its devoted citizens had built for her. The house there was so poor and simple that she promptly and happily named it "Bethlehem." She selected a small number of her best-trained nuns for its first community and named Sister Odette the abbess. Odette was the natural

daughter of the Duke of Burgundy, and on that account Sister Colette required a dispensation from Rome for Odette's installation.
She promptly appealed for and received it. The little girl in Corbie
who had reproached her mother for marrying a second time had
grown into the wise and sympathetic woman who did not scruple to
place a nun of illegitimate birth over one of her most fervent communities.

She left Ghent in late September, but her reply to the nuns who
begged her to stay a little longer was a prophecy: "I will return, and
I will remain with you a long time." Colette was to die in this monastery of Bethlehem, and the community which had her living presence
so short a time would become custodian of the saint's body for many
years.

It appears that the increasing consciousness of her approaching
end drove her back to Besançon after each new enterprise of these
last years. There was a sense in which the abbess-general of so many
monasteries was a pilgrim in them all. Besançon, the cradle of her
work of restoration, was "home" more than any other. When she
arrived there in the first part of October, she found John Capistran
awaiting her. He had a little sheaf of documents with him again, but
these were from the minister-general, Father William of Casal, granting her all manner of privileges. Father John had asked to bring them
to her personally.

Among other things, the documents confirmed previous permissions given to Colette to appoint personally the visitators of all
her monasteries. This was a delicate matter and one of extreme
importance for the endurance and prosperity of her restoration.
Canonical visitations of religious houses have a twofold purpose: the
removal of any relaxations or abuses, and the encouragement of
fervor. Religious are renewed in spirit or discouraged from strict
observance according to the views of the visitator. With many different schools of thought on Franciscan observance still prevailing
in the Order at this time, it was absolutely requisite for the continuance and flowering of the primitive way that the visitators to her
monasteries be always friars whose views she knew entirely accorded
with her own. Father William of Casal thus gave new and marvelous
proof of his respect for Colette and his trust in her. What he gave
her was a kind of blank check on the First Order. She could call any

friar she wished from any field or engagement, if and when she wished, and by her own authority. Here is the text of the all-important letter St. John Capistran brought to St. Colette:

To Sister Colette of the Order of St. Clare, entirely devoted to Christ our Lord, our very dear daughter in the heart of the Spouse of virgins, John Capistran of the Order of Minors, on the part of the Apostolic See and the Most Reverend Father General . . . wishes health and everlasting peace in the Lord.

Desiring, with paternal affection, to console you in the Lord, I ratify and I confirm by these letters present, and declare ratified and confirmed all the favors which the Most Reverend Minister-General has accorded you and your confessor, Pierre de Vaux, and the confessors of the convents of nuns which you have built and will build . . . I declare that you have power to appoint one or more friars of our Order to fill the office of Visitor of the nuns in the said convents, or of friars who live in monasteries [of this way of life]. To these friars so chosen, in virtue of these letters present, I accord and declare accorded the same faculties and the same power that preceding Ministers General have heretofore given these Visitators. I ordain, in virtue of holy obedience, that the friars so named accept the office of Visitor with respect, and that they fulfil it with diligence and piety.

Given by me, at Besançon, the eighth day of the month of November, in the year of our Lord, 1442.

Brother John Capistran,

Commissary General

But it is the postscript to this letter which is most revealing of John Capistran's shy tenderness for the abbess he had once tried to bend to his own will. "I have written this with my own hand," he carefully adds, in parentheses.

Father John Capistran had a plan to propose on this visit, too, but decidedly unlike the one he had laid before the abbess in 1439. They both knew that Duchess Bonne of Burgundy was eager to found a monastery of Poor Clares at Amiens. Why could they not attempt to restore the primitive Rule among the friars of nearby Abbéville at the same time? Sister Colette would thus be assured of having a confessor and chaplain easily accessible for her nuns. See what had been accomplished at the friary of Dôle, now called "the seminary of the reform"! John Capistran was certain that the same renewal could be effected at Abbéville. Colette agreed to try, and the two saints left Besançon together for Dôle.

Unhappily, the hoped-for restoration at Abbéville was never realized. Colette and John Capistran appealed in vain. Three friars from Dôle went to live for a time in the community at Abbéville, endeavoring to prove to their brothers the rewards of primitive observance. But their brothers wanted none of it. The sorrows and disappointments of her friends always affected Sister Colette more deeply than her directly personal ones. All the distress she had suffered over the hostility shown to Father Henri de la Baume years ago at Chambéry must have been renewed for Father John Capistran when she left him at Abbéville to journey on to Amiens with Father Pierre de Vaux. This indomitable little man, who in his seventies was to go to Hungary and fight with John Hunyadi against the Turks, later told his intimates that the spiritual defeat at Abbéville was one of the greatest sorrows of his life.

Colette found her own share of the disagreeable at Amiens. As it was, the town held some very painful memories for her. It was to Amiens that she had taken her first two postulants, Marie Sénéchal and Guillemette Chrétien, when she set out from the old quarry just outside Corbie to begin her work in 1406. It was at Amiens that she had been viciously calumniated and refused a hearing for her cause. Evidently the old monastery of Poor Clares she had visited, and where she had been so rebuffed, had been emptied of its community in the intervening years. Perhaps even the building was destroyed. At any rate, the old chronicles make no reference to it on Colette's return in 1442.

She was famous now, the spiritual mother of hundreds of nuns, many of them daughters of dukes and princes. Amiens could ill afford to persecute her as openly as it had thirty-six years earlier. In fact, Amiens had no wish to persecute her—if only she would keep her distance! She was a saint. They believed it. But many property holders, priests, and religious in Amiens preferred that the saint go elsewhere.

The kind of determined opposition that arose against Sister Colette's establishing a foundation in Amiens is a complex affair, compounded more of fear and selfishness than of active dislike. Someone is going to lose the rents on property deeded over to Colette by the Duchess of Burgundy. Some religious Order is afraid its prestige will be diminished by the coming of these penitential women. A bishop is nettled because the nuns will be less subject to his authority than to the friars'. And so it goes, on and on, until minds are seduced and vision perverted.

Opposition to St. Teresa's founding a tiny Carmelite convent in Avila in the sixteenth century was to be so violent that the Spanish reformer would declare it could better be raised against invading barbarian hordes than against four barefoot nuns. St. Colette's reflections in the fifteenth century must have been much the same. However, it is plain that the animosity in Amiens was more the result of propaganda than of calculation, for Father Pierre de Vaux was able to reduce its flames to a few low embers with some characteristic propaganda of his own. He drew up a document, a kind of open letter to the councillors and citizens of Amiens, and circulated copies of it throughout the city. This completely charming appeal, which is preserved in the monastery at Amiens, was free of the least strain of rancor; its friendly reasonableness succeeded where stern reproaches would certainly have failed. The last paragraph of it is sufficient to demonstrate its manner of petition; sufficient, too, to provide a character sketch of Father Pierre de Vaux:

Therefore, noble citizens of Amiens, do not reject or impede this work so pleasing to God, but for His love receive it joyfully. Sins are increasing, evils are multiplying, dangers are very great; and we must believe that we are greatly in need of help before our Lord. Do not be making complaints about a poor piece of ground where we wish to have a little house; it will be assigned to the children of our Lord; there are many other places which are profitable to no one. And, indeed, each one of us will own quite enough forever in a length of seven feet. And even if this house is in a fine street and on the great highway, no one should be displeased at this, but should praise our Lord. It is a happy exchange that for the possessions of this world, which are so soon left behind, we may obtain possessions in heaven which will last for ever.

Although she had already begun construction on her new monastery, Sister Colette had returned to Besançon when she saw the opposition at Amiens. But in the spring of 1443, Father Pierre sent her a joyous message to return and to bring with her the nuns she wished to make up the first community of her house at Amiens. She trusted him so completely that she began the return journey without further question, armed with a "passport" from the Duke of Burgundy, and accompanied, says Abbé Douillet, "by a numerous colony of religious chosen from the neighboring monasteries of the reform." Among these, he tells us, were the two daughters of Jacques de Bourbon and also his small granddaughter, the child of Eleanor de Bourbon and Bernard d'Armagnac, who, like Sister Perrine and Elizabeth of Bavaria, entered the cloister very young and made vows as a Poor Clare when she reached the proper age. The eldest of King Jacques' daughters became the first abbess of Amiens.

Sister Colette supervised the continuance of work on the building and spent weeks and months in tiresome interviews with public officials, the local chapter of canons, parish priests, and others of the private objectors, finally winning them all by her sweetness and humility. Father Pierre had put an end to the major hostilities; Colette herself now disposed of the petty remainders, and with such tact that Douillet declares she won "the veneration, the respect, the sympathy, and the co-operation of this capital of Picardy."

In January of 1444, everything was at last in order. The monastery was dedicated and community life begun. Sister Colette lingered with her nuns at Amiens until late spring. Did she know she would see them only once after this, and then very briefly? When she returned to Besançon with Sister Perrine and Father Pierre, the abbess spoke of it as her last homecoming.

So ill and exhausted she could often scarcely stand, she had the added burden of prophecy in these last months. She predicted the Protestant Reform. She told her nuns mournfully of how her southern monasteries would be destroyed, and she wept when she foretold the destruction of this loved nest of her restoration in Besançon, the great fire which would raze the house to the ground in the next century.

The nuns were horrified. They may have listened to her predictions of the Protestant Reformation as one hears of vague disasters in far countries. But their own monastery! Could they not prevent it? If they knew when the fire threatened, surely they could stop it! When was it to be? Colette shook her head. "When the big cross out there in the cemetery falls down across the graves, they will know the fire is about to come. Let them be warned and run out of the house. But they will not be able to prevent the disaster." The worried nuns wrote this carefully down in the monastery's archives for their Sisters of the next century.

It was in 1510 that the great cross toppled over the graves of the nuns who had heard this prophecy. Their successors were terrified, and set themselves to take every preventive measure against a fire of which they could see no sign at all. But their precautions availed them nothing. The first monastery of the reform burned down the next day, a mysterious consequent which we can only suppose was intended by God to show the indestructibility of the spiritual edifice Colette had built. For Besançon was rebuilt afterwards and flourishes even today.

This final sojourn at Besançon was a short one. There was only one more project Colette felt she must complete before her death, and she told her daughters of it as she prepared to leave them. "It is Corbie," she said. "I must make a foundation in Corbie before I die." It had been her first hope in 1406 when she was twenty-five. Now, at sixty-four, it was her last hope.

And now the abbess who had almost nothing which could be dignified with the name of possessions cast about for some little gifts to leave these daughters she would not see again. They knelt around her, weeping and protesting at her going, as she handed out her treasures. There was the breviary Pedro de Luna had presented to her after he had received her vows as a Poor Clare. "Always pray for him," Colette urged her children. Then she held out the tall wooden cross St. Vincent Ferrer had given her and committed it to their care. Finally, she drew out the little gold and pearl reliquary with its relic of the true Cross, and placed it in the hands of the abbess of Besançon. "Keep it and treasure it," she said simply, "for it is from heaven."

The poignancy of the moment must have become unbearable for the community. Typically, Colette eased it with a show of her old energetic practicality. "Now, where is that habit you made for the good Augustinian monk who is going to become a Franciscan friar?" The Sister who had shown her handiwork to Colette the day before ran for the habit and held it out to her Mother. "Now I shall just take that," the saint declared, "for our Augustinian friend will not need it." Evidently the nuns' eyes questioned their Mother at this, for we are told that Colette added: "He will change his mind soon enough. He will never enter our Order, and he will not need this habit. It is my size, and they can bury me in it. This one" (she looked down at the habit she had patched and mended for many years) "is too worn-out for heaven." And so she left them.

From the oldest house of her reform, she went to the newest at Amiens, fearing it might need some final ministrations of her love. While there, in February of 1445, she said plainly that she had only two more years to live. Her weakness at this time was so extreme that Father Pierre was for once inclined to doubt her word. It seemed impossible that she could survive for two years longer. At the same time, she gave him a confidence which summed up her life and her work: "Father, all that I have done, with the help of our Lord, I have done it; and even though I am a great sinner and full of faults, if I had to do it over again I do not know how I would do it, except in the way in which I have done it."

22 *Death*

With a supreme effort, the dying nun summoned her physical forces for the last spiritual campaign of her life: the erection of a Poor Clare monastery in Corbie. She wrote to the city councillors, and received a favorable reply on April 5, 1445. It was St. Vincent Ferrer's death day, and Colette said that she considered this a happy portent. The old slanders the Corbians had bruited against her years before were now long buried under mounds of shame and remorse. All France was acclaiming Colette as a saint. But, after all, she belonged to them, to the townspeople of Corbie. Only let her come home, and they would show her what they thought of her now! She handed the letter to Father Pierre. She was going home, and this time there would be no question of her not being welcomed.

We who seek to be detached from the thousand earthly ties that fetter us have not yet breathed the free air of that larger country which is sanctity. The saints get disentangled from a few things in order to embrace everything. While we paddle about in a shallow asceticism of negation, they plunge into the deep waters of affirmation, that is, into the ocean of God's love. For sixty years Colette of Corbie had been striving to love more and more. What a waste it would have been to have spent those years in attempting to love less and less. The suffering Corbie had caused her had been not so much endured as embraced. Now that Corbie offered her love, she accepted that just as simply.

Duke Philip of Savoy had obtained a bull of authorization for the new monastery from Pope Eugene IV. It arrived at the end of October, and Sister Colette assured Father Pierre she was quite well enough to begin the journey to Corbie. He agreed that she did look much better these days. Because of her feeble health, though, she had to forego her usual procedure of overseeing the work of laying the foundations of the new house. Father Pierre sent some of his most trusted lieutenants ahead to check every detail and to conduct to Corbie the nuns Colette had quickly chosen for the first community. This one time in her life, she let her daughters go on before her to a new beginning. Then, just as she herself was about to set out with Father Pierre, the opposition of the Benedictine monks in Corbie crashed down on their plans like axe-blows.

The old jealousies which Dom Raoul de Raye had bequeathed to the community of Saint-Pierre were as inflammable in 1445 as they had been in 1406. The present abbot himself declared that he was not against Colette's establishing a monastery in Corbie, but he had to make the humiliating admission that his prior and monks felt differently and that he could not control their opposition. This was Dom Michel Dauphin, third successor of Raoul de Raye.

In other like circumstances, Sister Colette would certainly have withdrawn at once. Her old horror of dissension and public scandal must have risen up suffocatingly, for the Benedictines had already appealed to the city parliament against her coming. (One wonders on what possible grounds?) But these were not "other circum-

stances." This was Corbie, her Corbie. And Colette's days on earth
were quickly running out. To Father Pierre's astonishment, she declared that she would not yield! Her loyal friend cast about for
a way to help her, but he knew well enough that the kind of letter he
had written to the people of Amiens would avail less than nothing
with the Benedictine monks of Corbie. Colette herself sat down and
began a letter to the Duchess of Burgundy.

Duchess Bonne was appalled at the attitude of the Benedictines;
and she wrote to them in her own hand, urging them to change their
views. The name of Burgundy was as powerful in France as ever;
it opened almost any door. But not the doors of the Benedictines'
hearts. The duchess then appealed directly to the King and Queen
of France, and Charles VII intervened personally on Colette's behalf. However, not even for the King of France would the Corbian
Benedictines put aside their invincible enmities.

Colette herself, at great cost to her fast failing strength, wrote a
long letter to the king which pathetically demonstrates the intensity
of her desire to see a monastery of the primitive Rule in Corbie before her death. Indeed, the very urgency of the dying runs through
this letter.

To our Lord the King: In humble supplication, the most useless
servant of Jesus Christ, and your unworthy petitioner, Sister Colette,
a poor nun of the Order of St. Clare. For the past year or so, the
Lord and Lady of Savoy . . . have wished to construct a convent
and a monastery of the said Order of St. Clare, and of our way of
living, within the town of Corbie; and for this purpose have obtained
a bull and mandate from our Holy Father the Pope, and in order to
execute them according to their authority, have presented them to
their lordships the abbot, prior and community of Saint-Pierre, of
the said Corbie, as was proper, praying and requesting of them that
they should be willing humbly to obey it.

To which a reply was given by his lordship the abbot, that he had
no intention of opposing the bulls of our Holy Father, and since then
has always been and still is satisfied; and the citizens, tradespeople
and inhabitants of this town are also satisfied. But the said prior and
community were not satisfied, and will not consent to it.

The said lord and lady, fortified by the authority of our said Holy
Father and the consent of the said abbot, have caused the convent
to be commenced and built, at great expense and outlay; and to

block the wall already commenced, the said monks have obtained an order from your parliament by virtue of which the work has been stopped: which is a great wrong, delaying the Divine Office and the good thus begun.

And when the Duchess of Burgundy was informed of the difficulties and obstacles raised by these monks, she caused remonstrances to be made, and begged of them and requested that they would give their consent. To which they refused to agree, finally and decisively; and because this is a very lamentable matter and concerned, above all, with the honor of God . . . we turn to you as to our last and sovereign refuge in this poor world.

May it please your gracious benignity . . . to grant your good will and such support to the good work commenced, that it may quickly attain completion, so that God's service there may promptly begin. May it please you also to free from all taxes the place and site where the said convent is to be built.

How can their rights be prejudiced or injured?—because the poor nuns cannot, nor ought not, at any time have any overlordship or jurisdiction, nor income nor revenues nor rents, but live on alms only, following the counsels of the Holy Gospel and of our Lord Jesus Christ. . . . May it please you, of your kindness and generous mercy, to arrange this; and you will be doing well and charitably and will place our poor Order under further obligation to pray for your high and holy intentions, a thing we always wish to do with all our poor powers. . . .

King Charles granted her the important tax exemption at once, so certain was the monarch that the inimical Benedictines would bow to his royal wishes. Reassured, Colette went on to Hesdin with Sister Perrine and Father Pierre de Vaux for a last visit with her community there before going herself to Corbie. She had a personal letter from His Majesty the King of France, assuring her of his intervention with the monks of Corbie. There was no further reason to fear, everyone agreed. The abbess-general appears to have been in very good spirits during the little sojourn at Hesdin. Both Father Pierre and Sister Perrine tell of a "very marvelous miracle" she worked there.

A certain lay brother named Andrew had been commissioned to make a new habit for Father Pierre. Maybe Sister Colette, with her own new robe that had first been destined for the Augustinian postulant of changing views, thought her confessor and companion should enter Corbie in like style. Father Pierre defends his confrère's work, saying that Brother Andrew "measured the material very carefully," before he tells of his running short. Brother Andrew knew that this problem was one for a woman to solve. He took the unfinished habit to Sister Colette, "showed it to the little handmaid of the Lord, and said it was impossible for him to make a habit out of such a little piece of material." If he expected her to produce more habit goods, he was disappointed. And Colette's answer must have held small appeal for a man. "Go and pray to our Lord," she told Brother Andrew, "and when you return, I'll pull on one end of the material and you pull on the other, to see if we can stretch it out long enough."

Whatever his personal opinion of the proposed solution, Andrew went off and prayed. When he came back, he and the abbess-general pulled mightily at each end of the half-finished habit. The results were so remarkable as to trouble Father Pierre's conscience. For, after recording with satisfaction that his habit was finished and "a good piece of material left over," he expresses some anxiety; his new robe, he said, was "so long and ample that it seemed against holy poverty."

This pleasant respite at Hesdin was abruptly terminated for Sister Colette when she received news that the Benedictine monks of Corbie had remained adamant even before the word of their king. Queen Marie of France herself wrote to the little colony of nuns in Corbie to stand firm against the opposition. Yet, what were they to do? The powerful Benedictines bent the parliament to their wishes and obtained fresh decrees against the erection of a Poor Clare monastery in their town.

Unable to take any stand against such bitter opposition, Colette at last bowed her head to this greatest sorrow in her life. Perhaps she found comfort in the words of our Lord that no prophet is honored in his own country. Yet it was no honor she had sought, but only that a humble house of prayer and penance should rise in her loved Corbie for the honor and glory of God and the good of the town. She could never appear in public now without people swarming around her in the hope of merely touching her poor garments. She was welcome in every castle in France and in the royal palace itself. Only in Corbie was there still no place for Colette. But no comment so poignantly describes her heartbreak as the letter she wrote from Hesdin on the second of March in 1446 to the Benedictine monks of Corbie:

To my most honored and revered lords, their lordships the prior and monks of Corbie:

As humbly as I can or know how, I recommend my poor soul to your holy prayers and devout petitions before our Lord Jesus Christ; and may it please you to know that I have received your letters. . . .

I declare to you that, not at my request, but at the instance of the Lord of Savoy, and by the permission and authority of our Holy Father the Pope, and with the consent and approval of the Reverend Father in God, the lord abbot of Corbie . . . I did consent to the construction and building of a monastery of our Order in your town of Corbie.

Not, truly, that I ever had any desire or intention or wish that the said monastery should be prejudicial to your rulership or jurisdiction; nor in any way injurious to the churches or to the poor. If this would really be so, and even if the said monastery were, with your consent and approval, completely constructed and finished, I would never occupy it or remain there, because that would be usurping the rights of others.

But, before God, I believe that the said undertaking would be to the honor of God and to your honor also, and to the credit of the abbey and even to its profit, and would be of great use to you and to all the inhabitants of the town. I have always seen and known by experience that this is the case in all places where our other monasteries were built, that is to say, in large, in medium-sized, and in small towns—some of these towns being smaller and poorer than Corbie, but through God's will, I never saw any which were not provided for without prejudicing or doing harm to others.

You call upon me to desist from the building of the monastery. This I am going to do, with great regret. But I doubt not, that once you come before the Lord who judges all things, you will have to explain why you thus hindered so excellent a work. Nevertheless, at your desire, I shall request the said Lord of Savoy that he depart from the monastery and give up the work, because we have all come to the conclusion that never while you live will you permit the said monastery to be built, as long as your resistance shall be of any avail.

Most honored and religious lords, I humbly pray the Holy Spirit
that He may always keep you in His holy graces, and finally grant
you everlasting grace.

Your useless petitioner,

Sister Colette

The affair was finished now. The "useless petitioner" was beaten.
However, her powerful friends would not give up so easily. In an
outrage of protest at the treatment given their saint and the insult
offered to their king, the Duke and Duchess of Burgundy appealed
directly to the pope. Eugene IV was himself scandalized at matters
in Corbie and wrote a letter to the Benedictines there which amounted
to a papal command and which bore the threat of excommunication
if they did not cease their entirely unwarranted opposition at once.
The pope entrusted this bull to three special commissioners, one
of whom was the Benedictine Abbot of Anverbade. The Lord Abbot
of Anverbade, sick at soul over the conduct of his fellow-Benedictines
in Corbie, declared himself glad to be selected by Pope Eugene as
one of the committee, that he might thus publicly proclaim that the
scandalous behavior of the community in Corbie in no way represented the feelings of other Benedictines.

It strains the imagination to the breaking-point to conceive of
these monks remaining obdurate before pope as well as king. Even
the threatened excommunication did not move them. And, in an
agony of fear, the abbot of Corbie presented himself to the town
provost and signed a public declaration that he yielded himself to the
wishes of the Holy Father and of the King of France, and that he
disclaimed all further responsibility for the actions of his prior and
his monks.

Only eternity will reveal what diabolic forces must have urged
these religious to such extremes of jealous hatred and insubordination. It was only Sister Colette's withdrawal of all claims which
saved the monks from excommunication. She sent word to her nuns
at Corbie to prepare to leave the town at once, and asked two friars
from Dôle to see that her daughters were safely returned to their
former monasteries. She then asked Father Pierre to take her to
Ghent. The foundation at Corbie had been her only reason for
clinging to the threads of life remaining to her. Now there was no

reason at all. She began the journey to Ghent only to keep her tryst with sister death.

Yet, for all her anguish of soul and weakness of body, the old sharp wit remained. When passing through Courtrai, she was regaled with accounts of a recluse there who never partook of any food. She was urged to visit this prodigy of sanctity, but politely declined. To the shocked amazement of her enthusiastic informers, Colette admitted she really had no desire at all to see the holy recluse. The credulous townsfolk were shocked from another direction when they discovered shortly afterward that their anchoress enjoyed good meals in secret. Sister Colette kept her powers of appraisal to the very last moments of her life, and exhibitionism had always repelled her.

Her gentle compassion for the suffering and her distrust of excessive zeal remained the same, too. Sister Perrine tells how the abbess, almost too weak to raise her arm, still managed to trace a sign of the cross over a young novice brought to her while she was en route to Ghent. The girl had lost the sight of one eye through an accident, and her community was preparing to dismiss her. Sister Colette restored the novice's vision, and found enough voice to express her displeasure with the superiors who had shown such lack of pity for their young charge. Humbly they confessed their error, and won the prize of a smile from the dying saint.

Word was brought to her that her friend, John Capistran, in an outburst of misguided devotedness for her and zeal for the reform, had asked the pope to pronounce that all violations of the primitive Rule which Colette had restored should be considered mortal sins. The abbess-general was not too ill to raise immediate protest to the proposed edict; and, of course, she prevailed. Doubtless impulsive Father John himself realized his mistake in short order, and Colette certainly knew that it had been a mistake of love.

Sister Perrine writes of two attempts on the saint's life by poisoning, but, according to her usual procedure, gives no dates. Perhaps dates would have been too revealing here, in any case, for Perrine says that "it was public knowledge among the Sisters, and they knew who had done it, but the glorious Mother lovingly pardoned them [the would-be murderers]." The abbess-general showed her secretary the swellings on her back which the poison caused, and Sister

Perrine declares that "it was only by the grace of our Savior that she was preserved from death."

Men's persecutions, however, were far outnumbered by God's favors. Once, Sister Perrine recalls, the abbess-general remained so long in ecstasy that the nuns feared for her life. They sent for Dr. Hugh Picotel. He examined the insensible saint and delivered his pronouncement: "God is the doctor here." Dr. Picotel, says Perrine, then knelt down before Colette and "repeated to the Sisters several times over: 'You are blessed indeed to have such a Mother.'"

Sister Perrine also relates how Colette's solicitude for the sufferings of her nuns remained to the end. One day Perrine hurt her arm, but determined to keep her suffering to herself. In true nun-fashion, however, she wound layer upon layer of bandaging around the injury. She tells us that, after fifteen days of this ineffectual treatment, she was washing Sister Colette's feet when Colette calmly asked her: "What is ailing you?" Poor Perrine, who had been in such pain that she could neither eat nor sleep for days, replied simply: "I have a misery in my arm." Colette insisted on seeing the arm, still swollen under its heavy swathing. "Off with all that," she ordered. "I took it off," Perrine concludes, "and I found myself cured."

Still another time, at Hesdin, Sister Perrine says she fell ill on Passion Sunday. "I was extremely sick," she remembers. "When our glorious Mother knew of it, she told me to go lie down on her own bed. I did as she told me, and after two or three days, she said to me: 'Go and do your work as secretary, and use your own bed in the dormitory.' And at these words, I was entirely cured. I did my work and lay down on my bed in the dormitory." The glorious Mother's gift of miracles was evidently very handy when work was plentiful and nuns wanting.

At the beginning of February, 1447, the abbess-general told her nuns that her death was very close. She also warned them, writes Sister Perrine, not to expect any final word: "Do not wait for me to say anything to you at my death, for I shall say nothing." It was apparently an affectionate reminder to them to ask any questions quickly. Surely they did. At last, on Friday, the third of March, she asked Father Pierre to summon all the friars who were near; and they crowded into her cell. The dying St. Clare had known the comfort of the friars' presence at her bedside; the pope did not deny

Colette the same consolation. The little cell at Ghent might have been the cell of St. Clare at San Damiano two centuries earlier. Brother Leo and Brother Reynaldo and the other faithful sons of St. Francis had wept at Clare's leaving them. Father Pierre and Father François Claret and their companions wept as bitterly to lose Colette. As for St. Francis and St. Clare, a friar read for St. Colette the Passion of our Lord. And the dying nun, says Sister Perrine, spoke to the friars "sweetly and comfortingly."

She heard Mass the next morning, and returned to her little cell for the last time. She walked unassisted to the shelf where she kept the veil reserved for special occasions. It was the one, records Sister Perrine, that Benedict XIII had placed on her head in 1406 when he had named her the abbess-general of all Poor Clares who would embrace her restoration of the primitive Rule. She had worn it on the greatest days in her life; now she had come to the greatest day of all, when she was going to render to her Divine Spouse an account of her stewardship and of her love.

She pinned the veil on her head and made a large sign of the cross over her bed of straw. As she lay down on it, she said with satisfaction: "This is the last time I shall lie down." At once she entered into her last agony, which lasted for two full days. Perrine says that the glorious Mother never lost consciousness to the end; she knew each time one of her daughters kissed her hands. Father Pierre stole in and out of the death-cell every hour, taking no rest during the two long days and nights. His loyalty was rewarded, for he was at Colette's side on Monday, March 6, 1447, when she opened her lovely eyes for the last time. Sister Perrine, who was bending over her, gives the hour as eight in the morning. It was just forty-one years since Sister Colette had held a newborn Perrine de la Baume in her arms. As she had foretold, the abbess spoke no final word. "In the presence of all the nuns in the monastery of Ghent and of her confessor and companion, she very humbly ended her days." This is Sister Perrine's brief description of the death of the saint.

The faithful secretary hurries on to relate that Sister Colette's appearance remained unchanged for twelve hours. Age and suffering marked the colorless face. The tired body was bent. "Then, suddenly," writes an exultant Perrine, "her body was transformed into a great and marvelous beauty; it was white as snow, and her veins showed through the white like fine azure; her whole body was so lovely, so supple, so fragrant, that it seemed entirely spiritualized, with an angelic purity." Father Pierre de Vaux has left us the same account.

For three days, the dead saint was visited by crowds of "the admiring and the curious," as Sister Perrine catalogues them. Then they buried her, with none of her unearthly loveliness diminished, as she had begged them many times these past months, without any kind of bier or coffin or even a winding-sheet. Her body, burned out like a pure candle in the service of God, was put down into a simple grave; and the friars built a flimsy wooden shelter above it. To this little sanctuary, the poorest shelter of the poor, the Queen of France and the Queen of England came on pilgrimage. The Duchess of York and the Duke and Duchess of Burgundy, the royal Bourbons, and the Duke and Duchess of Savoy knelt in the dust beside the grave which might have been that of any pauper of the town.

For nearly a century this humble grave remained untouched. The Bishop of Tournai then ordered the body exhumed, and the bones were enclosed in a reliquary about three feet long and placed in the chapel at Ghent. But even in death, Colette could not enjoy seclusion. During the Huguenot menace, again during the period of expulsion of all nuns from Flanders decreed by Emperor Joseph II, and still later during the French Revolution, the narrow reliquary was carried from one hiding-place to another. During the expulsion, the Carmelite Madame Louise of France begged the nuns of Ghent to entrust the treasure to her. Afterward, the great princess signed a deed of gift, restoring the precious relics of St. Colette to her own daughters in her favorite monastery at Poligny. There they still repose, along with the remains of Countess Blanche de Genève, the saint's first benefactress from the French nobility.

Francis of Assisi was raised to the altars of the Church only two years after his death. Clare of Assisi was canonized as quickly; in fact, she was very nearly canonized during her burial service by the pope who came himself to preside at the funeral and was deterred only by the distressed whispers of his cardinals that "such things are not done, Holy Father!" Colette of Corbie had never wanted any title save that of daughter of Francis and Clare. Her dearest wish was to lose herself entirely in the radiance of their glory. In death, her ambition was the same; and God appears to have yielded to her wish in postponing her beatification for nearly two hundred years.

On the very day of her death, Pope Nicholas V was elected to succeed Eugene IV. The accession of Nicholas V marked the end of the second schism and inaugurated an era of peace such as the Church had never enjoyed during all of Colette's long life. Perhaps the new pontiff felt he owed the portents of peace and spiritual prosperity in great measure to the humble nun of Corbie, for he opened the process of her beatification at once. Yet, by a series of complications both political and ecclesiastical, Colette was declared Blessed only in 1604; and the process of her canonization dragged out until 1807. Through all those years, many of the worldly great had petitioned Rome to hasten her exaltation; the most striking of their company was King Henry VIII of England.

Her life had abounded in astounding miracles, and prodigies continued at her grave. The only convincing explanation of the fact that official exaltation was delayed for centuries seems to lie in the heart of the saint herself. "I am only the servant of Sir St. Francis and Madame St. Clare," she had loved to declare during her lifetime. In death, she would not emulate their speedy glorification. Yet, after all, she did not have quite the last word.

Forty years before, St. Francis and St. Clare had looked down from heaven on a small anchorhold leaning against the church of Notre Dame in Corbie. Their prayers before the throne of God had drawn a humble recluse out of her seclusion into a welter of labor and misunderstanding, calumny and anguish, that she might restore their ideals and rebuild the Franciscan Order in France. On the sixth of March in 1447, Francis and Clare waited for God to draw her out of a little cell in the monastery at Ghent. With them now and forever, she reigns like a queen.

Did not St. Clare write in her Rule of the poverty "which has made you, my dearest daughters, heiresses and queens in the kingdom of heaven"? St. Colette has come into her inheritance.

Afterword

There are today nine monasteries of Poor Clares in the United
States, originating from St. Colette's foundation in Ghent. The
house at Tongres was founded from Ghent in 1845; Tongres sent
a colony of nuns to Dusseldorf, Germany, in 1859. When Bismarck's
Kulturkampf attempted to put an end to religious life there in the
1870's, the German Countess, Sister Veronica von Elmendorff, and
Sister Josepha Mungen brought the Colettine Poor Clare restoration to the United States from their exile in Holland. In 1877, they
established their first monastery in Cleveland, Ohio, where Mother
Maddalena Bentivoglio, an Italian countess, and her sister, Constance, had begun the observance of the first Rule of St. Clare
shortly before. The two founding groups attempted to merge their
efforts for a time, but differences of language, Constitutions and
customs made this too difficult for new beginnings in a strange
land. Mother Maddalena (whose cause for beatification is now
before Rome) invited the Colettine Poor Clares to continue religious life in Cleveland, while she and her companions would accept the offer of land and a new monastery in Omaha, Nebraska.
Throughout the years, relations between these two first foundations
and their daughter-houses have been of the closest.

From the Cleveland cradle of primitive Franciscanism in America
have been founded the Colettine Poor Clare monasteries in Chicago
and Rockford, Illinois; those of Aptos, Santa Barbara, and Los
Altos in California; that of Roswell in New Mexico; Warwick in
Virginia; and, as late as April, 1959, that of Kokomo, in Indiana.
Also founded from the Cleveland monastery in 1950 is the house
at Campina-Grande in Brazil.

Besides these Colettine Poor Clare monasteries of primitive observance, there are fourteen other Poor Clare monasteries in the
United States following the primitive Rule of St. Clare. These

houses, the oldest of them in Omaha, Nebraska, and the youngest in Greenville, South Carolina, stem from the Italian monasteries. Canada has five monasteries of primitive observance, three of them following the Constitutions of St. Colette.